In It Together
Making a Retirement Community

Half Meadow Press
San Geronimo, CA
2004

In It Together
Making a Retirement Community

Copyright © 2004 Montgomery Place, Inc.

All proceeds from the sale of **In It Together** *are donated to the* **Montgomery Place Care Assurance Fund.**

Printed in the United States of America.

Drawings by Alice Hayes.

Photographs courtesy IVY Marketing Group, Inc., Marilee Neihoff, and Carolyn Allen.

Reproduction of the First Annual Report of the Church Home for Aged Persons by permission of the Archives and Historical Collections, Diocese of Chicago (Episcopal), 65 E. Huron St., Chicago, IL 60611.

ISBN 0-9723269-3-6 (Hardcover)
ISBN 0-9723269-4-4 (Softcover)

Production by:
Half Meadow Press
PO Box 99
San Geronimo, CA 94963

Dedication

This book is a celebration of the courageous, hopeful people who live here and who still believe they can salvage and enjoy some part of the world they love and have helped to make.

Acknowledgments

The Montgomery Place Historic Book Committee would like to recognize the many who have proven instrumental in the creation of this work:

Bishop James Winchester Montgomery, the Montgomery Place Board of Trustees and administration, and especially Director Michael Apa and Chaplain Father Robert Petite.

Fellow residents, including Ann Lee for her excellent proofreading skills, and all those who contributed their stories and ideas.

Mary Alzina Stone Dale, author of *A Century of Church Women*.

Barbara Swift Brauer and Laurence Brauer of Half Meadow Press for their patient and peaceful wisdom in knitting the manuscript into its finished form.

Our endlessly optimistic editor, Carolyn Allen; and Debra Sheridan of IVY Marketing Group, Inc.

Contents

Section III: The Lives We've Led

Foreword

When I was ten years old and first given the task of mowing my parents' lawn, across the street sat an old man, Mr. White. From his front porch, he would watch me hard at work as he swayed back and forth in his comfortable old rocking chair, occasionally spitting out the remains of his chewing tobacco. I thought, *Man, what a life!*

By the end of that summer, Mr. White and I were good friends. He taught me how to catch a muskie on the very first lesson, and we would sit on that front porch relishing the joys of fishing. He'd spit out tobacco and I would have at it with my black licorice. I was ten and he was ninety-two, and life was good.

As years passed, we would debate new topics like the inequities of Social Security or the war in Southeast Asia, and I would gaze on him as the master of knowledge and wisdom. The mysterious old man had become someone I learned to admire, respect, and love. When he died at 104 years, I lost a very dear friend.

Looking back, I see that Mr. White opened doorway after doorway of information and in turn sparked my lifelong appreciation of the elderly. I've devoted my life educationally and professionally to long-term care and retirement housing. Now, thirty-three years later, I am honored to have been asked to write this foreword as the Executive Director of Montgomery Place retirement community.

In the spring of 2001, when planning began for Montgomery Place's tenth anniversary celebration to be held that fall, our residents played an active role. They wanted to tell the world of the community's first ten years, how they contributed to its birth and development, and the synergy that makes up its present-day culture. A committee compiled a book of the "best of the best" articles from the *Montgomery Messenger*, the monthly newsletter, and named it *The Magnificent Messenger*.

That fall, even while the world stood still, Debra Sheridan of IVY Marketing Group pitched the story of Montgomery Place, its residents, and the *Magnificent Messenger* to Chicago media. Werner Saunders, local news anchor with NBC News, saw a correlation between the shock we all faced in the aftermath of September 11, and the wisdom and insight a prior generation of Americans could offer. At Montgomery Place, he filmed a special segment on how earlier generations had dealt with fear and crisis in their lifetimes. Residents gave their personal accounts of the Great Depression, World War II, the Cuban missile crisis, the tumultuous sixties—where they were, what they accomplished, and how they persevered.

Following the anniversary celebration, at the suggestion of Debra Sheridan, several residents began planning a book about Montgomery Place, its origins, and their lives prior to and after moving here. Three years later, after much working, writing, editing and re-editing, it was completed in the spring of 2004.

In It Together: Making a Retirement Community is not a conventional textbook on how to design or build a retirement center. This book is written by individuals offering their personal stories about how they did not let age interfere with their ability to contribute to an organization's growth and development into one of the finest, most diverse retirement communities in the country.

If you are like me, reading this book will open a window in your mind. You will find yourself day-dreaming for short while of what you would do given the same situation or circumstance. It will press your imagination to place yourself at that moment in time, at that point of history. You will be with that author viewing his or her experiences with new respect and, in some cases, envy.

As the authors tell of the early days of Montgomery Place or recount a century's worth of life experience, I am back to those days on the front porch with Mr. White. All of these elders have been leaders in their respective vocations. They lived during formative times when America changed by the day and contributed to our culture, civil rights, and personal freedom. I am honored to present *In It Together: Making a Retirement Community.*

> *Michael Apa*
> *Executive Director*

P. S. One condition that all the authors put forth to me and the Montgomery Place Board of Directors is that all proceeds from this book, after publishing and legal expenses, are to be placed into a restricted fund designated solely for use by future residents in need of financial assistance. The fund was established and is referred to as the Care Assurance Fund. The authors will continue to leave a lasting impression.

Preface

Before the Industrial Revolution, elders held a revered place in American families. They were teachers and mentors, the champions of tradition. When families started to splinter and younger generations sought urban opportunities, elders' role as contributors diminished. We began to provide "care" and to choose what we considered "best" for this segment of our population. Gradually, the aged came to be seen more as a drain on society than a wellspring of knowledge and experience.

Working with retirement communities since 1990 through her firm, The IVY Marketing Group, Debra Sheridan has often seen facility administrators trying to establish policies, create efficiencies, and impose programs they believed to be in the best interest of elderly residents. When the first directors of Montgomery Place attempted this, however, the activist seniors living here were no more willing to be told what to do and when to do it than they had been earlier in their lives.

In the spring of 2001, Debra presented the residents of Montgomery Place with the outline for a "historic book" to be written in time to commemorate the community's tenth anniversary that fall. (With the clarity of hindsight, Debra concedes her naïveté in believing the book would be finished in a mere six months!) There was immediate interest in the idea, and a group of eight fiery individuals accepted the challenge. The only question was how to bring to fruition a committee-produced work written by a group of people in their ninth and tenth decades of life, people for whom "retirement" is often a mere figure of speech.

As a writer for over thirty years and the initiator of the concept, Debra assumed her role with the committee would be significant: she would provide multiple literary contributions and would act as committee leader. In no time, she realized that she had committed the same folly as many a well-meaning administrator. This group did *not* need anyone else to do their work.

An important role in the project remained: the book's Cheerleader! Debra prompted, prodded, and encouraged the committee to keep working, to meet weekly. She set schedules and kept detailed minutes that helped everyone fulfill their commitments from week to week. Meetings convened on Wednesdays at 10:15 A.M. in the Activity Room and lasted about two hours. Typically, the time was divided equally between planning and reviewing material for the book, and laughter and discussion of myriad topics peripherally related to the task at hand. This combination of work and play brought everyone to the meetings anticipating both entertainment and creative accomplishment.

Also vital to the project was the role of Sidekick, which was readily assumed by Carolyn Allen. Coming from her position as layout artist for the monthly newsletter *Montgomery Messenger*, years of friendship with many Montgomery Place residents, and a conviction that nothing is more entrancing than a life story, Carolyn was drawn to the *In It Together* project as a moth to the flame. Offered the position of amanuensis/editor, she could not resist.

So while Debra was cheerleading and coordinating at the meetings, Carolyn was persistently at the side of committee members, encouraging rewrites and improvements. In addition to attending and enjoying the camaraderie of the committee meetings, Carolyn spent hundreds of hours gathering materials: talking with individual residents, transcribing tales, and editing and circulating preliminary versions of the book to the always eagle-eyed committee members. Many hilarious comments and serious changes later, a final draft was ready for publication.

Now, years removed from the original proposal, we are awestruck by the final product. However much we both contributed to the realization of this book, neither of us is responsible for the words, energy, drama, and entertainment you will find in its pages. That credit goes entirely to the book's many authors.

Sometimes old things become new again, and so it is in the twenty-first century with the resurgent respect for the elderly, the keepers of our traditions, our teachers and mentors. As volunteer Cheerleader and Sidekick of the committee who wrote this book, we feel eminently qualified to speak to the topic of admiration for the oldest generation.

What lesson is to be drawn from our experience? Truly it is this: listen to your elders; you never know what you may learn or what fast friends you may make. Anyone who aspires, as we do, to be successful in old age, should read this book and beam.

Debra Sheridan
Carolyn Allen
October 2004

Lake Michigan and Promontory Point viewed from Montgomery Place.

Introduction:
The Story We Are Writing

Today, all kinds of retirement communities are springing up. Montgomery Place is an unusual one. Since 1991, it has grown from a place where the administration and the Board expected to run a kindly institution to care for dependent old people, to a place where the residents have taken responsibility for creating an active and partly autonomous community within the framework of a building, facilities, and staff provided by the administration and the Board.

The story we are writing is about how the residents of Montgomery Place created the retirement community they want to live in. The story will be of interest to the growing number of people entering existing retirement communities or starting new ones, as well as to their families and the many professionals, administrators, and others who work with them. Expecting that many in our own and subsequent generations will face similar choices, we hope that sharing these experiences will be of some value.

Montgomery Place succeeds the Church Home for Aged Persons established by the Episcopal Church of Chicago in the nineteenth century. The Church Home was located in Hyde Park, a part of the city where citizen initiative and the University of Chicago created the first urban renewal area in the country and a stable, integrated community. When the Board of Trustees of the Church Home decided in 1985 to replace it with a retirement community, they elected to stay in Hyde Park and to name the building in honor of the retiring bishop, a strong supporter of

1

integration. They also believed that a retirement community in Hyde Park would better meet the needs of the coming century than a suburban community. So they built a fourteen-story building on the lakefront of Chicago, where retiring city dwellers could continue to enjoy the life that only a city provides. The symphony orchestra, museums, the opera, theaters, good stores, great hospitals, and, for some of us, our old offices—all are no more than a half-hour bus ride away.

Those of us who moved in during the first few months soon discovered that we had very pleasant, well-designed apartments, an inviting Dining Room, and space set aside for activities, but no plans for the activities themselves. A person called the "Activities Director" had her office in a room designated the "Activity Room," which she locked every time she left her desk. The only activities she initiated were a bingo game every Saturday afternoon, and, when we acquired a bus, shopping trips to malls and grocery stores. There were empty bookcases in the Library, and nothing but a mirror and an exercise bar in the Exercise Room.

We weren't expecting or wanting a "cruise director" who would provide us with constant amusement, and we found the vacuum actually gave us the opportunity to fill the void ourselves. We organized the legally mandated Residents Association in our own way and started a variety of activities.

Old age is a place to grow to. When still-active people retire, it is important to them to continue to use their talents and abilities. Having a creative role in planning, running, and participating in activities and programs is a way of continuing to feel a valuable part of the world. The pattern of resident initiation of programs was set in the first few months of Montgomery Place, and it continues as some old programs change and are revitalized by new residents, and new activities are added by incoming residents with fresh talents and capabilities.

As important as making use of old skills is the chance to experiment with new ones. To find that one can act or paint or write poetry can be an exciting surprise. To find that one can teach or become deeply involved in music or can be a successful journalist is an unexpected and very satisfying experience, an extension of oneself in old age!

This book is itself such an experience. It has been generated by a group of us who began working together at the time our community's tenth anniversary celebration was being planned. We wanted to write a book about how we came to create our unusual retirement community, and how that has affected the quality of our lives. While it has been a group effort, individual committee members have taken on primary responsibility for particular parts.

During the three years it has taken to complete this project, changes have been ongoing as various staff members have come and gone, and residents, too. Some activities, policies, and practices described herein have been altered or replaced. By the time the book is produced, published, and distributed, further changes will have occurred. Above all, Montgomery Place is a work in progress; an institution designed to meet the needs of the people it serves undoubtedly will change as need arises.

The book is divided into sections: The first, "How We Got Here" begins with "Meeting the Challenges of Old Age: Then and Now," which looks at how the lives of older people have changed in America over the past 150 years, and how this particular institution came into being in the context of those changes. Chapter 2, "Transition: Making the Decision and Making the Move," recounts residents' reasons for and experiences in coming to Montgomery Place.

The chapters in Section II, "In It Together," describe the various social structures, committees, and activities that have been started and run by the initiative of residents; how working together on these has made our lives richer and more satisfying; and how sharing in them has affected our personal relationships and built a real community.

Partly because of its Church Home background, and mostly because of its location in the liberal, integrated university community of Hyde Park, Montgomery Place has a marvelous mix of residents. We come from diverse backgrounds and have a wide variety of experience, needs, abilities, and expectations to draw on as members of the Montgomery Place community. Many have worked in service professions as doctors, lawyers, teachers, or social workers.

In the third and final section, "The Lives We've Led," more than seventy of us tell in our own words about the times, places, and events of our lives. Some of these memories reach back almost to 1900. These individual stories have been put into the larger framework of events shared by everyone who lived in the twentieth century.

Those of us who have worked on this book believe that most human beings, regardless of sex, race, or social background, desire to live in friendship and harmony with their neighbors. All of us enjoy getting to know new people, sharing our pasts with one another. When our neighbor has problems, we want to help; when he grieves, we want to share his grief. It is natural to care for others, and we are enriched by our mutual relationships. Our experiences reported in this book confirm this belief.

Elizabeth Jones Borst, Emily Ellison,
Jack Ellison, Aileen Howell Gordon,
Albert M. Hayes, Alice J. R. Hayes,
Allen Lang, Joan Swift

Section I:
How We Got Here

FIRST ANNUAL REPORT

OF THE

Church Home for Aged Persons

4327 ELLIS AVENUE

1890.

1

Meeting the Challenges of Old Age: Then and Now

In December of 1888, the Church Home for Aged Persons opened its doors at 4331 South Ellis Avenue to its first residents. In September of 1991, Montgomery Place, a modern continuing care retirement community and successor to the Church Home, opened its doors at 5550 South Shore Drive. One a modest three-story apartment house, the other a fourteen-story building overlooking Lake Michigan, they shared the mission of serving the needs of the elderly. Both institutions were established and operated under the auspices of the Episcopal Church of Chicago, both were located in the Hyde Park–Kenwood community on Chicago's South Side, and both represented the most popular model of a senior group-living facility of their day.

While the century that separates the establishment of these two institutions has seen many changes in all aspects of American life, one has not changed: Growing old is a fact of life.

Whether you subscribe to Robert Browning's optimistic words of Rabbi Ben Ezra:

> Grow old along with me!
> The best is yet to be,
> The last of life, for which the first was made. . . .

or Shakespeare's more pessimistic final stage of man

> Sans teeth, sans eyes, sans taste, sans everything

old age presents a challenge to individuals, to their families, and to society as they strive to meet elders' changing needs.

Aging is a process that starts before we are born and accompanies us throughout our lives, from applause for our first tooth, our first words, our first steps, to sighs of regret as age dulls our vision and slows our stride.

Like any stage of life, old age brings many benefits: a wealth of experience, accumulated knowledge, and, for many, freedom from earlier duties and responsibilities. It also has its vulnerabilities: loss of physical strength, vision, and hearing, and often the loss of spouses, colleagues, and friends.

Although it reaches us later today than in previous eras—when sixty was considered "old" and "three score years and ten" the most we could hope for—old age still presents a challenge.

Beyond the basic needs shared by all living things, we human beings have developed a number of social and psychological needs as well: Meaningful accomplishment, social contact, and personal independence and control of our lives. A baby needs the encouragement and involvement of his parents to learn to talk; as a growing child, he works hard to master many skills that bring a sense of accomplishment: the two-year-old's "me do it!" as he rejects a parental helping hand brings the sense of being in control. For the elderly, these needs remain important to a satisfying life.

The Industrial Era

Communities organize around the needs of their members. All societies provide for the weak and the vulnerable, the very young and the old, within the physical, social, and cultural conditions that prevail. The nature of this provision is a reflection of many factors, and changes with conditions in the larger society.

The nineteenth century was a time of major change in America, as the Industrial Revolution brought about a whole new way of life. The change from an agricultural to an industrial economy resulted in the breakup of many family farms that had constituted a major way of life for a large portion of the population.

The family farm provided roles for all ages: simple tasks for the young; hard labor for able adults; and less strenuous jobs for the elderly. There was room for the maiden aunt, the orphaned nephew, and disabled brother-in-law. The elderly played an important role in the household, passing on skills and knowledge acquired over years of experience and practice. Even the frail could feed the chickens, watch the pot, or quiet the baby. Family celebrations, community events, and social affairs included all ages; there was no need for "senior activities."

With the passing of the family farm and the advent of urban living, there was less opportunity for families to absorb members of the extended family. The elderly, the orphaned, and other needy individuals became the recipients of the charities that, fueled in part by the Protestant Evangelism of the end of the nineteenth century, were established by many religious and ethnic groups to meet the needs of their constituencies. The number of orphanages, poorhouses, and homes for the elderly grew rapidly during this time when few public programs were available, and those that were, were often punitive and demeaning.

Montgomery Place resident Mary Brock describes the efforts of religious leaders and of her own grandmother, a former slave, to meet the needs of elderly people at the turn of the twentieth century:

> After the huge catastrophe of the Great Chicago Fire in 1871, the city was rebuilt, and people began to pour in from all around the world, looking for work. Lawlessness and petty crimes increased as more and more African Americans arrived, unprepared in every way to live in the big city. When things began to look hopeless, the ministers of the two religious giants Quinn Chapel AME and Olivet Baptist Church joined together to attack the problem.
>
> Classes were organized to teach newcomers how to adjust to city life. Soon, responsibility for groups became a goal. Since the number of homeless old people had increased, one young woman donated her house for an old folks' home. It was called The Home for Aged Colored

People and was located on the corner of 29th and Dearborn streets. As the city grew, the home moved several times and was last known as the Jane Dent Home.

When I was a child living with my grandparents in the very early 1900s, Gramah felt the old, old people were neglected by the church. The government didn't do anything for them in those days, and young people sometimes got tired of the elders. So Gramah started the Old Mothers Circle. She met with them every Wednesday. The mortician—Chicago's first black mortician—would send his carriage to pick up the ladies and bring them to our house. They sewed quilts and talked about times when they were young. We would have a luncheon. Then after lunch, these old ladies would go out into the backyard and play tag, play "Drop the Handkerchief," try to jump rope, and play all the games they played when they were young. They had the best time!

By the late 1800s, the Episcopal Church of Chicago had already established several institutions in and around the Hyde Park–Kenwood area: an orphanage, the Chicago Convalescents Home, and, as early as 1861, the Home for Indigent Females, later called the Old People's Home.

The Old Church Home

The Church Home for Aged Persons, a three-story brick house on a quiet residential street, opened in 1888 to accommodate three old ladies of the parish, so that they "should not have to go to the County Poor House."* More formally, the Church Home for Aged Persons was established to meet the needs of "gentlewomen who had outlived family and friends, home and fortune, glad to find a refuge in which to end their days in peace."** It was the intent of

---

* Dale, Mary Alzina Stone, *A Century of Church Women: The Story of the Board of Managers of the Episcopal Church Home for Aged Persons.* Nappanee, Indiana: Evangel Press, 1996, p. 1.

**Ibid., p. 1.

the home to provide "all the comforts, if not all the luxuries, which may have been theirs during their earlier days."*

An admission fee of $300 was charged and the resident (initially referred to as "inmate") was required to turn over all personal property of value to the Church Home. In return, the individual received lifetime care and a burial plot. Single women, men, and couples were accepted. Though trustees were required to be members of the Episcopal Church, there was no such requirement for the residents.

Hyde Park–Kenwood in the 1880s was a quiet, upscale residential neighborhood, comfortably distant from the business section of Chicago's Loop, but close enough for easy commuting for business or shopping. It was characterized by large homes surrounded by spacious lawns.

The Church Home itself was not a poorhouse, as a contemporary description makes clear. "A stranger passing along Ellis Avenue . . . would never imagine that the brick houses midway in the long block . . . were anything . . . but the private residences of well-to-do citizens. . . . [N]o cozier room [than the Church Home parlor] could be found, [with] soft carpets, the walls prettily tinted, and hung with good pictures. Books and easy chairs abound."**

The Church Home was administered by a Board of Trustees (men) who handled the financial affairs of the home, and a Board of Managers (women), who tended to the day-by-day affairs of the home. From the first, the women assumed responsibility for obtaining the donations, in-kind and monetary, which covered the expenses of the institution.

It is clear from the descriptions of its work that the Board of Managers, and the many women volunteers from parishes throughout Chicago who assisted the Board, was the force that kept the institution running. Donations of all kinds were accepted. One listing from 1890 includes a half ton of coal, matting for the floor, screens for the windows, a bed, a mattress, a pillow, a comforter, a washtub, four sheets, and six mason jars. To "pound parties" for children, donors each brought a pound of something, ranging

* Ibid., p. 12.

**Ibid., p. 13.

from toilet soap to foods such as sugar, prunes, raisins, crackers, rice, flour, oranges, and eggs.*

Volunteers played a major role in all the daily affairs of the home's residents. Around 1941, one volunteer reported: "'[W]e took the residents shopping, to vote, out for drives. . . . [For] residents without income we formed the members fund and took pocket money to them each month . . . to provide things . . . the Trustees did not. We planned parties in the home . . . and we went with them on once-a-month outings, boat trips, bus trips . . . and even . . . an airplane ride over Chicago in a DC-3.'"**

The residents of the Church Home were cared for well and thoughtfully by the members of the Board of Managers and the volunteers they enlisted. The major (and most minor) decisions that governed the lives of these residents were made for them; they were almost entirely dependent upon others. It was a life of being "done for" and being "done to." Decisions not made by the Board of Managers were made by those who gave in-kind donations, or the Superintendent or the Matron.

Despite the seeming ability of the Church Home to attract residents, the dedication of its Board of Managers, and the fact that many of its patrons were individuals of stature in the Chicago community, the Church Home's history reflects a series of ups and downs, periods of prosperity and periods of financial stress. Funds to pay off the mortgages on the original Ellis Avenue buildings were early concerns. As time went by, funds were needed to cover the mounting costs of running the home.

The most serious—and persistent— concerns were reflections of the health and safety requirements pertaining to institutions like the Church Home, changes in codes and in enforcement that demanded expensive remodeling of the existing structures. The first of these resulted in the abandonment of the original Church Home buildings on Ellis Avenue in 1916 and their replacement with a building at 5445 South Ingleside Avenue.

The new building on Ingleside Avenue, built specifically to meet the requirements for facilities to care for the elderly, housed

*Ibid., pp. 3, 4.

**Ibid., p. 57.

seventy-five residents (more than doubling the capacity of the Ellis Avenue buildings), had an expanded infirmary and an occupational therapy room on the third floor. Sun porches on every floor as well as open porches and a garden, brought the Church Home to a state-of-the-art standard for the day.

Montgomery Place resident Elizabeth Jones Borst describes visiting the Church Home as part of the expected round of charitable activities in the 1920s:

> When I was a young bride, certain benevolent activities, such as visiting the institutional elderly and bearing gifts on designated holidays, were considered obligatory. My "obligations" extended to three such institutions: The Home for the Incurables, the Baptist Old People's Home, and the Episcopal Church Home.
>
> I remember the interior of the Church Home on Ingleside Avenue, as having long halls with linoleum floor covering. It was a sunny area, broken at intervals with clusters of rocking chairs. The chairs were often occupied by the elderly residents of the home.
>
> This backward glance reflects the age of the visitor, not of the visited. At about age twenty-four, I saw it as a sad scene and was moved by the silence of the rocking chair occupants and, indeed, of the home itself. My present interpretation, at age ninety-one, is a more intelligent and sympathetic one. I now know those rocking quietly were probably having their afternoon rest even a nap. They may have seen my presence, and the small gift I brought, as a disturbance. But they were gracious and cordial in their welcome. Only once did someone voice any complaint, and then the cross words concerned the slipperiness of the linoleum floors, and the single bathroom that had to accommodate the whole first floor. Any silence observed was a courtesy to a visitor, not a common state of affairs.
>
> Montgomery Place today emulates the Church Home in some respects, but differs in others. We are not always quiet, and we have no rocking chairs or linoleum floors.

A Century of Change

The hundred years that separated the establishment of the Church Home for Aged Persons and Montgomery Place witnessed tremendous changes in the political, economic, scientific, and social lives of Americans. While all segments of the population have felt the effects of these changes, none, perhaps, have felt them more strongly than the elderly of today.

These were the years that marked the lives of the early residents of Montgomery Place and others of their generation. The lessons learned through such events as the Great Depression, World War II, the Cold War, and the turmoil of the 1960s significantly shaped the attitudes and expectations of those who endured them.

With the 1930s came bank failures, unemployment, and economic hardship. Elizabeth Wissler remembers what it was like to be a teenager in the Great Depression:

In 1935, when I was a freshman in high school, my father suddenly found himself out of a job. Income was scarce, farmers didn't buy any more overalls, and then my father was completely out of work. My sister and I could see that he was worried and that made our mother worried, so of course we were worried. I was four years older than my sister and I felt responsible in some strange way for the family when I saw my father was getting shaky and my mother was wondering what next.

I guess I thought that it must be somebody's fault that there was a depression and I should talk with someone about it. One Saturday afternoon I secretly got my courage up and went to see my father's partner in their clothing business. I said to him, "What did you do that made my father lose his job?" The man said, "Well, I lost mine, too, and we are all in this together." I wanted some better reason why this had happened; it was scary.

With my father out of work, I got three jobs. Selling popcorn was the most adventurous. My sister and I ran a lively popcorn and peanut business that brought some income. We roasted the peanuts in our oven at home and sold them with the popcorn in a stand next to the only theater in town. The peanuts were warm and people liked them that way. I can still remember my mother roasting the peanuts, making sure she didn't burn them, but that they tasted "roasty."

Then I got a job washing dishes in a restaurant. I always washed dishes at home, but the pans at the restaurant were so big! I'd never seen such big pots and pans. I didn't mind dirtiness; it was a good thing to do. They let me eat supper at the restaurant for free also, so I liked that.

My third job was typing letters for my uncle, who owned a stationery store. I was fifteen or sixteen years old, and my typing was good enough to produce good-looking business letters. My uncle was very glad because he could pay me less than he would pay someone else, and he knew I liked to do the work.

For Leslie Orear and his family, the Great Depression was a time of pulling together:

Full of eager anticipation, I had entered college as a freshman in September of 1929 pretty much on a shoestring. I had my savings from a year's work as an office boy at fifteen dollars a week, and my dad had finally landed a pretty good job in public relations for one of utility tycoon Samuel Insull's pet projects, so, not to worry.

It was a crisp October afternoon as Alan, my new roommate, and I were walking back to the dorm from an afternoon with a fraternity that had invited us to lunch for a once-over by the brothers. There, on a newsstand, was a big headline about a stock market crash. I knew that would mean problems for the stenographers and clerks in the office I'd been working in. They were all "in the market," and forever calling their brokers, or gossiping with one another about American Can. But, no worry of mine, or so I thought!

Two years later my money was gone, my father's job wiped out with Sam Insull's financial collapse. I had to come home and look for a job to support my parents and two young brothers. Dad was broke, depressed, and alcoholic, and it was going to get worse.

The family upstairs in our South Side Chicago apartment house was in deep trouble, too. That winter, Mr. Dodd had been fired and sent to jail for stealing some turkeys at the Fulton Street market where he worked. Both families were about to be evicted, so we consolidated our miseries by moving together into a five-room apartment around 63rd and Cottage Grove. The Dodds were a mother, two very large teenagers, and a big German shepherd. There wasn't space for me, so I rented a sleeping room nearby. I was the one with a job. Dad provided what he could by borrowing money from relatives and friends. Fortunately, that ordeal only lasted a few months until Dad got a job on the Federal Writers Project of the WPA.

Less than a decade later, World War II interrupted the lives of millions across America and around the world. Alice Hayes was a young wife:

By the time my husband was drafted we had a baby, the first I had ever held. When her father went off to basic training, the baby and I became camp followers.

Every day I washed diapers, made supper, fed the baby and waited. Sometimes Ned came home and sometimes not. Once he came home saying that the sergeant had told him to have his hair cut before he came back at six in the morning, so I got out the scissors and cut. When I was through there were little round bald spots all over his head, but the army wasn't after beauty.

After basic training, because he knew French and a little Italian, Ned was sent to Columbus, Ohio, to learn German. Susan and I followed and settled in two rooms on the second floor of a ramshackle frame house. I was very lonesome, but of course Susan was company. She learned to walk and jump up and down on the bed and talk. I put up three jars of pears and set them on the windowsill, not to eat, but for reassuring decor. During the day I rarely had a chance to speak to an adult so I relied heavily on a radio soap opera called *The Guiding Light* for companionship.*

Like so many other future Montgomery Place residents, Willard Masterson was in the service:

When the clouds of World War II engulfed Europe, Uncle Sam decided that his enlistees would be given one year's training at the great salary of twenty-one dollars per month. Oh yes, our clothes and food were furnished, but once we paid our insurance premium of ten dollars a month and laundry charges, take-home pay was about eight dollars.

I went to Fort Benning, Georgia. While I waited for assignment, the Army decided I would become a wireman. A wireman straps a huge roll of wire on his back and runs to the future location of the new command post. In actual battle, this area has just been taken from the enemy, who are angry and do not like you trespassing on their property. This makes it a dangerous mission.

We were training with General George S. Patton's tank division, and I was ordered to take my wire to the new location of the training command post. I obeyed and reached the new location before General Patton and his staff arrived. I did my work and was hooking up the field telephone when General Patton looked at me on the ground and said, "Soldier, get to hell out of my way!" I stood up and said, "Yes, Sir!" and got out of the tent. I am proud to have had a conversation with such an outstanding war hero.

From Fort Benning I was transferred to the Huntsville Arsenal at Huntsville, Alabama, to fill an existing Table of Organization. We installed and maintained all communi-

*Excerpted from Chapter 8, "Word War II"

cations for this huge arsenal, which did nothing but
manufacture and transport poison gases and explosives
of all known kinds and filled special shells with the same.
After several months our company commander received
a communication that they were seeking Signal Corps-
men to go to Fort Monmouth, New Jersey, for officer
training. My statistics were right as I was a noncommis-
sioned officer and had a civilian background in telephone work. My company commander was very
democratic about the transfer. He said, "Masterson, you
are going to New Jersey." Soon I was in the big war.*

The Great Depression and World War II not only altered the
individual lives of Americans, but also brought about monumental changes in the political field—resulting in greater government
involvement in economic and social affairs affecting the elderly
and other populations. Social Security ensured that workers and
their wives or widows would receive benefits for life, based on their
lifetime earnings. A combined pension and life and disability
insurance, Social Security serves as a safety net for the majority of
workers. Such additional benefits as workman's compensation,
unemployment insurance, and federal guarantees on savings have
afforded further economic protection. Years later, Medicare,
second only to basic Social Security benefits, has eradicated a major source of economic insolvency among the elderly.

    With its return to normalcy and increasing affluence, the post-
war era saw continuing advances in medicine and science that have
eliminated many diseases that plagued us a century ago. Immuni-
zation, antibiotics, and improved treatment techniques have eradicated or markedly reduced the effects of many diseases at all stages
of life. Understanding of nutrition has helped in the prevention
and control of heart disease and stroke, two serious threats to the
elderly. Even diseases like cancer, long considered a death sentence,
are proving responsive to treatment. In addition to the general
advances in all areas of medicine, geriatrics now provides the elderly
with their own specialty.

*Excerpted from Chapter 8, "Word War II"

With broadened provision of welfare benefits for the needy of all ages, the role of private charity itself has changed. Its province is no longer a matter of supporting the basic survival of the unfortunate, but providing more specialized services to individuals or groups with special needs.

The role of women in American society has changed as well, since the cult of True Womanhood no longer holds sway, affecting philanthropic work. Within the last four decades, women have entered the workforce in increasing numbers, earning their own pension funds. A woman of the type who joined the Board of Managers of the Church Home as a volunteer in former times is more likely to be involved in her own career. For Montgomery Place resident Ruth Lang this included a job at Argonne National Laboratory:

> I spent the spring and summer of 1963 writing letters of application for jobs. Finally I had a call from the employment agency to set up an appointment with Dean Dalquest at Argonne National Laboratory. I had two daughters living in Chicago and I had wanted to live there for years. Most of all, I was between husbands: I could go anyplace my heart desired. So I made the appointment. I was instructed to go to the University of Chicago to meet a man who drove out to Argonne every day. I started looking for the place on the map—it was way out in the sticks! It was a long way out on the Stevenson Expressway, which was still under construction. I kept thinking, "I don't want to work there! I like my job at Whirlpool, I like my boss, and I haven't given notice yet."
>
> Bob Buchanan interviewed me for a job in the Chemistry Division. He made clear what was expected and explained the functions of the division. He made little pretense of looking at my book of sample illustrations and drawings, which had taken me so long to assemble. I felt at ease when I had my interview with Mr. Dalquest. Perhaps it was because I had already made up my mind I didn't want to work there. For the first time in my life I wasn't nervous at a job interview!

Finally, after several weeks went by an offer was made. So I went back. Mr. Dalquest assured me that he preferred a man. As a matter of fact, he had been interviewing men but he couldn't find one with my qualifications. In the meantime, I had been thinking about Argonne. It would be nice to live in the city and to work in the country. And, too, I could look for another job while working at Argonne. I thought I'd give myself about a year.*

Other changes taking place in the century of the Church Home's service to the community directly affected the Church Home itself. Legislation and statutes designed to protect the public presented a challenge to older institutions and agencies. New living standards, lifestyles, and tastes required changes in the institutions that had to accommodate them.

Lifestyles enjoyed by today's elders reflect the advances and encounters of the twentieth century. With improved health care and nutrition, and increased life expectancy, the term "elderly" no longer includes people in their sixties. At the beginning of the twenty-first century, more men and women are living into their eighties, nineties, and even hundreds. They are healthier, wealthier, and more independent than earlier generations. They are, in general, better educated, have traveled more widely, and have more demanding expectations from life—including "old age."

Changes in the Neighborhood

Hyde Park–Kenwood underwent a series of major changes over the years, beginning almost immediately after the Church Home opened. In 1891 the University of Chicago was established, and in 1893 the World's Columbian Exposition was held. The World's Fair of 1933 helped to further change the nature of the neighborhood. The Museum of Science and Industry, a legacy of the Columbian Exposition, today brings visitors from all parts of the world. The university, with a number of specialized libraries and museums and a major medical center, draws a diverse population

*Excerpted from Chapter 9, "Getting Back to Work and Family"

of scholars. Townhouses and apartments have replaced the magnificent mansions of the millionaires and city leaders who once occupied them. These large homes have been divided into smaller units to house a less affluent population of students and employees of the university, as well as migrants from the South seeking employment. Many of the communities that had supported charities like the Church Home were also subject to "white flight" to the suburbs, and they are no longer available to attend to the support of the Church Home.

In the 1950s and 1960s the urban blight that was encroaching on the Hyde Park–Kenwood neighborhood became the focus of a major urban renewal effort, which in turn brought about further changes in standards and requirements for institutions like the Church Home. Montgomery Place resident Albert Hayes was among those who participated in these events:

> In the spring of 1950 we bought a third-floor apartment containing five bedrooms, four baths, a mahogany-paneled dining room, and forty-three windows to be washed. It was a three-family co-op, and the second-floor owner, who was the chairman of the English Department, insisted that the third floor could be sold only to a person who had permanent status in the community. Hence the price was only $11,000. The reason it had become available was that during the winter of 1949–50 the Supreme Court had declared restrictive covenants illegal. We had never known of these covenants, which prevented African Americans from buying property anywhere in the Hyde Park–Kenwood area. The seller was unwilling to live in a block where African Americans were expected, and indeed the first black family moved in one week before we did.

> In Chicago real estate lore, it was a "certainty" that when one black moved into a block, all whites would leave the block within one year. This principle was not accepted as certain by either the university or the residents of Hyde Park. The university set up a program for neighborhood protection, which included

drawing up laws for the federal government to create "urban renewal" areas. This included provisions for purchase of property that was deteriorating and reselling the land at a loss for specified uses that would "renew" the community. It also provided that the university could supervise the drawing up of plans for the renewal and could get credit for property it purchased in pursuit of its general aims for renewal.

The citizens of Hyde Park took a different stance from the university. They organized the Hyde Park–Kenwood Community Conference. Its principle aim was to encourage new residents to join in preventing the creation of slums. The whole community was divided into block groups to welcome new arrivals as persons seeking to get out of the slums and urging them to join with the established residents in enforcing the laws that were intended to preserve the character of the neighborhood.

During that period, I had a treasurer's responsibility for some several hundred thousand dollars of endowment money belonging to the Western Unitarian Conference. The man who served as the broker to help me make appropriate investment decisions in those years was an Episcopalian, Francis Butler, who happened to be a trustee of the Church Home at Ingleside and 54th Street, three or four blocks from my home. In 1952 or 1953 he mentioned to me that his Board of Trustees was about to decide to sell the Church Home and move to a whiter neighborhood because they assumed Hyde Park would soon be all black. I immediately told him about the way we were working through the Community Conference to create a really integrated community. He thanked me for the information and apparently was able to persuade his fellow trustees to keep the Church Home in Hyde Park. For this reason, I feel that I had some part in the later decision to build Montgomery Place in its present location.

The urban renewal process induced the citizens of Hyde Park to take responsibility for the community they lived in. All of us are inclined to have strong opinions about national and international problems—problems we cannot resolve ourselves—but Americans too often forget that the problems of our own community are the only ones we can really expect to solve by our own activities. Many of us have learned this lesson and have brought this kind of responsibility with us into Montgomery Place. I think, in fact, that our training in working on local problems is one important source of our success in making Montgomery Place a community where residents assume responsibility for each other and for our common life.*

With the acquisition of the land for the garden and a large parking lot, acquired as part of Hyde Park's Urban Renewal Plan, the Church Home came under the requirement that all agencies utilizing urban renewal funding must be open to all ethnic groups. During the 1970s a small number of African Americans became residents of the Church Home. Montgomery Place resident Joan Swift remembers:

Some time in the 1970s my husband and I drove an elderly friend and professional colleague home at night from a meeting. She had been ill with heart trouble and as we dropped her off at her dark apartment I exclaimed about her living alone at this time. She said that her son was urging her to enter the Church Home, as he was also worried about her living alone. She was considering it, she said, and added that the home's director was also urging her to come; he wanted her as an active, involved person who would help bring more life to the group. It turned out that she did become a resident, one of the first African Americans to be admitted. At that time it never occurred to me that the Church Home was not integrated; this was Hyde Park!

*Excerpted from Chapter 10, "Community Involvement and Troubled Times"

The Closing of the Church Home

The factors that had triggered the inauguration of urban renewal in Hyde Park affected the number of parishioners from citywide Episcopal parishes supporting the home as well as the number of visitors to the home from other neighborhoods. By the 1970s the Church Home was no longer one of the Diocese's most favored institutions, as it had been earlier. It was having to strive to attract a new clientele. The appeal of lifetime care and protection was replaced by an appeal to a new generation of more independent seniors to "enjoy the privacy and freedom of a normal independent life . . . in a contemporary age group . . . in a facility where a spacious garden has been added for the enjoyment of the family."*

Further alterations to Church Home policies were needed to respond to the changing times and to the demands of a more affluent group of residents. Modifications in admission fees and financial arrangements were made. The original admission fee of $300 had been raised over the years to $1,000, then to $5,000. By 1967 there were two admission plans. Under the original plan, the resident paid an admission fee and conveyed all assets of value to the home. Under the second plan, the resident paid a moderate admission fee and a monthly fee but did not convey all personal assets to the home. By 1975 a further change required the resident to have individual medical insurance as well as paying an admission fee and a monthly fee; no personal assets were turned over, however.

In the end, it was the health and fire codes, upgraded over the years, that brought about the closing of the Ingleside building and the search for a new location. The purchase of land adjoining the Ingleside building was required to meet the newer standards, but the land was owned by the University of Chicago and not available. The Ingleside Avenue building was bought by the university, and the Church Home Board of Trustees was left with the decision of where to build a new Church Home.

The decision of where to locate the new building was a difficult one. The Hyde Park of the 1980s was not the Hyde Park of

*Dale, op. cit., p. 77.

1888. The constituency that had supported the home in its prime no longer lived on the South Side of Chicago but had moved north or to the suburbs. Finally, however, the decision was made to stay in Hyde Park. Bishop James Winchester Montgomery, for whom Montgomery Place was named, describes the decision:

> An important part of the reason to remain in Hyde Park was to take a stand in support of its diversity. The vast differences of religious, racial, and social economic backgrounds that have always prevailed in Hyde Park spoke to the Church Home's mission. This is where our Christian service began and where it was still needed.
>
> The 1980s was an era of "urban flight," when many prosperous white families fled from the city to the suburbs, leaving the less fortunate in the city. Remaining in the diverse community was an issue discussed among the Trustees of the Church Home Board because we knew that many Episcopalians had never lived in the city and would not consider Montgomery Place as a location for their retirement years.
>
> However, suburban Episcopalians would always have the option of choosing Montgomery Place if they wished to do so. Ultimately, the Board determined that continuing in Hyde Park was the most appropriate conclusion to meeting our mission.

The opportunity arose to acquire a prime piece of real estate on the lakefront, and the plans for a modern high-rise building overlooking Lake Michigan were drawn up. In keeping with today's trend in senior housing, the new facility was to be a continuing care retirement community (CCRC), offering both 165 apartments for residents wishing independent living units and skilled nursing care on two floors through its Health Care Pavilion (Health Pavilion).

Among the fastest growing industries in America today, CCRCs were originally limited to the Sunbelt states. They are now found in all parts of the country, in cities large and small, in suburban and rural areas, and vary in their sizes and in financial arrangements. Some are developed by large commercial chains, some are individual endeavors, and others are sponsored by religious organizations. Many of the latter, like Montgomery Place, have their roots in homes for the elderly that were established in the late-nineteenth and early-twentieth centuries—a far cry from the continuing care communities of today. (More information about CCRCs and the populations they serve are found in Appendix A.)

The decision to build and maintain Montgomery Place as a rental retirement community for independent elderly with no commitment for long-term care, was again a major change in concept and role for the Church Home. As in 1888 and 1916, the Board of Trustees aimed to provide a state-of-the-art accommodation to their prospective residents. It is to be anticipated that what constitutes the state of the art will continue to evolve, and Montgomery Place will continue to adapt to keep pace.

On September 14, 1987, the Church Home closed its doors and its remaining residents were placed in nursing homes, assisted by the then-current Board of Managers, until a new building could be built.

2

Transition: Making the Decision and Making the Move

Gradually it came over us that it was time—time to move out of houses and apartments we'd lived in, some of us for many decades. We began to feel the weight of the world on our backs, which were a lot weaker than they used to be. Our children began worrying about us. The basement needed cleaning and the roof started to leak again. We began dreaming about elevators.

For some, it was a matter of health: Stairs that one could go up two at a time forty years before had become a serious barrier to the bedroom; lugging groceries up to a third-floor apartment was now a misery. One resident confided, "I didn't know whether I could ever get up again if I sat down to rest on the top step of the second floor." Fear of an accident or a serious illness can erode confidence in living alone, or a spouse's failing health may make it desirable to have care nearby, allowing as much time together as possible without having to provide more physical care than one can manage. Some of us wanted to move closer to children or friends. Many hoped for company during the years when old friends were disappearing or becoming incapacitated.

So it came to us: the idea that we could move into a place where some of the difficulties of age were made easier, where we could still have independence and go on living our lives.

Then, in 1989, the word got around, first to people in Hyde Park and South Shore, of a facility to be built right here in Hyde Park, where every apartment would have a view of the lake and anyone over sixty-five would be welcome. Montgomery Place was in the works.

Resident Elizabeth Wissler was among those who took part in the planning stages:

> During 1989 and 1990 there was newspaper publicity about plans by the Episcopal Diocese of Chicago to build Montgomery Place on a 56th Street and South Shore Drive corner lot with a history of a good restaurant and a good motel that had changed hands and deteriorated into a poorly managed coffee shop, a motel frequented by prostitutes, and, later, a halfway house used by the state for homeless teenage boys. Neighbors were delighted at the prospect of a "respectable" plan for the corner.
>
> Public meetings were held in the neighborhood to tell about construction plans and interior designs for apartments and nursing home floors. Two of the tallest apartment buildings on the block sent representatives to protest Montgomery Place blocking their views of the lake and also adding to parking problems. After much discussion, architects were able to reposition plans for the building on the lot to the general satisfaction of all concerned. Space in the proposed parking garage would be offered to neighbors.

The site also pleased many prospective residents who identified with the Hyde Park community and felt at home in familiar streets. One longtime Hyde Parker recalls:

> We came to Montgomery Place with clear expectations of what life would be like: a fresh new modern apartment, a view of the lake, housekeeping service on a regular basis, one meal a day in the Dining Room to eliminate major cooking responsibilities, maintenance

duties cared for by someone else, indoor parking and the security of the Health Pavilion as a backup in case of need in times to come. I looked forward to all the free time I would have. My husband, who maintained his office at the university, looked forward to extra time freed up from maintenance and home ownership chores.

Sound reasons for moving overcame our very serious concerns about uprooting ourselves. For those who had lived a long time in the same place, the move may have felt as though it signaled the final end of an active life in the world. Retirement from a job may have meant a new kind of responsibility as a grandparent. Grandma's house may have been the family gathering place for birthdays and holidays.

There were worries, also, that living in a retirement community would mean the loss of independence. There would be rules. Someone would tell us what was good for us all the time, what to do and when we should do it. They would expect us to be amused by things that did not amuse us and grateful for things we didn't want. Dependency is a specter that haunts reasonably healthy and capable people, so freedom of choice about almost everything felt vitally important.

Then there was the big bugaboo: living with the aged. We are like the tourists who don't want to tour with other tourists, or those who say all people of a certain age look alike. (Just wait! You may never have had a chance to get to know such a variety of interesting human beings.)

One woman who had led a busy and adventurous life observes:

> I once took a course in child psychology. Among the terms that I remember is "developmental tasks." There were apparently exact times in one's life when it was appropriate to learn to eat, to ride a bicycle, to play football, and even to arrange for a wedding. I learned that these tasks do not stop at age forty. There is retirement and finally "downsizing" as one decides to move into a retirement community.

Some residents, like Joan Swift, had long anticipated the eventual need to downsize, as she writes:

Our decision to come to Montgomery Place was based on a number of factors, some immediate, some of many years standing.

The immediate: a ten-room house, three floors and a full basement; steep front steps with no handrail, a front lawn and hedge to be tended. We had lived in the house for forty-three years, climbed those steps, mowed the lawn, and clipped the hedge with enjoyment. But the time came when the steps were a challenge—and in the winter a menace—the lawn mower a struggle. It was time to move on.

When the plans for Montgomery Place were announced in the local newspaper, our decision was immediate. The building would meet our criteria for a replacement home: elevators for arthritic knees, a lake view, respite from major housekeeping chores and daily meal planning; indoor parking.

The major factors in our decision went much farther back, to our parents' experiences. My parents' experience provided us a "worst-case scenario," my husband's parents' with a "best-case scenario."

My grandparents on both sides of my family had lived in cities some four hundred miles from New York, where my parents made their home. On my mother's side, there was my grandfather, who lived in the home where he had grown up and then raised his own family. He lived close to his church and to the university he had attended and for which he had worked for fifty years. His wife managed the household with the aid of part-time help, who came in to take care of the cooking and cleaning. When my grandmother died, my mother was faced with the worry of providing for her aging father. He was in reasonably good health, but not able to cook for himself or handle the laundry, cleaning, and upkeep of the house. As my grandfather, deaf and becoming more and more forgetful, required supervision as well as housekeeping services, finding someone completely capable and trustworthy to take on the task was a problem and constant worry for my mother.

There was no question of bringing my grandfather to New York to live with us in our two-bedroom apartment, severing his ties to his church and friends. Frequent overnight visits, phone calls, and letters were the best my mother could do.

My father's mother presented many of the same problems. She lived in Niagara Falls, New York, in a good-sized house, in which she insisted on living alone after my paternal grandfather died suddenly. Fiercely independent, she resisted any suggestion that she have live-in or even daily help. My parents went through a period of looking for a house that we might buy in the city that would provide space for her to live with us, but it was clear she would never willingly accept this arrangement. The worry that she would fall down the steep stairs to the basement and lie there unconscious for days hung over my father. Keeping in touch with her next-door neighbors was the best he could do. When she developed heart trouble, his concern became acute.

My husband and I were determined that we would not subject our children to similar distress.

My husband's parents retired from their New York home to a retirement community for theologians and ministers in Southern California. Our experience of their retirement was an important factor in our decision to come to Montgomery Place.

In anticipation of retirement, they had bought an old farmhouse ninety miles north of New York City and used it as a weekend retreat. It was a lovely place with beautiful old trees shading a broad lawn, lots of space for gardens, and a dammed-up brook for a swimming pool among the trees beyond the rose garden. My mother-in-law, a writer, divided her time between writing and nurturing the rose garden. Her husband, a former professor, turned farmer and

planted corn, tomatoes, and a variety of green
vegetables, for possession of which he fought an
ongoing battle with the local woodchuck population.
In spring, summer, and fall it seemed an ideal retirement house—though the steep stairs and arthritic
knees limited use of upstairs rooms, and the weeds in
the gardens became harder to keep up with as time
went by. Winter was more difficult. Snow and ice
storms covered the roads and shut down telephone
and electric service for hours or even days at a time.
The isolation of the farm, anticipated with such pleasure in the midst of a busy, pressured city life, became
oppressive when the only neighbors became ill and
moved away.

My in-laws' move to the retirement community in
California proved a more satisfactory solution. They had
a small house with a rose garden and a compatible group
of fellow residents. My father-in-law taught a course or
two at a nearby college and used his administrative skills
in resident affairs in the community. As time went on,
and ill health became an issue, the move to assisted living
for one and to the nursing unit for the other met their
needs. For us, so many miles away and tied to a demanding home life, the knowledge that we would be notified
immediately if anything was needed made their decision
a tremendous comfort for us.

In making our own decision to come to Montgomery
Place, a major consideration was the solution it offered
for our children as well as for ourselves.

For other residents, the choice to leave longtime residences
for a new life at Montgomery Place required the careful weighing
of pros and cons. As Elizabeth Jones Borst describes it:

It was time to make a decision. My husband's life had
ended. My daughter, living in a distant city, responded
promptly to my brief hospitalization, but it was time to
make new and independent plans.

In my neighborhood was an attractive retirement community where many of my old friends were living. I made an appointment, visited, applied for admission, and was accepted. I sent a check to cover my security deposit with the assurance that this would be refunded if I changed my mind. (They never should have told me!)

Soon thereafter, the opportunity to travel more than a few blocks was suddenly offered and was more attractive. A brochure invited me to emulate Lewis and Clark on board a Columbia River ship. It was too good to miss! A telephone call to the retirement community retrieved my deposit, paid for my trip, and I was off. After all, I wasn't that old!

Once home after the trip I again needed to make a decision: Shall I continue to live alone in more space and with more responsibility than I need or want? Or shall I seek this protected setting with friends to join in many accessible activities?

Transition won: I moved. I find my energy needn't be spent on taking care of a big apartment and making elaborate plans to see friends. And this means I can travel more easily than before. I get high marks all around for making a good decision!

Badonna Reingold and her husband Haim also came to their decision over time, as Badonna relates:

I was born in 1934. My husband, Haim, was born in 1910. We married in 1968, when I was thirty-two and he was fifty-seven. In 2003 we faced the reality of degenerative aging in the form of several health crises occurring close together.

We were fortunate to have in our neighborhood a community retirement facility that offered a temporary option of renting a furnished apartment on a monthly basis, for a maximum of three months, without having to commit to a yearlong lease. After living there for six weeks, temporarily we thought, we experienced an epiphany-like crossover to make the move a more permanent one.

We had been planning to try to upgrade our three-story townhouse to make it more accessible and secure. I consulted an expert who recommended an outside elevator as a more enduring and efficient solution than a chair lift on our stairway. Haim, however, was determined to continue practicing stair climbing with the goal of being able to return to our house within the three-month time frame of our contract at Montgomery Place. Knowing this was his plan, I had not fully shared with him my anxieties and other reservations, wanting instead to encourage his positive, goal-oriented posture.

One evening we had dinner with friends facing similar dilemmas. One of them, a ninety-year-old retired psychoanalyst, recovering from his third stroke, was soon to be discharged from the rehabilitation service at the Health Pavilion. As we discussed our views of Montgomery Place, I blurted out that I would really prefer to stay permanently. Haim, in utmost surprise, asked me why I had not told him this before. He further questioned how I could, at my age, want to consign myself to a place where people are coming to die. It was to him a *moshav skanim*, a home for the aged, signifying the last stop on the way to death.

I launched into a spirited defense, talking about the glorious range of vitality and energy of the residents, saying that I couldn't categorize it as a place only of decline. I appealed to our friend the psychoanalyst to help me in addressing Haim's glum view. He wisely replied, "You know, this is really a matter of feelings, not reason." He talked about his own view that we are all facing aging and dying, and that many at Montgomery Place are dealing with these issues quite gracefully. By the time we parted from our dinner companions, I had a heightened awareness of the profound pain Haim was experiencing faced with the possibility of staying in a place which threatened to take away his hopes for returning to a life of independence, freedom, control, and fullness.

Back in our apartment, we continued our conversation. Haim said that he was not prepared to make the decision to stay or leave since he believed the weight of the choice was on me. As it was expected that I would outlive him, I would be facing the issue of living beyond the fact of our home's dissolution. He clearly didn't think it made sense to keep the house if we chose to stay at Montgomery Place. Furthermore, since I was his primary caretaker, he would respect and accept my choice if it meant more of a sense of safety and comfort for me. I confirmed that I was prepared to accept the responsibility for making the decision, and that my choice was to stay and settle into life's opportunities here.

He accepted my position and began to employ his more usual ways of coping. He talked about trying to get a larger apartment, planning ways to map out space for order and separateness. We also started planning how to begin to disassemble the overflow contents of our house of twenty-eight years. Even as we were thus engaged, he sadly talked of how he would give up the house with a heavy heart as it had great meaning to him.

For me, the decision signifies more peace of mind— the awareness that we are now in an attractive, modern place, set next to Lake Michigan, with the availability of service and care, giving me a level of safety not possible in our independent home and having the freedom to come and go without fear, knowing that help is there for us wherever we are on the premises.

Looking the Place Over

In 1989, a deep hole in the ground appeared on the corner of 56th Street and South Shore Drive; Montgomery Place was underway. Those of us who knew what the hole was for watched with interest. As the building grew, a temporary rental office appeared on the street outside. Some of us stopped by to get floor plans and took them home to study. The steel frame of the building took shape and we imagined our apartments nestling inside it. One eager resident remembers deciding on the tenth floor and imagining himself high on those naked girders. He wondered if his beloved piano, all half a ton of it, might have to be hoisted up ten floors by intrepid workers operating a complex arrangement of pulleys. Undaunted, he rented that tenth-floor apartment for himself and his wife. Pioneer residents, they moved in October 1991, and even today as you walk down the tenth-floor corridor you can sometimes hear him playing Beethoven or Bach or Scott Joplin on his treasured piano.

Someone else, a person addicted to good views, writes:

> While the building was under construction, I walked up and down the lakefront, siting with binoculars to see what floor we should try for. We wanted to see the lake and the beach and the park, but not the Outer Drive, while sitting down in our living room. We wanted to see the tops of trees but didn't want trees to block our view of the lake, and we wanted to be low enough in this four-teen-story building to see picnics and bicycles and swim-mers and lovers. The sixth floor turned out to be the end of the site line. We were lucky and got exactly that.

Since the apartments are of various sizes and shapes, having the floor plans was extremely convenient. Once we had decided to move we could see how our furniture would fit. Those so inclined could even make a scale drawing of the apartment and cut out little scale sofas, chairs, tables, and beds, and move them around on the scale drawing. This was fun and helped to avoid unhappy surprises when the furniture actually arrived. Some people just took their chances.

Packing Up

Having decided to move and having reserved an apartment, the grueling work of actually moving began. Sorting, deciding, parting with cherished objects, books, pictures, clothes, furniture, dishes, pots and pans . . . sometimes this is an acutely painful process. And then to

top it off, there is packing! At this point almost everybody thinks they've made an awful mistake: better to have stayed and moldered peacefully away in familiar surroundings, living on peanut butter sandwiches and cottage cheese, and watching television all day.

However, we pulled ourselves together, and, for the sake of our heirs and descendants, we got to work. Grown-up children can be good at deciding what to throw away, and homes were found for usable discards. If we were lucky, we had grandchildren just moving into their first apartments or children who had houses with attics.

Everything packable was packed, and moving day finally came. The boxes and furniture huddled all over the old living room floor were ruthlessly carted away. Although many different kinds of people have moved into Montgomery Place, and although we come from many different lives, all of us have been through the ordeal of moving.

Being a Resident at the Start

Alex Coutts remembers his historic arrival at Montgomery Place:

On September 16, 1991, I became the first resident of Montgomery Place. I was greeted by the Bishop and the Director, and immediately suggested that they had forgotten the red carpet, the brass band, and the photographers. I was joined by Ralph and Calla Burhoe that afternoon, and by Don and Barbara Fiske the next day. We usually ate together in the nearly empty Dining Room and looked out on the top of the garage. We watched the contractors haul in all the dirt, and plant the ground cover and trees that became the garden. For about two weeks we ate catered food—pretty good too—because the Chicago Health Department hadn't gotten around to inspecting and approving the use of our kitchen.

So it was in the beginning, and I should mention that it was the first time I was first in anything!

During the early months, Alex welcomed new arrivals. Sitting in a chair in the front hall, he was the greeter, and before long he was known to everyone as "the Mayor."

While early residents were ready for Montgomery Place, the building itself was not completely ready for them. Elizabeth Wissler describes the situation:

Tony Bale, who became the first Administrator, was determined to open on the exact date announced to the public. Some surprises turned up. Kitchen equipment was not in place, resulting in having to bring in food from nearby restaurants. The front desk was a card table and two chairs. A male R.N. from Rush Homecare checked in twice a week. Handrails did not exist. There were only a few grab bars. Washers and dryers were coin operated with no source of quarters.

These and other deficiencies had an upside! Resident initiative and participation were a necessity for the twenty-odd initial residents (the second and third floors were not yet appropriately licensed). The first Director of Housekeeping had a hard time making it through the day in her three-inch heels and tight skirts. A resident who was still a licensed physician responded to various emergencies and anxieties at night.

By Christmas every one of the eleven residential floors was at least partly settled, and residents were looking out their windows at the lake and beginning to assess their new lifestyle. The building itself was pristine and comfortable: clean white walls and light-colored carpets; plenty of bathrooms and ample closets; cords to pull in an emergency; heat in winter and air conditioning in summer; blinds to let in as much or as little light as struck the fancy of each apartment dweller, and everyone's own furniture neatly disposed in their own living rooms and bedrooms.

The architect designed the building so that every apartment has at least a glimpse of the lake. The windows on the south look out on the 57th Street Beach, Jackson Park, and the Museum of Science and Industry, an imposing relic of the 1893 World's Columbian Exposition. On the north the windows look over the garden, planted with young locust trees, and east to Promontory Point, a mecca for walkers, bicyclers, joggers, and baby buggy pushers all year round, and for kite flyers, swimmers, and picnickers in summer. The east windows have a 180-degree view of the lake with all the activities of the park and beyond, the Outer Drive in the foreground.

An underground garage, entered from the basement, lets cars quickly reach the Outer Drive and thence to all highways in every direction. The Health Pavilion on the second floor provides for those with Alzheimer's disease and other dementias and on the third floor accommodates patients needing nursing care temporarily or permanently. Thus a couple can live here in the same building and see each other daily, even though one has needs that the other cannot meet.

For a while we were all very much occupied with the stacks of boxes and bundles blocking the open space on our apartment floors. When we changed our minds about the arrangement of furniture, we could get someone from the Maintenance Department to move the sofa or the bed. They even helped hang pictures in those early days. Finally, after much bending and lifting and folding and losing and finding and lying down to rest, we had stowed our possessions.

So there we were: the original settlers. We'd unloaded our covered wagons and staked a claim to our share of the rest of our lives. And what happened?

We noticed there were no books in the Library, no paints in the Activity Room, only an exercise bar and mirror in the Exercise Room. We looked at a bleak schedule of activities: one movie a week (selected by who-knows-who?), regular Episcopalian services in the chapel, Bingo, meals, a moderately large television near the jigsaw puzzle in the Lounge, and, in warm weather, the garden to sit or walk or dig in. So the original settlers began having ideas.

We were, by and large, people who had led active, creative lives. We were teachers, social workers, doctors, economists, ministers, scientists, and a sprinkling of artists and businessmen and -women. (This is still pretty much the mix.)

Meanwhile, the administration was valiantly trying to run a benign home for dependent old people. It would take a while for these well-intentioned administrators to give up the Mommy-knows-best way of dealing with our suggestions and to learn what kind of retirees they were dealing with.

Section II:
In It Together

First Floor, Montgomery Place

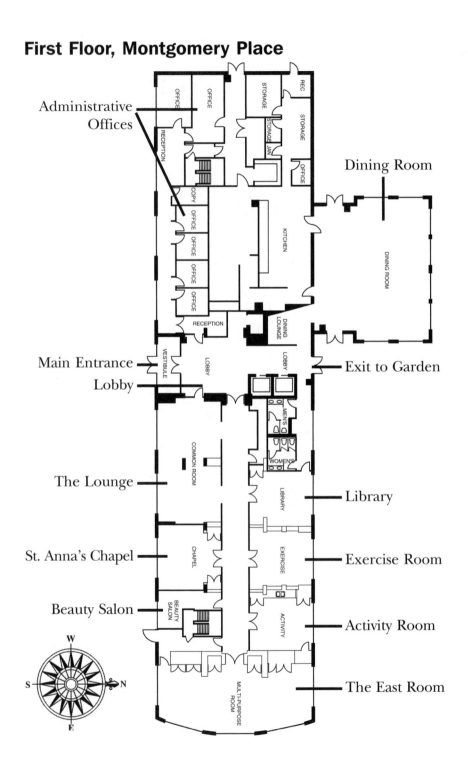

Administrative Offices

Dining Room

Main Entrance

Exit to Garden

Lobby

The Lounge

Library

St. Anna's Chapel

Exercise Room

Beauty Salon

Activity Room

The East Room

3

Taking Charge:
Making a Community

Getting old is a different ballgame from what it was when the Church Home began. Lifestyles are very different, the sources of help are different, the very concept of old age is different.

There is a new kind of space to fill between retirement and incapacity, a limbo between taking care of and being cared for, and, although it is an ambiguous place to be, we still need opportunities for meaningful accomplishment and creative activity. We still need to make as many of our own decisions and to live as independently as we can. We still need friendly contact with other people.

Residents Association

The original Montgomery Place administration had come from the old Church Home, a kindly paternalistic place for "helpless" old people, to a retirement community for people with some independence left. So at first there was some conflict between us residents, who were trying to do things for ourselves, and the old-style administration, which thought it knew best what would make us happy. We, on the other hand, had moved into a building where the apartments were designed for independent living, and we began working to make a community out of it.

So it was a surprise when, in December 1991, the Activities Director suggested that we organize a Residents Association. This was the first sign that the administration recognized that this retirement community was different from the Church Home. A group of seven residents emerged as a steering committee. A small subcommittee was appointed to draft bylaws, and chairs were appointed to organize committees for some other essential jobs.

On January 22, 1992, the Residents Association convened for the first time to talk about plans and to contribute further suggestions. The temporary committee chairs reported on their activities and solicited members.

The Bylaws Committee consisted of three retired professors from the University of Chicago, and the results reflected their experience with faculty structures at the university. Their work began with a request to half a dozen retirement communities scattered across the United States for samples of their bylaws. This is what resulted:

Section 1.02, states the purposes of the organization as follows:

To encourage and promote an atmosphere of general concern and friendship among the residents of the association.

To initiate and implement, in conjunction with the staff of Montgomery Place, programs contributing to an active, enjoyable, and useful community life in a healthful environment.

To initiate and implement in an effective way, with the staff of Montgomery Place, in conjunction with the Board of Directors, changes that reflect the environmental concerns of the residents that are valid and need changing.

The bylaws provide for a Council of eleven members and two alternates. Six Council members are elected in even-numbered years for two-year terms, and five are elected in odd-numbered years. The two alternates are elected for one-year terms, and are available to vote in the place of absent Council members and to replace any Council member who cannot finish out his term because of illness, death, or any other cause. The present rule requires a nomination (by one person) and a signature of the nominee that she or he is willing to serve.

The bylaws were discussed at a meeting on April 22, 1992, and formally approved at a meeting on May 5, 1992. The first election was conducted in May, and in June the first Residents Council took office.

Committees defined by the bylaws distinguish between those dealing with matters that affect all residents (food, garden, health, housekeeping, and maintenance) and committees related to special interest groups (art, book discussion, music, needlecrafters, poetry, playreading, etc.). The Council appoints the chairs of the first set of committees, and the groups of the second category choose their own leaders. The Council elects its own president, vice president, and secretary.

The Council has proved very useful. Four times a year it conducts a meeting of the whole resident body, at which committee chairs report on their activities and address any issues raised by members of the association. This has been a good way to let off steam and enables residents to call attention to matters that may not have been sufficiently dealt with in committee. Meetings of the Council may be open to the general association, if the Council so desires, or closed, if that seems best in view of its agenda at a particular time.

At the time of this writing, all residents at Montgomery Place are renters, but we do not have easy access to our "landlord." Management stands between us and the trustees, who obviously cannot deal with the problems of each individual tenant. Some of the matters residents become concerned about cannot be changed by management because they come from decisions made by the Board of Directors. The Council has turned out to be the one tool we can use to communicate with the Board. The Board has consented to have two representatives of the Council as non-voting attendees at trustee meetings and they have been able to convey some of our concerns. The Council representatives are barred, however, from the Executive Committee meetings and from some parts of some Board meetings. Board membership remains a desired, but so far unattainable, goal for residents. However, it is still possible to say that the Council and its several committees have played a major role in developing a community spirit at Montgomery Place, and some of the Trustees have worked hard to familiarize themselves with residents and their needs.

Committees of the Residents Council

Quality of Life and Health Care Committees

The Board of Trustees realized early on that creating a state-of-the-art continuing care retirement community involved more than a new building and revised fee structure. Elizabeth Wissler was on the committee to assure residents of a compatible environment from the start:

> Beginning in 1989 and 1990 the Board set up an advisory committee co-chaired by Tony Bale, manager of the old Church Home, and Jean Stephens, a member of the Board who was the Director of Bowman Center, the geriatric rehab arm of Rush Medical Center. Among others on this committee were Dr. Christine Cassel, Director of Geriatric Medicine at the University of Chicago; Rev. Bernie Brown, an Episcopalian and dean of Rockefeller Chapel; the chaplain of the old Church Home; a lawyer from the Rush Medical Center; an R.N. director of one of the V.A. hospitals; the administrator of a retirement complex in Hinsdale; and me as representative of the Hyde Park Community.
>
> The purpose of this committee was to listen carefully to experts in fields relating to the care of the elderly and to put together quality-of-life recommendations for the Board. This committee met monthly and then weekly in 1991 until Montgomery Place opened in September.

As early residents unpacked moving boxes to hunt for winter gloves or a favorite paring knife (both of which might turn up in a box marked "picture frames"), various other needs began to emerge that seemed to be related to the concept of "continuing care." For instance, a resident needs help after falling out of bed twice in one night, then tripping over an unpacked box.

Then, there were the questions:

"Why aren't the grab bars in the right places in the bathrooms?"
"When will we get handrails in the hallways?"
"What about a massive nosebleed on the living-room carpet after midnight?"
"How can I get help with my eye drops four times a day?"
"Is my sudden chest pain at 2:00 A.M. indigestion?"
"Who will show us how to use the exercise machines safely?
"What about flu shots?"

Greatest needs always seemed to come at night, on weekends, or on holidays. Although a resident couple (medical doctor and social worker) helped to respond to night calls for some weeks at the outset, it became clear that one part-time registered nurse provided by Montgomery Place through Rush Homecare Agency was not enough to meet the promises of continuing care.

Rather spontaneously, a group of residents with professional expertise in nursing, social work, physical and occupational therapy, psychology, nutrition, and geriatrics assembled as a Residents Health Care Committee. Our Administrator, Chaplain, and Medical Director, and a representative from Rush Homecare were invited to meet monthly with the committee, and we became vital partners. Two members were liaisons with the Health Pavilion to keep the committee informed of developments.

The Health Care Committee strongly supports the concept of preventing illness through resident education and participation. Over the years, many experts have talked in our East Room about health matters such as diabetes, strokes, heart attacks, and falling; how food and medication needs change with age; and other topics such as incontinence, exercise, hearing aids, low vision, Alzheimer's disease and other dementias, and sleep.

Residents' participation in fitness opportunities has increased steadily through the years. Chair-exercise classes are held three times a week, and strength-training sessions are offered twice a week. There is a water aerobics class at a nearby pool one day a week, and those who love to walk can do so Monday, Wednesday, and Friday mornings at the neighboring Museum of Science and Industry before its doors are opened to the public. Another option is walking in the park across the street or along the shore of Lake Michigan.

The committee has worked hard over the years to establish detailed plans for coping with emergencies, so that residents, their families, and staff can be assured that "continuing care" has predictable meaning. The addition of a public health Wellness Nurse and a Director of Resident Services has been invaluable in coordinating services of caregivers and assessing the changing needs of residents as we age.

For example, we discovered that although we had emergency cords in our apartments to pull, occasional accidents made further checking necessary. So the residents improvised a door-check system to make sure everyone was okay each morning. You had a tag to hang on the outside doorknob when you got up in the morning. A volunteer on each floor checked the tags, and if there was no tag out by nine o'clock, the volunteer knocked or telephoned to check up. Though this was a worthy and thoughtful plan, it didn't work very well. People forgot to put out their tags, or they overslept. Sometimes, alas, even the volunteer checkers forgot their job.

Management was alerted to the problem, and now we have little acrylic tags attached high on the doorframes. They are flipped up late at night by a security guard and fall down the next morning with a reassuring little click when the door is opened. The guard checks in the morning, and if the tag hasn't flipped down he knocks to make sure all is well. If nobody answers, the receptionist at the Lobby desk telephones the apartment. If the phone isn't answered, Security enters the apartment to check on the resident's well-being. It's reassuring to know that somebody will find you if you're lying on the floor.

Bit by bit, the administration has appropriately taken responsibility for many health care needs at Montgomery Place. Nevertheless, the Health Care Committee finds that ongoing vigilance and monitoring are necessary. The committee's focus will continue to change as we age in place and function increasingly as an assisted living facility, while still others of us need skilled nursing care, rehabilitation, and long-term care in our Health Pavilion.

Food Committee

The Montgomery Place Food Committee is composed of individuals whose backgrounds, education, and experience make them especially suited to their positions. In addition, the members all like food, all must eat, and most have firm opinions that they are eager to share. Meetings of this committee are held monthly, chaired by a physician, a resident with special experience and knowledge of nutrition. The Director of Food and Dining Services joins them to give information and advice. The committee members come prepared to present specific requests from some of their neighbors.

"The chicken and dumplings for late diners was mostly dumplings. The early birds got the chicken."

"There is a pressing need and an unfulfilled desire for three-bean salad."

"Please remove the skin from all potatoes served." (The chair and committee members pointed out the nutritional value of the skin to the complainer, but in vain. At a later date, he brought news of his extended trip to an exclusive resort where "not one potato was served with the skin on.")

From the beginning, the resident Food Committee has worked with the Director of Food and Dining Services to make suggestions and to monitor the healthfulness as well as the tastiness of the food we eat. It was the committee's early efforts that removed salt and much fat from the menu. (There's plenty of salt on the tables, and those who want it can shake it on.) Our menu always includes a vegetarian dish among the five entrée choices, and, if nothing suits your individual diet, you can always order an omelet made with cholesterol-free eggs. If you don't want the cake, pudding, or pie dessert-of-the-day, you can always get fresh fruit or a dish of ice cream. Thanks to Catrine Guzik, our present Director of Food and Dining Services, who comes from Paris, we now have very good food, and, thanks largely to the years of effort of the Food Committee, we can not only eat well, but can eat without damage to our hearts or stomachs.

Another important decision was in the arrangements for meal service. As apartments began filling up, the Director of Food and Dining Services suggested dividing the population into first and second sittings. The residents, speaking through the Food Committee, insisted that everyone should be free to come to the Dining Room whenever it is open and to choose whomever they wish to share a table with. This system has made it possible for residents to get acquainted with a larger proportion of their fellow residents and thus has fostered a sense of real community.

Recycling, Housekeeping, and Maintenance

One policy introduced on the initiative of a committee is the collection of paper, cans, and bottles for recycling. Garbage and rubbish in secure bags goes down a chute from each residential floor near the west end of the building. At the east end, every floor has a room where the service carts for housekeeping and market baskets can be housed. The Housekeeping Committee realized these rooms had space for containers to receive recyclable materials. Since the City of Chicago requires owners of buildings with more than three residential units to pay for removal of trash and recyclables, management found this suggestion financially feasible, and residents gained the satisfaction of being socially responsible citizens.

The Housekeeping Committee found that residents and management did not always agree on what kind of service should be provided in the biweekly visits of the cleaning staff. Meeting with the Director of Housekeeping, the committee arrived at a written description of what was expected and how much time could be available for what size apartments. Suggestions were made about the laundry services provided by the building, and the quarter-eating washers and driers in the residents' laundry room were replaced by machines that operate at no charge.

The Maintenance Committee struggled with various items that troubled residents. During the first year of operation, many complained about a steady dose of dust particles that continued to appear every day. Gradually the dust diminished, and

Kiyo Hashimoto takes advantage of the
recycling facilities; one room is available on every floor.

eventually disappeared altogether. The general consensus was
that the carpets laid over the concrete floors had been the real
source of this annoyance. Problems connected with hot water,
heating and air conditioning, and the care of the garage, as
well as the establishment of a woodworking shop in the basement, have all been dealt with by this committee, with the
cooperation of the maintenance staff.

The Welcoming Committee

During the first three months of operation, new residents were visited by the Activities Director on the day they moved in. Soon, resident Aileen Gordon took over the job, meeting and orienting newcomers and answering questions: "How in the world do you turn on this shower?" "How does the heat work?" "What can I do with all these extra books?" Later, Aileen and another resident created a booklet that also answers questions.

More importantly, for the ten years she lived here, Aileen made newcomers feel that there was a familiar person in a strange place. Aileen talked with them about their past experiences and wrote a thumbnail sketch for the next month's *Montgomery Messenger* news-letter. Her warm manner and her arranging for introductory din-ners became a major way of making new residents quickly feel welcome. She also introduced them at the quarterly meetings of the Residents Association so that others could identify them.

While Aileen was the friendly moving spirit for this project, other residents have been inspired to help. Although she is gone, the Welcoming Committee she started continues, and biographies of newcomers continue to appear in the *Messenger*.

Another device for helping residents to connect with one another is a photo directory of residents that enables people to associate faces with names. Originally we had a professional portrait photographer, but he could come only once a quarter, which was not often enough. Then he moved away from Hyde Park, so we asked for help. The volunteer resident photographers who answered the call have ranged from talented amateurs to noted professionals. The directory is kept in the Library for general consultation. As one resident says, "If we think about not having the albums to consult, we begin to realize their value in binding us together as a community."

Montgomery Messenger

Even before the organization of the Residents Association, the *Montgomery Messenger* began to take shape. A group of residents met in December 1991 to determine what our various interests were, who had skills and expertise to share, what new directions might be explored, and what needs could be met. They saw that

MONTGOMERY MESSENGER

May 1999
Volume 8, No. 5

The Newsletter of the Residents of Montgomery Place
5550 South Shore Drive, Chicago, Illinois 60637

RESIDENTS COUNCIL ELECTED

Residents re-elected Betty Borst and Hewson Swift and elected new members Phyllis French, Ben Meeker, Frank Wagner, and Virginia Bensema for two-year terms to the Residents Council. Charles Greene, now serving on the Council, was elected first alternate and Margaret Walters was elected second alternate.

Elected last year, and with another year to serve, are Albert Hayes, Elizabeth Jacob, Evelyn Kitagawa, Lester O'Dell and Ben Spargo.

After the May Annual Meeting of the Residents Association, the new Council will elect a President, Vice President, and Secretary.

Participation in the election was 98 out of a possible 164, or 60%.

HOW WE VOTED FOR ALDERMAN

In the April 13 run-off election for Fifth Ward Alderman, 267 people voted in our precinct, a 47% participation and 14 fewer than voted in the February 23 city election. Barbara Holt, the incumbent alderman, got 104 votes, 25 less than in February. Leslie Hairston, the upset winner, was a winner in our precinct as well, with 153 votes, 22 more than she got in February.

RUMMAGE SALE BOOSTS DANCE FLOOR FUND

The second Montgomery Place Rummage Sale was held on Sunday afternoon. April 18, in the East Room and netted $251.85 toward the purchase of a dance floor. We now have about 65% of the money needed for the dance floor.

In addition to the rummage sale. we collected $135.44 from the lost penny jar at the front desk. The "50/50" raffle sold under 25 tickets but made a small contribution

The first hour of the sale was the busiest—we took in $200 in the first hour. Special thanks go to all the staff who helped gather, set up and take down the items: Tina Johnson, Kineta Riley. Jackie Sheperd, and Gloria Johnson. Residents Camille Raimondi and Iola Slade were terrific checkout ladies and salespeople. Residents were very generous in donating items for the sale. Items that were not sold are being donated to a charity which helps the homeless

Many residents suggested that we have a sale every other month, and I think this is a good idea. It will not only help us buy a dance floor, but also will help residents do a little spring cleaning in their apartments. **The next sale will be Thursday, June 11,** from noon to 7 p.m. in the East Room

Carrie Jaksic

Do you want to grow plants and/or vegetables?
To reserve a garden plot, pot or planter, call Frank Wagner at 4035.
Gardening is BYOT (Bring Your Own Tools).

The monthly Montgomery Messenger, *written and edited by residents, has not missed a single issue since its inception in January 1992.*

all needed an organ of communication within the building, and so on January 1, 1992, the infant *Montgomery Messenger* was born. It was named by a resident newspaperman and edited by some enthusiastic editors. The layout was cut and pasted and photocopied by the few residents who had computers on which they could more or less process words. The first proud issue, four pages long, told of potential groups and meeting times (further development was up to the groups themselves). Thus began a newsletter that hasn't missed a month for over twelve years.

Gradually this has become a more sophisticated publication and an important channel of communication, information, and entertainment. The *Messenger* prints a complete schedule of coming events in the building, both regular monthly activities and special events. The Administrator has a column in which he can make announcements and explain whatever is on his mind. Sometimes the *Messenger* includes articles by a resident biologist on subjects like birds in the garden or ladybugs in the apartments, or a series on adventures on public transportation by a journalist-historian who goes to his office every day on the bus. As a major road construction project began just outside our windows, one couple became our roving reporters, and for three years they reported their observations and conversations with the hard hats about what the great yellow dinosaurs below were doing. We waited eagerly for each new copy of the *Messenger* to soothe our fears that what we watched was simply the creation of chaos.

Every month, although the editors remain stable, a variety of people are listed as contributors since it takes the efforts of a dozen or so residents to produce this newsletter. In the beginning, before the building had filled up, there were 100 four-page copies printed each month. Now the *Messenger* goes out to families and friends as well as prospective residents and trustees, and we publish 600 twelve- to fourteen-page copies every month.

The Library

The Library has been entirely created and operated by the residents. In a sense it is a major activity, but one with an established place. It is used by nearly everyone at Montgomery Place, including staff and caregivers. We were lucky to have had an English professor to set it up, and then a resident who has become a skilled amateur librarian to run it since.

When the first residents arrived at Montgomery Place, the Library was a handsome, empty room. On the east wall, bookshelves had been created from pressed wood and a mahogany veneer. There were no books and no plans by management for getting books. In front of the windows was a table with a lamp and two easy chairs. The principal furniture was two long tables parallel to each other, each surrounded by comfortable chairs. It was explained by the management that this room was intended to be a private dining room. One door led toward the Dining Room for easy service.

We decided we would see what we could do with contributions of books from people who were moving in. We also decided that the smaller section of bookshelves should be reserved for reference use. One of the Church Home residents who moved into Montgomery Place had been a reference librarian. Her efforts ensured that we got two sets of encyclopedias as well as other important reference books.

As the books appeared, we cataloged each in the simplest possible fashion: author, title, and category. The Library Committee met once a week, sorting books into different categories and then writing up the data for the cards to be produced before the next meeting. Categories were limited to large groups: fiction, mysteries, poetry, social science, art, history, biography, and perhaps one or two more. By having a catalog, we could avoid accepting duplicates.

It did not take long to fill up the limited shelf space. A Hyde Park resident who specializes in making bookcases was asked to bid on building new bookcases to match those already supplied, but with sturdier wood. When this bid was taken to the Administrator, he hit the ceiling, saying, "When I am ready to buy more bookcases, I will have my architect design them. You are usurping my authority!" His bookcases arrived several months later and did not fit the space available for them.

Among the many interesting and amusing episodes involved in assembling the Library, one deserves to be mentioned specifically. A well-known psychiatrist, Maria Piers, decided that she would not have room in her apartment for all her books, so she carefully divided them into two sets of boxes: those for her apartment she labeled "MP" for "Maria Piers," and the others she labeled "MP" for "Montgomery Place." Only after the moving men had completed their work, did she discover that many of the books she wanted in her apartment had been placed in storage in the basement for the Montgomery Place Library.

We soon found that in addition to duplicates, we had to start eliminating books that were unlikely to be useful for Montgomery Place residents. So we found other agencies that might welcome the books and also made a collection of books to be passed on to the Hyde Park Co-op's annual book sale.

The Activities Director had funds adequate to supply cards for the card catalog and cards for sign-ups to be placed in each book on the shelves. Additional needs were met by using income from an endowment given the Library by resident John Rust in memory of his wife. The first purchase was a magazine rack wide enough for at least three magazines in a row, and five or six tiers of such rows. The magazines themselves were contributed by residents after they had finished reading them. Another purchase was a carousel to accommodate paperbacks. Our endowment fund has proved very handy for maintaining the Library's independence.

In the first years of the Library, residents also contributed newspapers. Now the Library's income is used to subscribe to newspapers, and the Library has become a place where people spend hours every day reading the *Chicago Tribune*, the *Hyde Park Herald*, the *Chicago Sun Times*, the *Wall Street Journal*, the *New York Times*, and the *New York Times* large-print edition. Many people subscribe to newspapers that are delivered daily to their apartment doors, but the subscriptions can be expensive, so as world news becomes more and more engrossing and controversial, the newspapers in the Library are devoured. A computer is available to residents for e-mail and Web viewing.

Our concern for those with failing vision has led to an impressive collection of large-print books, many obtained from Chicago's Newberry Library by a resident who is a longtime volunteer there. Others have contributed to the growing collection of audiotapes available. Also in the Library, we have a closed circuit television which magnifies print up to twenty-five times on its screen and makes reading possible for many who can no longer read in any other way.

Col. Ed Johnson with visitor Darius Brooks in the Library.

In 1995 or 1996, resident Barbara Fiske took over the running of the Library, which has more than doubled in size since that time. Bookcases have been placed in the hall toward the Dining Room and along the wall of the corridor leading to the East Room. Barbara succeeded in getting each section of books arranged alphabetically by author or, in the case of biographies and histories, by subject. This has greatly facilitated finding books.

A substantial and growing category of publications—books written by Montgomery Place residents—is kept in the hallway. Both professionally published and self-produced, their contents range from poetry, memoir, and autobiography to the scholarly and professional.

The Library Committee believes that books create a homelike atmosphere in any room. Some books and magazines have now moved across the hall into the Lounge. Art books are in a separate closet in the Activity Room, from which they may be rotated to table space around the building. Children's books are in the Exercise Room for visiting children to use; and some overflow of light reading now sits on tables outside the elevators on each floor. Although small as libraries in the great world go, our Library is an amazing collection with something for every taste, and is a valuable part of our lives.

Garden Committee

Early resident Alex Coutts remembers sitting with John Rust in the empty Dining Room and watching trees being planted in the garden. The little locust trees had to be established on top of the underground garage on piles of dirt dumped to make small hills for their roots to spread in. The trees have taken to their hillocks and have grown large and leafy in spite of the thinness of their soil.

The basic plan of the garden is a checkerboard of squares lush with pachysandra, each with a tree in the middle and surrounded by a border of bright colored impatiens. There are walks and benches and a small green for croquet or quoits. There is also a statue of St. Francis, who, with the help of our chaplain, Father Bob Petite, presides over the annual blessing of the animals. For this event, dogs and cats are brought out by their owners in arms or on leashes. They eye each other uneasily; there is an occasional growl or hiss, the blessing is said, and all hurry back into the safety of their own apartments. Some animals, cats in particular, have been known to attend the blessing ceremony in a snapshot held by their owners rather than risk the great outdoors.

The residents loved the garden from the beginning, particularly the wide border beds available for their use. Elizabeth Wissler writes a lively account of the arrival of Betty Wagner, who was a devoted gardener:

Gathering for the annual blessing of the animals is Ginny Bensema with Amy;
Esther Meyer; Faye Dickerson with Calico; and Montgomery Place
Chaplain Father Bob Petite with Brodie, as St. Francis looks on.

It was a sparkling fall day late in October of 1991.
Longtime friends were moving into Montgomery
Place. This involved the moving of nearly all the
Wagners' backyard plants. It took three trips in their
station wagon to transfer the many perennials, includ-
ing some bushes and an abundance of wild flowers.

I was in the garden when I saw Betty carrying boxes of
plants. That morning she had asked the front desk where

she could plant her garden. She had been told that she could not plant anything yet even though she had been promised a lot of good dirt.

So Betty proceeded to plant everything and said she was delighted with the results as well as being dirty and tired: "Nobody stopped me and I would not consider living here without my garden!" Thus the Wagners *and* their backyard moved in without front-desk approval, but with great pleasure to themselves and the rest of us.

The Wagners' garden flourished for eight years. Betty was always out there in gardening weather, wearing her wide straw hat and apron, and her husband Frank was the first chairman of the Garden Committee.

We also have many vegetable gardeners and the committee has provided a small shed for gardening tools. In the spring, the Garden Committee assigns the available lots and planting begins. Every summer the beds at the west end are loaded with tomatoes and other highly edible delights. (An avid vegetable gardener regularly leaves baskets of goodies in the late summer on the little table opposite the elevators.) People in wheelchairs can garden in pots and flower boxes. One year there was a box with a charming mixture of real and artificial flowers planted by residents from the Health Pavilion.

Probably the crowning achievement of the Garden Committee came when it persuaded management to have an automatic sprinkler system installed. At first, the system came on just as people were taking a stroll after supper, and, although it is not unpleasant to be watered on a very hot day, it was felt that most people might prefer to stay dry. Soon thereafter, the timing was changed so that the sprinklers now come on automatically at midnight.

Resident Vinnie Orpen reflects on what gardening means to her:

Having my own garden plot while living in a retirement community in the city is a great gift to me. I was able to bring some plants and a couple of young trees from my previous garden and planted some spring bulbs even before we moved in. There are also links with

previous residents' gardens: a sundial, an iris, and some
bulbs. These connections with the past delight me.

Later on during my first summer as a resident, I was
allotted a much bigger plot. I was told it had been a glorious garden, but it had been neglected for the last three
or four years. Climbing vines were winding their way up
many plants; bulbs had become overcrowded, and plants
that had not flowered in several years were thickly
spreading. I had dug up all the grass in our front and
back "postage-stamp" size city yards, so I enjoyed this
challenge. As autumn approached with dropping
temperatures and stronger winds, my determination to
dig up all the roots of the weeds and other undesirable
plants was shaken by doubts about my willingness to finish the job and get the bulbs I dreamed of into the
ground. I was greatly encouraged by the many residents
who stopped by and talked with me: "What *are* you
doing?" "What are you going to plant?" "How wonderful
it is to see this garden becoming more civilized, more
cared for!" "It's been so long since I've been able to get
down on the ground to garden like you!"

We'd talk about their gardens, their favorite flowers,
and how much we were all looking forward to spring and
flowers again. The garden has been put to bed now; the
bulbs, both new and old, have been planted. In a few
months I'll start dreaming of what may bloom and what
plants I may add. A wonderful thing about a garden is
that there are always new things to do in it—and there
are always going to be surprises.

Resident Doug Anderson, an ornithologist, planted some
nursery-stock trees of a flowering species that bear seeds to attract
birds. Unfortunately, before they had a chance to grow, some helpful soul, probably thinking the small seedlings were dead, pulled
some of them up. (Helpful souls should be aware that some nursery stock is delivered in a dormant state.) So to our garden rule "If
you didn't plant it, don't pick it" should be added: "Don't pull it
up without direction of the gardener."

Alice and Albert Hayes and Davina Wong in the garden.

Birds are not our only visitors. We have squirrels, of course, and lately a veritable infestation of little bunnies that grow up to be full-size rabbits, thanks to the delicacies available in flowerbeds and vegetable plots alike. Keen observers may find other types of wildlife, as Margaret Matchett relates:

> I like to sit in the garden at dusk. It is a quiet time, but it has surprises. In early summer, clouds of lightning bugs arise from the ground. Recently, as I sat, I was aware of a disturbance in the impatiens flowers nearby. Its cause was a creature I did not recognize. It was about the size of a hummingbird, and had the same way of fluttering its wings rapidly so it could hover over a flower. It explored each blossom with what appeared to be a long bill. Later I asked a new resident, whose knowledge of nature is encyclopedic, about the stranger. He was sure from my description that I had seen a hummingbird moth. Certainly the name seemed appropriate. What I

had taken for a long bill is really the tongue, used by the moth to forage for nectar.

From summer until late in the fall, the big windows of the Dining Room are full of green and dancing locust leaves. People walk up and down the paths and sit on the benches to talk or rest or occasionally to eat a picnic out of a bag packed upstairs in their own kitchens. It is not necessary to plant a single flower to get full benefit from the garden.

Art Classes

From early in the life of Montgomery Place, the Activity Room, with its sink and cupboards, has been used by the artists and craftspeople among us. There have been art classes, painting groups, and open studios. For a few years, a potter's wheel occupied one corner of the room. A volunteer pottery teacher brought us ready-to-use clay and fired our pots at the Hyde Park Art Center half a mile away. A small loom is available for weavers. The uses of the room have varied over the years, depending on the artists and would-be artists in residence at the time.

Jean Bowman, a distinguished economist, was remarkable for her enterprising exploration of new talents after eighty. She participated in the Poetry Group, took a four-year Great Books course at the University of Chicago, traveled on a sailboat in the Aegean Sea, and went to Chile and Easter Island. She went to India with her son to attend a student's spectacular traditional wedding, where she was treated as an honored elder.

Another discovery was painting. Jean describes the first art class at Montgomery Place, taught by Hal Haydon, a Chicago painter. Though he was handicapped by severe Parkinson's disease, students found him an inspiring teacher:

It's all Hal's fault!

Here I am at fourscore years and four, and here is the result of my very first adventure with a paintbrush.

Some people at Montgomery Place were just starting a painting group. I had no intention whatsoever of joining them, but about halfway into the first session I happened to pass the door of the Activity Room, and, being mildly curious, I poked my nose in. Ann asked me to join them. *Me!* I'd known I was a dud since my nine-year-old sister kept asking me (then fifteen) to draw what she was drawing because her drawings were so very much better than mine. After all, if your little sister could do that, wouldn't you know you were a dud? But since I had no ambition to paint I was quite willing to please Ann.

That's my big advantage. Since I don't expect to do anything professional, I can just have fun. So I figured that perhaps for this one time I could do something—a Charlie Chaplin with a top hat and Ross Perot ears so big he would have to cut slits in the brim to accommodate them. I didn't know how to get flesh tones, but what did that matter? Lime green would do very well. Ann sat me beside Hal Haydon, and that was fatal. I quickly gave my Charlie a lime green collar to match his hair. And of course his black tie chose to fly.

I guess Hal was interested because everyone else was working so seriously, and I was just going at it in a slapdash fashion. I gave Charlie eyebrows and a sweeping mustache, just the right expression (quite by accident, of course—but I knew it would spoil things to add eyes and mouth). Hal gave me a rudimentary lesson, "Leave space for highlights on the hat," and then, "put some red on his cheeks." "How about a red nose?" By now my Charlie had turned into a clown. His jacket and pants, which I had outlined with paint, could *not* be black.

"You haven't given him any hands." Done.

"He needs a background." Sky duly provided.

"How about giving him some flowers?"

I decided the first flower had to be blue, but the only thing I knew how to represent was a daisy, so he first got a blue daisy. (Yes, I know there are blue asters but that didn't occur to me at the time, so it's a blue daisy.)

The feet are reminiscent of Charlie Chaplin. I'm glad
I put some ground under his feet, but not too close to
them. It would never do to bring him too close to earth,
don't you agree?

That's how it all started. I had no idea what else I
might do, but I came again, and now Hal has me hooked.
He's dangerous!

After this initiation, Jean took painting classes at the Art Institute and became an enthusiastic painter.

Much later, after a hiatus in art groups in the Activity Room,
another artist, Jane Overton, moved into the building. Soon she
found herself the head of a new art program.

When I first came to Montgomery Place, there was no
arrangement for carrying out artwork on a regular basis,
although there was a pleasant, spacious room with a closet
bulging with equipment that had been used in the past. A
friend who had been attending music classes at the Cultural
Center downtown but could no longer make the trip asked
me if I would start an art class. I was a bit hesitant since I
had never taught art, but then I learned that the most
successful classes here have been those with minimal instruction, so that is the way things work now. Equipment,
help, and suggestions are available. Angela Lee and I run
the class with two volunteers from the University of Chicago
Laboratory Schools. They take out suitable materials from
the closet, occasionally act as models, and seem particularly
to enjoy choosing and putting up arrangements of the
residents' artwork. We are provided with an abundance of
material: watercolor, acrylic, chalk, pastel and oil pastel,
charcoal, and a variety of sizes and types of paper.

Portraiture is the main interest of some participants.
Angela brings her mother, Marie, with her to class, and
seats her comfortably in the middle of the room, where
she is a willing and favorite model. A second major interest is still life. There are a number of plants and flowers
around, and I always bring a bunch of fruit chosen for

color. One resident brought her own subject, a favorite teakettle. We have also had some acrylic abstract art, and drawings of things remembered such as mountains, camels, and elephants. A resident who produced one of my favorite pieces sat for a long time doing nothing, then outlined each of her open hands on the paper together with what looked like the path of a fly.

Our first sale of paintings by people at Montgomery Place occurred spontaneously several years ago at a time when a very special occupational therapist was working in the Health Pavilion with dementia patients. With his encouragement, some of them painted such wonderful pictures that our first art show and sale was held in the East Room that year. Every painting sold.

A number of years later there was another show, this time of pictures painted in Jane Overton's art class. She and some helpers, while clearing space in the supply closet, decided to turn the Activity Room into a gallery and sell artwork to visitors at the bargain price of one dollar each. Some of the exhibitors were pleasantly surprised to see their previously discarded pieces looking quite professional, and some even bought back their own work!

Music Committee

Musical programs have been very popular events at Montgomery Place almost since the beginning, thanks to musical Hyde Parker Mildred Ries. She writes:

On a day in March 1992, I popped into Montgomery Place to check whether plans for my moving in were in order. I was feeling happy about coming to the community. Into the room came Ann Parks. She greeted me with: "Oh, you are coming! Now we can have music!" She had touched my "bliss" and I replied, "Sure!" I had been a program director of the Hyde Park Music Club so I was familiar with many fine local musicians. We could have live concerts from time to time, and I could offer regular recorded programs. I started with recorded music each Wednesday evening after

dinner. Live concerts were planned for some Sunday afternoons. Preparing tapes and records for Wednesdays was a
delight. I used my own collection and added visits to the
Chicago Public Library Music Department, gathering
material for short introductions.

The white- and gray-headed listeners became a regular
audience. Occasionally Ann and Bob Parks brought a record player
downstairs to play somebody's treasured old records, and they often
sounded as good as the latest CD. An active Music Committee
evolved from this beginning, and now on Wednesday evenings
members of this group take turns sharing the music they love.
They also arrange for our live Sunday afternoon concerts.

An enthusiastic member of the committee, Jack Ellison,
recounts his experience:

It never occurred to me before we came to Montgomery Place that I would become addicted to music. But I've
done that—and with great pleasure. When we moved in,
I learned that there was a musical program scheduled for
one hour every Wednesday evening. A genuine interest
in music is all that is necessary to become a member of
the Music Committee.

Soon I found I had the responsibility for a program. I
had been listening to piano sonatas of Schubert and of
Beethoven, both played by Alfred Brendel. These were
two of the only ten compact discs we owned at that time.
I thought it would be interesting for the audience to hear
one movement from each of the two composers. Two
songs of Schubert and a few words about Alfred Brendel
would round out the program. Playing these CDs over
and over again taught me how to listen with more care
and greater perception.

Over three years I must have done fifteen programs,
ranging from Haydn to Poulenc. In each case there was
music included which I had never been aware of before.
Looking back over the programs, I realize how much I
learned from the planning process, which involves choices,

organization, timing, and awareness of the audience. The music, of course, is central. At its best, this process includes elements of creativity. Older people need opportunities to feel they can still be creative in different ways. Montgomery Place nurtures such creativity. We all need it.

At first our sound system didn't live up to the high standards of the Music Committee. Hewson Swift, then head of the committee, writes:

By 2000, the original hi-fi equipment, purchased in the early 1990s, was limping along. Only half the amplifier was functional and one of the tape decks was beyond repair. A member of the Music Committee compared the situation with past troubles with the Montgomery Place bus—repairs promised for the future but not today. Another member felt the television screen was too small, and suggested we get a bigger one. These comments stung us into action. We visited eight different electronics stores, one in company with Father Bob Petite, and finally got the equipment we needed.

Now we have a wonderful sound system to use, and the Wednesday producers play and talk about all sorts of music. It's interesting that two of our regular music producers are blind, but someone stands by to keep the hi-fi in order and to help change the tapes and CDs as required.

Recorded music isn't all we've had. As Mid Ries recalls:

I wanted us to have a piano for the concerts. We had only an upright. With the memory of my husband in mind, I visited Steinway in the Loop, chose a grand piano under reconstruction, and offered it to Montgomery Place. That very day, Maria Piers moved in and brought along her magnificent old Steinway grand piano. I returned to the Loop and canceled my order, and Maria's piano was put in the East Room where large audiences could enjoy it.

The September 1992 *Montgomery Messenger* reported:

> The first of a live concert series planned by Mildred
> Ries for Montgomery Place will be on September 20 in
> the East Room. Martha Faulhaber, a well-known Chicago
> pianist associated with the Chicago Children's Choir, will
> present a unique program, which she entitles "The Call
> of the Birds." For this she has chosen from piano litera-
> ture music inspired by birds, works of Rameau, Daquin,
> Messiaen, Schumann, Amy Beach, Ravel, Granados, and
> Liszt—music spanning the centuries.

Mid Ries was acquainted with all the talented musicians in Hyde
Park and some farther afield, and the concerts she arranged were
played by professionals or talented students. They have been willing to play for us without fees. We are a very appreciative audience
with a good piano to offer—plus lemonade and cookies after a
Sunday afternoon concert.

Music was an abiding interest for resident Alex Coutts. He had
a beautiful bass voice, and although he had sung in choruses and
church choirs all his life, he didn't have a chance to begin serious
voice training until, in his eighties, he cut down on the amount of
time he spent at his office and began taking voice lessons. On his
ninetieth birthday he gave the first of three annual concerts in
Chicago's Fine Arts Building. The hall was packed. He walked
briskly onto the stage, wearing one of his tartan ties, fully in
command of his audience. He sang familiar American music, Scot-
tish folk songs, spirited show tunes, and operatic numbers. Because
he had been a staunch member of the Unitarian church choir for
many years, and the leader of the small group of singers at the
monthly Unitarian services at Montgomery Place, the church
celebrated his ninetieth birthday by having a professionally
recorded tape of his first downtown concert made.

Alex continued singing right up to the time of his death. At
one rehearsal his caregiver joined in and was discovered to be a
promising tenor. After some practice, he and Alex sang a duet of
"Amazing Grace" at the end of Alex's final concert.

The Saga of the Piano

In September 1997 the following notice appeared in the *Messenger:*

The Steinway grand piano, owned by the late Maria Piers and lent by her for our use in the East Room over the past four years, will remain as a permanent possession of Montgomery Place. The instrument has not been well maintained in recent years, but Montgomery Place has now contracted with Steinway and Sons to have the piano completely refurbished in their factory in New York.

The considerable funds needed for the rebuilding have been most generously donated by a few residents, who have also provided for the purchase of a matching artist's bench. Our old piano should now look better and sound better, and when it is settled back into its old surroundings we plan to arrange a concert of piano music in its honor.

The Piers piano, a rare C size no longer manufactured, was built in New York in 1921. Steinway estimates that the repairs will take about six months. On completion we should have a really excellent instrument, with modern action, but with a case and keyboard representative of the fine workmanship of a past generation.

The June 1998 *Messenger* published this progress report:

As most of you know, the Piers grand piano was sent in October 1997 to Steinway and Sons in New York for reconstruction. This included completely new action, restringing and refinishing, and the installation of a new sounding board. This work was finally completed in mid-May. We now have a superb "like new" instrument. We have sent the final payment to cover the rebuilding and

Renowned pianist Amy Dissanayake is one of the many musicians to perform in the East Room.

the piano will be shipped back to Montgomery Place as soon as possible.

We have been blessed with many concerts using our marvelous piano. It has been played by professionals and talented amateurs both as a solo instrument and in chamber groups. It has been played in recital by Hyde Park piano students. It has accompanied school choruses, concert singers, all sorts of instrumentalists, and singing groups of various kinds. And for our piano-playing residents, it is a treasure beyond price.

Sitting together and listening to music is not only a very great pleasure but has a mysterious way of bonding a group of miscellaneous people. Quietly sharing the same sounds does something to our feelings for one another.

Poetry Group

Alice Hayes, the longtime facilitator of the Poetry Group, writes:

The Poetry Group began a few months after Montgomery Place opened. I had written poetry all my life but had never taught it. I risked announcing that anybody who loved poetry could meet in the Library on Monday mornings. To my delight, a half-dozen residents showed up on that first Monday morning and read poetry to each other. More came, and that liking has been powerful enough to keep the group going for a dozen years.

We have read a lot of poetry: Keats and Byron, Gertrude Stein, A. A. Milne, and Shakespeare. We have read our grandchildren's poems, and poems we read as children and to our children. Very soon we began writing our own poems.

Although nearly everybody who joins the class has begun by announcing that they love poetry but have never written any and would certainly not begin now, they have mostly become hooked on writing it. They tried writing about what a small smooth rock sitting on the table sounds like, or a blind man's description of a meadow. Every week we had an assignment—voluntary homework—write a poem that is a letter or a list, or your earliest memory. Write one using only words of one syllable; no adverbs; no adjectives; no rhyme. We experimented with traditional forms: sonnets, villanelles, sestinas, haiku.

Over the years these non-writers have produced several home-published books of poetry that are on a shelf

Elizabeth Jacob, Ann Parks, Marion Murphy, Phillip Harley, Lillian Century, Alice Hayes, Grace Bibler, and Barbara Fiske of the Poetry Group.

in the Library right next to Wordsworth. Several members of the group have collected entire books of their own poems. After Natsuko Takehita died, her friends outside Montgomery Place printed a collection of the haiku she had written in the class. Here's one:

> If one hears old age is coming
> Lock the door and reply
> No one at home.

Jean Bowman, the economist who learned to paint and began traveling extensively after she moved to Montgomery Place, also continued her lifetime habit of writing poetry. For her ninetieth birthday she compiled a book of poems written at different times in her life and gave a copy to each of the guests who attended her party. Here's one of her Montgomery Place poems:

Lost Again

I cannot find it.
Could it be
That it is in the library?
Perhaps I left it on a chair, then where?

I may be wrong but I don't think
I'd stick it in the kitchen sink.
But now I'm wondering what I lost
And at what sort of mental cost.

I say—could I have lost my brain?
Ah, there it is! It's just my cane.

Mary Brock was writing the life of her grandmother, who was born into slavery and came north as a very small child after the Civil War. Mary also wrote many wonderful poems. Here's one of them:

Wind—A Sonnet

With bold demonstrations capricious and sly
The wind masks his mood and intent.
He soars and sings then seems to die
Ready to pounce then relent.

Wee baby breezes like to tease
They whisper and giggle and sing.
But wind waits in deep gullies
Or on pinnacles ready to spring!

See pushed back curls of cloudlets' hair
Wind tossed and rain storm free
Just to nuzzle the neck of a shoreline,
Fond lover the wind can be.

Wind can be soft, loving, and kind.
Wind can be harsh and hard to define.

From Alberta Gray there were ballads about the black experience in Chicago:

Hungry Black Children in the Hood

Through the window across the way
Not just on Sundays but every day

The neighborhood children could easily spy
Fried chicken, collard greens, and apple pie

Black children so hungry they could hardly bear
To smell that magnificent bill-o-fare

The lady next door was a very good cook
Whenever they could they would take a look

At that fine dinner she made for her man
He had a steady job we understand

Black men with steady jobs were really quite rare
And that wonderful aroma was everywhere.

He would cut a slice of apple pie
Taste the juice of the apples then mutter, "My! My!"

That fortunate man could eat and eat
When his lady performed her culinary feat

He did not look up at the many eyes
That watched him dine on those apple pies

Though they hoped, still they knew
There was nothing to gain

By pressing their noses
To the windowpane.

Grace Bibler, an energetic Quaker, who started the sewing group at Montgomery Place and ran the Friday night series of talks for many years, wrote in response to the assignment "Write one of your earliest memories":

Going to the Museum

Mother's hand is there for me
With a light clasp she guides me.
She can see the way
I can see winter coats and pant legs.
She steps over puddles
But I stump through them.
As she looks down at me
I say, "I'm sorry," but inside I smile.
When we reach the big steps
She slows down a bit.
She knows I need two feet on each.
It's a "together" trip for two
And a holiday thing to do.

Laurie Fish, who claimed at first to be no poet, had lived in Israel with her husband. She wrote this:

The Way to Jerusalem

1
Up to Jerusalem from the sea
even the unchurched special journey
Canaanites climbing high places.
Across the plain of Sharon and up
bare hills, their woods lost to old wars,
look mowed.
Long cropped by sheep and goats
The thin earth almost gone.

2
An old forest whose branches shed gold
joined each year by a new crop of youngsters.
Now in spring the birds stop by
and the voice of the turtle is heard
while under the trees the cyclamen grow
as on the plain the storks stalk to and fro
before the land goes dry.

We also have written group poems for various occasions. Going around the table, each person contributes a line on a given theme, and surprising doggerel results. Here's a contribution to the *Montgomery Messenger:*

Senior Citizen Month
[a group poem]

"Senior's" an evasive way to say
We are getting old and gray,
But, though we're old, we are not cold,
And we are canny but not sold.
And though I'm in the golden years
They sometimes seem rusted with tears.
The world moves faster, faster, faster.
Sometimes we need a comfort plaster.
Age means I cannot go so far
Because I've given up my car.
And all the old familiar vices
Are lost amid forbidding voices.
And yet, although I'm aged now,
I look for moonlight on the bough.
For in the end there's nothing to rival
The tranquil joy of mere survival.

Alice concludes:

Lately we have spent more time reading poetry than writing it. We have listened to recordings of poets all the way back to Tennyson, captured on a wax disk by Thomas Edison in 1881. As I write, we have just spent an hour listening to Gertrude Stein.

I have learned more about poetry by leading this group than in all the rest of my life put together. This is one of the remarkable things about this place: septa- and octogenarians have a chance to use what they know to embark on freshly remodeled careers within the community. Their skills are needed and can be put to fruitful use. For me, learning to teach poetry by teaching it has been a wonderful experience in my old age!

The Writers Group

In the summer of 1996 a new activity group was formed, initiated and led by resident Ann Parks. The Writers Group met once a week to share their writing. Several were already involved in writing projects and, for the most part, followed their individual agendas. One was working on a biography of her great-aunt's life as a missionary in Burma under the British Raj; two members of the group, sisters, were writing their experiences as refugees from Hitler's Germany and their early days in America. Another, whose grandmother had been a slave as a child in the South, was writing the stories her grandmother had told her about life in Chicago around the time of the Chicago Fire; one participant was recording the events of life in the Englewood neighborhood of Chicago during the protests and riots of the Civil Rights Movement. Other projects involved a romantic piece of family history and a description of life in the bayou country of Louisiana when the author was a child. Other people joined for briefer periods to share their writing. On occasion, all members took on a single topic as a challenge and change of pace.

The group met weekly for several months. The two autobiographies were finished; illness reduced our numbers and the group ended. For a writer, the opportunity to share one's words with a non-critical audience is always a treat. To have the enforced motivation of group expectation each week helps one plow through cases of temporary writer's block. The need to write something that would hold one's audience for the informally allotted time slot—not too long, not too short—brings a measure of self-discipline to the process. Perhaps the most enjoyable aspect of the group experience is the sharing—of life experiences, of common goals, and of vulnerability as a writer—with other members of our community.

Playreaders

The Playreaders Group offers an opportunity for those who like to play at being actors without the hard work of memorizing or staging a play. Anyone who has eyes to see and can read "character" into the words is welcome to join this group that meets the first and second Tuesday of each month. The producer decides on the play and selects the cast. Individual microphones that enlarge small voices have been a great boon to the group. And for those who can't see or don't care to perform, there's always the role of Audience. Playreaders has a place for all. Priscilla Higgins documents the group's early years:

Montgomery Place Playreaders Group
A Dramatis Historiae

In Hyde Park there lyes the Scene: from Iles of research
And teaching and computing of records
The princes of academe have brought to the halls of
Montgomery their mimes and perceptions,
Vowing to ransack their brains and create
A Continuum of the drama of history and culture.
All this was in Anno 1991, and has continued in its
Name as the Playreading Group of Montgomery Place.

From another venue came The Shoestring Theatre,
With a hallowed three-year Grant, and in combination
With Montgomery Place, a merger devoutly enjoyed
On the boards of Montgomery Place's East Room.
And our Argument will tell you (faire Beholders)
What may be digested in a Play bi-weekly for ten years
Under the chairpersonship of the fair Ann Parks.

When Shoestring's fiber and funding ran out,
The Library of scripts was transported to
Montgomery Place to provide a Rich Source of plays
For our volunteer Producers to replay.

The Playreaders sometimes provided a quick entrance into the life of Montgomery Place. Jack Ellison describes the "playreading greeting" he and his wife received when they first moved in:

> As we were unpacking box number nine in our new apartment, the phone rang. It was Barbara Fiske, who wanted to see us in the Lounge "at our convenience." Of course, it was very convenient to do anything other than unpack our boxes.
>
> When we arrived in the Lounge, Barbara made it very clear what she had in mind. There was a group of residents who met regularly to read plays aloud. Two members of the current cast were going to be absent even though they had read the first act. Didn't we see this as an opportunity to become part of an activity right away?
>
> We agreed with some hesitation that, though we had never been in a playreading group before, we would be foolish to turn it down. So, script in hand, we returned to our apartment, eager to see just what this experience would be like.
>
> The reading the next evening went unexpectedly well, with the woman who had the main part inspiring us with her performance. When we got to our apartment that evening, two thoughts came to mind. First, what a great way to be involved in a community project, and second, how good the feeling was that at one's advanced age one could learn something new.

Playreaders Become Playwrights

At the 2002 Christmas party for employees' children, Mila Meeker and Ann Parks were frustrated by the late arrival of the puppeteer. While fretting over the problem, they concluded that tardy or absent professional entertainers wouldn't be a problem if the residents could develop and present their own puppet show for the 2003 party. The idea was so appealing that it soon blossomed into an organized activity that wouldn't wait until Christmas.

A crew was assembled under the inspired leadership of Ann Parks. She wrote the script and the talented residents of Montgomery Place performed the show. Some designed and built the stage and proscenium, some imagined and crafted the puppets, and others wrote humorous new lyrics to old familiar tunes. In short order, the puppet show became more a fun activity for the participants and less a project to entertain kids.

The resulting humorous one-act sketch, *Daze of Our Lives*, was loosely based on life at Montgomery Place. Continuity was provided by a talking spectacle case that morphed into a character called Fat Rat, who sat on a perch above the stage and kibitzed with the "actors" as they appeared. His banter included conversation with a pair of animated cardboard elevators that lurched unsteadily up and down the side curtain and admonished everyone to "Take the stairs!" The metallic voice of the elevators was expertly provided by a resident who spoke with a Servox Electrolarynx.

The puppets included Generic Cleric, representing the retired pastors who live here; the Absent-minded Professor, inspired by the number of educators in residence; and a charming Widow named Merry, as there is no shortage of those in any retirement community. Balancing the residents was a puppet called Solicitous Staff, an amalgamation of the hardworking crew who attend to our needs, as well as the Admirable Administrator, who directs the staff.

The open dress rehearsal and first two standing-room-only performances were so well received that the company was asked to give a performance for residents of the Health Pavilion, and yet another in the East Room for the local grade school students to whom residents read each week. To be certain that insider jokes from *Daze of Our Lives* wouldn't be lost on those audiences, a new play was written. In addition to the fresh script, songs and lyrics were revised, and a Tin Woodman puppet—whose voice suggests he's a close relative of the elevators—was added.

Friday Evening Speakers

From the beginning, it didn't take long to discover what a wealth of information and entertainment existed within our walls, and soon Grace Bibler initiated the Friday evening talks. These have included many of our residents talking about all sorts of things: from bugs to life in Saudi Arabia; Chinese politics to birds in Jackson Park; a Bible tour in the Holy Land to primates in the Lincoln Park Zoo. A psychoanalyst talked about the mourning process. Our visiting children have spoken on topics we know little or nothing about: being a casting director for A-list movies, life as a Buddhist, and patterns of stereotyping around the world.

Because we have the good luck to live near a great university and in a great city, and because residents have a wide range of contacts, we have heard from the editors of *Poetry* magazine, the head of Special Collections at the U. of C. library, and the executives of two great philanthropic nonprofit organizations. The son of the original director of the Chicago Urban League talked about Al Capone, and a paleontologist described the digging up of a giant crocodile.

Wallace Rusterholtz, a historian among us well into his nineties, writes of the pleasure it gave him to present a series of talks about aspects of American history:

> When I moved into Montgomery Place, Grace Bibler asked me to give lectures. I had not known her before, and I don't know how she knew that I would be any good at it. But it has been a favorite activity of mine ever since my mother started me with elocution when I was a small child. So I gladly accepted. The first year my five lectures were on "Highlights of American History." The second series, in 2001, was on "Freethinkers in America." The 2002 series was "Our Ten Best Presidents." Each series

was also given at Chautauqua, New York, the summer after I had presented it at Montgomery Place.

So I am very grateful to Grace for pushing me into
doing something that I love to do, and to my fellow residents for their apparent pleasure in listening to me. My
Chautauqua audiences have been large and enthusiastic,
too. I am glad that I can be of some use and justify my
continued existence at the age of ninety-three.

Activities Committee

As these other groups flourished, it became useful to organize an
Activities Committee to meet regularly with the Activities Director to
coordinate times and to deal with problems of space use. It has also
proved of value in other ways. When one Activities Director thought
we would enjoy having an occasional dance if only there were a por-
table dance floor, she suggested that a rummage sale might provide
the needed funds. The residents contributed items, and after a few
sales, enough money was raised to purchase a suitable floor.

The rummage sale has become popular with employees and
neighborhood residents, and is now a regular feature every few
months. It also serves management as a way to dispose of furniture that has been replaced. The money, controlled by the Residents Council, has provided for the purchase of other items desired
by residents, such as tabletop microphones, a clock in the East
Room, and a digital camera that is used by the photographers who
keep the residents photo album up to date.

Exercise

Entering the room just east of the Library, a visitor might think
he'd wandered onto the set of a horror movie. Eight machines are
lined up there, all clearly designed to stretch, test, and toughen
human muscles. This is our Exercise Room*. In the wintertime,
the exerciser can pedal her stationary bicycle while watching the
snow pile up outside. In summer, she'll look out onto the impatiens

*now moved to the fourth floor

bordering our locust trees. As another exerciser lifts the stack of weights on the Nautilus compound-row machine, he can watch squirrels running across our broad green lawn, or maybe see a cardinal perched on the east fence.

Resident Allen Lang reports in the *Messenger* on how he uses the exercise machines and communes with nature at 6:00 A.M., six days a week:

> Once I watched a squirrel gnaw for thirty minutes through the plastic cap of a bird feeder, then dive head first into the column of birdseed. I worried that the thief might overeat, cork himself in tight, and that we'd have to call the Fire Department to free him. Today my prize for patience goes to a gull. This bird—white-headed, navy-gray body, yellow spectacles—rummaged through the pachysandra under a locust tree to tease out and drag to the sidewalk a hot dog, truant from our Fourth of July picnic.

> The gull wrestled with the weenie, demonstrating how tedious it is to dine without using one's hands. First the bird posed with the sausage sticking straight out from its bill, Churchill-style. Then the gull flipped the dog to grab it crosswise, giving it a Groucho Marx effect. "You'll never get it down," I told the bird through the window. It glanced my way, sneered, and in ten seconds had snapped the weenie in two. In another five, the dog was gone.

> I recalled the English schoolboy saying "Patience and perseverance/Made a bishop of His Reverence." Meanwhile, my patient and perseverant gull had flapped over our garden fence, off toward the parks and the lakeshore, yellow-ringed eyes searching for some more savory souvenirs of the Fourth of July.

The exercise machines serve one person at a time. More sociable are the five classes each week. These classes were started at the request of residents and are immensely popular. Our strength-training coach, Amr Elzeidy, has his classes of some twenty residents lifting free weights and strap-on leg weights two mornings a week. Activities Director Dana Witta leads three half-hour midday classes each week. The aim of these classes is to improve mobility and balance. Some members of the class do their "band practice"—stretching rubber loops—sitting in their wheelchairs.

The Museum of Science and Industry, across the park from Montgomery Place, makes it possible for us to get exercise out of the sun and rain and winter cold. The Montgomery Place bus picks up walkers at 8:00 A.M. on Monday, Wednesday, and Friday to take them to the museum, and at 9:00 A.M. takes them back home. Each walker logs in at the museum entrance, then strolls past the coal mine and the German submarine U-505 exhibits, on the way to the great balcony. Each circuit of the balcony is a quarter mile. Before leaving, the exerciser enters mileage earned on a personal chart. One Montgomery Place walker puts pennies in her pocket, and transfers one to another pocket for every circuit around the balcony. She says she seldom goes further than a dime's worth. No wonder museum-going is so exhausting!

We also have a weekly water aerobics program at a nearby pool. And in the summer, visiting children and grandchildren often swim in Lake Michigan from the beach across the Outer Drive.

Lately, some golfers have begun to use the public course in Jackson Park, and every Saturday afternoon during the cold months the Carpet Bowlers take over the East Room. Don Fiske describes it.

> This activity began when a tiny announcement appeared in the December 1994 *Messenger* saying that carpet bowling—lawn bowling moved indoors—would begin that month, and everyone should come to the East Room to watch and maybe to try it out. A reasonable number came to watch and others worked seriously at learning the game.
>
> It was about our second spring that we were invaded by a dozen or more of the members of the Lake Shore Bowling Club. They had come to bowl with us. The next Saturday that they came, they said, "How about doing it in the Lounge, too?" We replied, "Let's try it." (On Saturdays there

were very few residents in the Lounge.) So they moved the furniture to the sides to clear a path down the middle of the Lounge. We found padding to provide backstopping. We had a lot of fun even though the Lounge course was only perhaps one-third the length of an outdoor course. But, understandably, the residents began to get annoyed about these intruders. Fortunately the weather turned favorable and so our friends departed for the summer world of lawn bowling.

Some exercise opportunities aren't organized at all. A recent newcomer to the use of a wheelchair has discovered that walking the chair to where she's going is wonderful leg exercise, and wheeling herself with her arms is a tremendous biceps developer. She is happy to note that even those with crippled backs need not despair as long as they have a wheelchair. And the opportunity to exercise the brain, in the privacy of one's own apartment, is an activity all can enjoy, as Alice Hayes reveals:

The old lady in 615 is doing her exercises. She lies on the floor and kicks. She bends in different directions, ignoring all the little dancing pains. When she has stretched everything except her memory she gets back in bed and begins.

She has resolved to remember three things each morning before breakfast.

Yesterday it was three small mountain ranges. She started with the first letter of the first range. She knows it begins with an *O*. She does a small pirouette with her memory and makes her brain relax. Then after a minute she pops out from behind forgetfulness with her butterfly net: Ozarks. She impales it on a pin and goes on to the second range: *P*. Relax. Swing the net—Poconos. *C*. Relax, swing, miss, associate . . . Rip Van Winkle. Got it! Catskills!

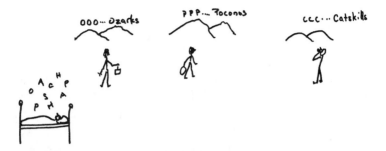

Then she can get up and have breakfast.

Today she is remembering the names of three diseases: sciatica, Parkinson's, anorexia. Tomorrow she'll do Greek Gods: Hephaestus and Hera, and finally Athena will pop out of her head instead of Zeus's.

All down the hall on the sixth floor, letters of the alphabet are rattling behind the doors as people with weak synapses grope for the names those letters begin.

The Historic Book Committee

There is one more activity initiated and carried through by the residents of this community, which we haven't yet fully described. That is the long, hard, sometimes impossible-seeming, often humorous, and finally rewarding making of this book. We want to tell you the saga of how it was put together by brave residents who volunteered to be on a committee to discuss the possibility of writing a book about Montgomery Place.

At the time of the tenth anniversary celebration, it was agreed that this retirement community was exceptional enough to deserve a book about itself. Eight interested people found themselves volunteering to write it, although they had no idea of the epic labor that they were undertaking. Once started, however, they went doggedly on, writing and rewriting, planning and organizing and reorganizing. Sometimes they met every week, making decisions about the organization of the book, and in between they wrote and thought and changed their minds and collected material from other residents. This went on for a long time. As everyone knows, any project done by a committee multiplies the difficulty of it by a factor of at least ten. Great minds do not have single thoughts.

One member of the committee describes the group in a typical meeting:

> The writers had had active lives, participating in and often leading other activities both before and after moving to Montgomery Place. We were talented, often compatible, and sometimes gifted in executing our tasks. We met in the Activity Room, a space meant to accommodate groups of thirty or forty. Since ours was a group of eight or ten, and since we didn't all hear very well or speak loudly enough or see well enough to read or recognize faces (being in our eighties and nineties), the first order of business at each meeting was furniture moving. Tables were moved as close together as possible, the better to see and hear each other.
>
> In its other lives the room also served as a greenhouse for discarded plants or arrangements of dried weeds. These, together with remnants of needlework and art projects, were tidied away, leaving room on the tables for manuscripts and doughnuts. The youngest and most agile member of the group (he had two knee replacements while we were working on the book) would go for coffee, and we were ready to work: a university professor of humanities and English literature, a poet, a teacher of linguistics, the headmaster of a distinguished private school, a child psychologist, a housewife and secretary, a social worker, and an environmental protector. All retired, all with strong and various opinions, and fortunately, all with a highly developed sense of the comic.
>
> Even with the difficulties of communication caused by our physical incapacities and our different convictions and approaches due to our varied backgrounds, who do you suppose we are, now that the book is finished? Best friends!

So at last the book got organized and members of the committee took on responsibility for different parts of the job. There was the background of Montgomery Place to be dealt with. How did it come to be a fourteen-story high rise in Hyde Park? How was it affected by its location? Why is it such a diverse community? What was it like when it opened? How have the residents changed both the atmosphere and the available resources? And how has it become a place where it's possible to live a creative old age?

One member of the committee took on the job of describing how the community developed and the work the residents have done to shape it into a place where their lives could expand in old age. This required getting help from residents who had started programs and activities, or worked on them later. It meant putting this information into a narrative, and attempting to explain how this made the quality of the place where we live richer and more humane.

Because this book is an example of a resident-initiated activity, we wanted to have as many residents as possible participate. We asked for help and got a wonderful response. One member of the committee took on the task of organizing this material. It was shuffled and sorted. Its organization went through many phases as the book developed. While some stories were used for specific illustrative material in earlier sections, the majority are grouped in Section III according to their time in the century and their place in the lives of those who wrote them.

We think these wonderful tales will give others in their seventies and eighties and nineties a sense of solidarity with those who shared the same century and who have contributed so generously to this book. These stories will also offer a firsthand glimpse of the twentieth century for those who follow us—our children's and grandchildren's generations and beyond.

Aboard the S.S. *Montgomery*

Over the years, committees, resources, and activities have evolved to reflect the unique needs and interests of Montgomery Place residents: from health care, food, and other management committees to activities such as gardening, music, art, and poetry writing. Our physical environment, a modern high rise on the shore of Lake Michigan in a large city, further contributes to our one-of-a-kind retirement community. Jane Overton likens our situation to that on an ocean liner:

Looking east toward the horizon from Montgomery Place on a gray November day is surprisingly reminiscent of transatlantic travel in the 1920s and early '30s. You are inside a box looking out at clouds and gray-purple water. There are no whales or dolphins, of course, but there is bird life.

Within, there is the same sort of serious effort to provide continuous entertainment. On board there are shuffleboard, quoits, and badminton; there is 11:00 A.M. bouillon and biscuits, card playing in the Lounge, a lending library and the Purser's Office for minor business and shopping. There is a dinner seating, for which many people change to something more formal, and usually a ball, and, of course, the inevitable Captain's Dinner.

One also finds a similar emphasis on exercise. On shipboard one counts out loud to mark each turn around the deck, while here many of us count out loud the steps we take up and down the long hallways. On the ship there is likely to be a sort of exercise room with a mechanical horse capable of giving you the feel of a trot or gallop, and a saddle that purports to give you the gaits of a camel. Although our equipment here is more diverse, I am sure many of the same muscles get a workout.

Furthermore, on shipboard one often meets old acquaintances and can always make new and lasting friends, while frequent transatlantic travelers can even be surprised by finding a distant relative aboard.

Lastly, even though our box never pitches or rolls, unfortunately sometimes we do. When this happens, we can grab the convenient rail along the hall, just as on a liner, when the weather gets rough, one lurches from rail to rail.

Sail on, *Montgomery!*

4

Staying Connected: Relationships with the Larger Community

While there are many things to do within our own community, we don't want to break off connections with the outside world and live on an island. We are still active; many of us still run meetings, and make talks. We still teach and drive and take long walks. We go to plays and concerts and movies. We go to occasional weddings and frequent memorial services.

Some residents continue to go to offices and laboratories, or they enjoy volunteering in churches and schools and museums and hospitals. People go to visit their children, who live all over the United States. They travel and bring back slides and tales of faraway places. During just the first ten years of Montgomery Place, inveterate travelers among us went to China, India, Easter Island, the South Pacific (in a sailboat), Scandinavia—including Spitzbergen and the North Cape—Russia, and even across Mongolia and Siberia on the Orient Express.

Many residents have been involved with local politics and community groups that meet in the East Room. The League of Women Voters meets here twice a month, as do the East Hyde Park Association and the Friends of the Parks. The East Room is also used as a polling place for two precincts, and Montgomery Place residents act as judges for our precinct.

Candlelight vigil, 2003

Because we are part of a great city as well as of Hyde Park, we have all the resources and some of the worries of Chicago at our fingertips. We are definitely part of that community, too.

And we are part of the United States and the world. We worry about them a lot. We vote and write letters and read newspapers. This picture shows residents holding candles in our garden on a night before the war in Iraq started in 2003. That night we were joining in the candlelight vigil for peace taking place all over the world.

The City of Chicago Connection

Leslie Orear regularly provides reports in the *Montgomery Messenger* about his experiences traversing the city of Chicago on the No. 6 Jeffrey Express bus. His dispatches began in June 1999 with a reflection, "On Becoming a Pedestrian":

Birthdays are to be celebrated, even by the elderly; but if the birthday is the day you lose your driver's license, then it can be a bittersweet occasion. When that day came to me in May, I picked up my briefcase as usual and headed for the office. I refrained from punching elevator button "B" for Basement and Garage, and sauntered boldly out the door for the No. 6.

On the way downtown I caught a ride with a friend, but going home it was pouring rain as I joined the throng waiting for the bus at State and Jackson. I did get the last seat; so far, so good. But not good enough. The windshield wiper went kaput as we neared the Outer Drive. Hailing an approaching (and already crowded) bus, our driver put us back in the rain, to squeeze aboard the rescue vessel. It was standing room only, but just a few minutes to 56th Street. That could be endured.

Then, what a pleasant surprise as I stepped to the curb and saw that the raincoated figure ahead of me was a delightful fellow-resident. So arm-in-arm we dodged the whizzing cars on Everett and safely strode into the welcoming arms of Monty—and a dry change of clothes.

The University Connection

Even though we can't see it out our windows, many of us think of the University of Chicago as part of the larger community we are closest to. Many residents have worked there, some for all their working lives: in offices, in classrooms, in laboratories, in libraries, or as students. A few still go to their offices or laboratories, or teach an occasional course.

Whatever our former connections with the university, it is a kind of extension of Montgomery Place for all of us. The U. of C. geriatric clinic two blocks away provides us with medical care. Many residents attend chamber music series, plays at Court Theatre, and lectures and courses in the university's adult education program. We go to exhibits at the three marvelous museums on campus: the Smart Museum, which has a wide variety of temporary exhibits and a fine collection of its own; the Renaissance Gallery, which, in spite of its name, shows contemporary artists; and the Oriental Institute, an archaeological museum, which has one of the world's foremost collections of Middle Eastern art and artifacts. There are movies and all sorts of student performances, musical and theatrical, at which we are welcome. We are very lucky to be connected with such an institution!

The League Of Women Voters

The League (L.W.V.) is an organization predominantly with women members, though it is not a "women's issues" organization. At Montgomery Place it has grown and prospered. Early on, a number of League members who had met at each other's houses came to live at Montgomery Place. At first we met in these residents' apartments, but we soon outgrew those spaces and moved the meetings into the East Room. The 1990 list of members of Unit 74 (one of two Hyde Park units of the Chicago League) shows twenty members and an average attendance of eleven. In 2003 the list of people at Montgomery Place to whom organizer Barbara Fiske sent meeting reminders had forty-eight names (including four men), and another twenty-two people (including one man) who don't live here came to meetings. Our average attendance, depending on the subject being discussed, is about thirty to thirty-five. The group is unselfconsciously racially integrated.

What do we discuss, if not women's issues? In recent years, we discussed the death penalty (against it), election laws, campaign finance legislation (for it), the city budget, school funding, tax equity (for that, too), the United Nations (it should be strengthened), foreign trade, health care funding (we're for a single-payer system), affordable housing, social welfare, protection of the environment, prison reform, the city park system. Those are women's issues, all right, and men's issues as well. We also tell people how to register to vote and how to find out about candidates, and we conduct candidate forums. We do not recommend candidates. We do take positions on the issues that we study, and we urge our members and others to make their views known to governmental officials.

Little by little, we are making ourselves heard. A favorite L.W.V. quote is, "Governmental reform is no sport for the short-winded." And so we keep on trying even into our seventies, eighties, and nineties, for the sake of our children and grandchildren of both genders.

Teaming Up with the East Hyde Park Committee

Once a month Montgomery Place hosts a breakfast meeting for the East Hyde Park Committee, a group of neighborhood notables—a sort of real-space chatroom. Our dining staff provides coffee, juice, and muffins for the group. Recent discussions have centered on the plan for shoring up the lakefront at Promontory Point, right across the Outer Drive from Montgomery Place. The original plan showed a cold, rectilinear, glaring white cement series of steps replacing the friendly jumble of natural-looking limestone blocks leading down into the water.

The Point is a part of the park with trees and benches and a field for kite flying and ball playing. The lake laps or crashes around it, and in the summer swimmers lounge on the limestone blocks of this promontory created by landfill built into the lake in the 1920s. Since the late 1990s, the Army Corps of Engineers has been reinforcing the whole lakefront with a cement revetment. When the project proposed to continue the line of cement steps and remove the old limestone blocks around the Point, the Hyde Park community rose in arms.

We wanted our natural-looking shoreline, and we didn't want trees cut down in order to get big machines to the water's edge. A community task force was formed to face this problem, and the upshot was that an engineer hired by the group made a plan to preserve and protect the Point, using limestone blocks rather than concrete. Many of our residents have spent time and energy on this project. We definitely think of ourselves as part of the larger Hyde Park community.

Alice Hayes writes,

> I moved here a few years ago, partly to have a view of something that made me feel part of the natural world. There was a perfect tree. The lake was wild and wonderful. Ducks dove. The strip of park was narrow between the water and the Outer Drive. It contained the four seasons, with people using them. The tree blazoned each season against sky and water: white,

yellow, green, brown, each with its own birds and exercisers. People swam in the green, walked in the brown, skied in the white, and in the yellow they stood around hugging each other, and through each color there were bicycles—even in the snow. The different times of day succeeded each other, calmly switching the lighting so there was always change. The different kinds of weather affected the tree and the grass and the lake and the texture of the air.

I didn't know exactly what I'd see when I looked out the window morning or evening, but I'm not trying to describe the views, only to tell you how having them there, coming and going, changing like a movie day after day, enriched my old age.

It was late winter when the machines came and cut down the crow trees to make room for themselves. They said they were going to dig a tunnel under the Drive so we could get to the beach without going up and down stairs. There was a pedestrian bridge across the Drive, which in summer they trimmed lusciously with flowers, but it did have many steps, so a tunnel seemed like some sort of compensation for the mess they were making.

At first they said of course they wouldn't cut down the perfect tree and they put a flabby red plastic fence around it and began chopping up stones to make white heaps and digging holes and hammering long steel things into the ground. There were pipes laid, and before they cut down the tree, the incomprehensible digging and filling went on without producing any sign of a tunnel.

The day I saw men standing around the perfect tree beside a truck that said "TREE WORK," I put on my coat, took two canes, drove to the old tunnel two blocks away, and hobbled through it as fast as I could. As I approached the scene of the threatened crime, the truck was coming toward me down the sidewalk, so I stood in front of it and waved my canes and called *"Stop!"* like a demented old hag, which I was. The frightened truck driver stopped before he hit me, rolled down his window, and leaned out.

"Ma'am?"

"They promised not to cut down that tree. Are you going to cut it down?"

"We just want to be sure it's the right tree," he said.

I went home and called our alderman and the local newspaper. I got polite responses from the people who answered the telephones at each place, but it was nearly five o'clock, too late for any deus ex machina to appear that day.

The next morning, early, when I looked out my window there were already two men with chainsaws up in the tree and most of the upper branches had been amputated. It was too late to chain myself to the trunk. When we asked questions, we were told the big yellow dinosaurs needed more room to maneuver.

When you're old, what you see out your window is an important connection with the real world, and you can't help relating to what goes on. It took me a while to get used to the absence of my beloved tree, but another resident gave me an excellent photograph he'd taken of it, which I stuck in the corner of the window through which I had always seen the tree when it was there.

There is still wildlife to watch. Sociable crows, occasional ducks and even swans, and once a peregrine falcon sitting on a streetlight plucking the small duck he'd caught, white feathers floating down like snow onto the cars below. The construction equipment across the street makes for a temporary non-natural interest out the window, and even the birds watch curiously. Yesterday a large goose led a tour group of smaller geese swimming along the shore with heads turned toward the construction site. Two small geese broke away from the group and swam right up under the crane to get a closer look. As the work goes on month after month, the machines begin to have personalities of their own. Although it starts work early, the front-end loader always stops when the oil

truck arrives, and the loader hurries over for its breakfast, fed to it through a tube to its stomach.

Gradually I began to be interested in the construction
site itself and to watch eagerly for any sign of a tunnel.
It's like watching a very long play which never comes to a
climax. And on days when there's no pounding or
squeaking of backing trucks, I feel nothing but frustration. Will they never be done?

Priscilla and Colin Higgins act as roving reporters for the
Messenger, working mostly on the construction beat. They have made
friends with some of the supervisors, who come in white pickup
trucks. This couple, who are good walkers, tramp over to the construction site (quite a distance once the pedestrian bridge was gone
and before the tunnel was built) and report back with their inter-
pretations of the craters and mountains they see. Here is one report printed in the *Montgomery Messenger:*

Hard Hats and Iron Pipes

Over the holidays our construction site was the recipi-
ent of hundreds of husky iron pipes, each twelve inches
in diameter and almost fifty feet long. What for? On the
fourth of January, after no apparent activity for several
days, we spot two closed pickup trucks near the
excavation's mud puddle.

On a truck tailgate, a man sits diligently sawing wood,
a four-by-four, turning it into thin stakes to give to the
man with the surveyor's transom for his orange quiver.
Then both vanish. Two days later, white pickup trucks, a
tall crane nuzzling up to a praying mantis-like machine,
square red generators, a front-end loader with prongs.
Many hard hats stand about, staring into the hole: four
white hats, a yellow, two reds, soon joined by two browns
and another white.

Clanging noises as a pipe is snared by the crane and
hoisted to the mantis, which turns out to be an elongated
three-sided cage just as long as the pipes. Up to the top,

and then the hammer goes to work: BANG! *Puff* BANG! *Puff* for about twenty minutes, until the pipe hits bedrock. So, at probably 200 more pipes, you can figure out how many more early-morning BANG! *Puffs* will get us up and rolling. (The *puff* is exhaust.)

On the morning of January 16, the trucks and hard hats are all there, but by 4:00 P.M. the whole place has been cleared except for the crane. Each pipe sticking out is wearing an Afghan turban: two Arabic armies facing each other.

After two conversations with "I'm not sure I'm the one you should talk with" hard hats, suddenly from a white pickup truck comes our friendly engineer, John, grinning, to talk with us. His testimony corroborates the others. Yes, indeed, the iron pipes that are now driven into the ground, some of them fifty feet down, will be filled individually with a cement compound. The turbans kept debris out of them. This will support the bridge, keep it from collapsing under heavy traffic. The tops are protected with barbican wreaths of prickly metal, which they call "Top Shelling." They have between 100 and 200 more pipes to pound.

"Do we wake you up in the morning?"

"Oh no, we love watching you work."

Our most jovial workman is the fellow of Local 151 of the Operating Engineers who mans the folding crane, which shoots a stream of cement into each pipe. We find him just after he had folded the yellow crane down, and ask him about the mad angles of the pipes driven into the ground. One of our neighbors has suggested she wants a tax rebate because they weren't in straight.

"Oh," hand sweeping toward the white pickup trucks, "They design all that."

And cement freezing?

"Not with those plastic covers and tarps. That cement will be 180 degrees tonight. Just like summer."

And the Paris green outhouse has been moved from its precarious position at the edge of the abyss to more stable ground. What next? We're following up.

The Coast Guard Connection

A few years after Montgomery Place opened, the United States Coast Guard, meeting with reduced government support, launched a new service: the Coast Watchers. Some of the occupants of high-rise buildings along Lake Michigan were asked to serve as watchers of the shore and the lake, and, after proper initiation, to report any departure from the norm to an assigned Coast Guard telephone number.

Two of our residents who had long been owners of sailboats made inquiry of the Coast Guard, which resulted in a Coast Guard volunteer arriving at Montgomery Place to initiate and instruct nine volunteers. This involved the assignment to each volunteer of a compass properly calibrated for each household. Once the compasses were in place all was ready for observation and reportings. Action followed soon, when the next day one watcher who owned not just binoculars but also a powerful telescope mounted and adjusted for action, called to say there was a naked man swimming in the lake. Before action could be initiated, the nude swimmer took refuge in a cabin cruiser nearby.

The daughter of one watcher felt proper recognition should be made of these ancient aides of the Coast Guard. She went to an Army store and purchased nine commodore hats and shipped one to each watcher. The second recognition came when one watcher was given an official citation. Her brave act occurred one dark and stormy night when a lifeguard rowboat that had not been pulled up high enough on the 57th Street Beach went back to sea on its own. A phone call gave the Coast Guard the precise location of the boat, brought a rescue vessel to capture it, and, according to the citation, saved the taxpayers the cost of a replacement.

Some of our families delight in telling their friends that their parents are now in a retirement community and have joined the Coast Guard.

The Museum Connection

Over the years, the Museum of Science and Industry has provided extraordinary surprises in the view seen from our windows. Holiday decorations always feature outdoor light shows: Once there was a fifteen-foot gorilla in the classic porticos, cavorting among the caryatids; another time a huge spider scaled the front of the museum. One winter there was an inflated twenty-foot penguin on the roof. Watching his efforts to stay blown up in the winter chill was a special pleasure. We have seen a DC3 arrive across the lake to its new home in the museum, and we watched the huge old Santa Fe steam engine No. 2903 towed away on track laid down, section by section, across the park toward its new home in a railroad museum.

During renovations at the museum, from 1997 through 1998, we watched as the large outdoor parking lot that had once been an exhibit in itself, with cars displaying license plates from everywhere (sometimes on a busy weekend, all fifty states and Canada) was moved underground and the asphalt turned to grass. It was a long and interesting transition.

On the now-grassy field where cars used to park, we have had kite-flying contests, the start of solar cars races, and, in the summer of 1999, five members of Chicago's famous Cows on Parade, as explained in an article from the *Messenger*.

The Sheep's in the Meadow, the Cow's . . . on the Lawn?

Just across the street—looking out of your south windows—are cows! They are multicolored and strangely adorned. If you go to look, you will discover that each cow refers to an exhibit at the Museum of Science and Industry. The one carrying an upside-down table represents a castle, the "Cowleen Moore's Doll Cowstle" ["Colleen Moore's Doll Castle"], and the cow emerging from an egg refers to the popular exhibit of baby chickens hatching. Also moo-vingly present are cows representing the submarine, the train exhibit, and the space exhibit. Note the udderly charming bouquets.

These cows are part of a herd of 300 now on the streets and in the parks of Chicago. They are in front of the Civic Center, the Art Institute, and the shops along the Magnificent Mile. They are not, however, part of a conventional Guernsey or Holstein herd. Rather they are fiberglass, multi-decorated (some by distinguished artists) members of Chicago's latest passion: Cows on Parade.

The Hyde Park Community Connection

As members of the larger Hyde Park community, we like to stay in the swing of things. One glorious Fourth of July, a dozen residents participated in a festive parade through the neighborhood. The Montgomery Place bus was festooned with balloons. We waited in air-conditioned comfort inside the bus while hundreds of children finished weaving red-white-and-blue bunting into the wheels of their bicycles. Then our driver, Freddie, eased the bus into the queue of pedaling youngsters. Behind us trotted nine horsemen, the end of the parade.

Going down Lake Park, we sighted a traffic accident: a baby carriage had thrown a wheel, but driver and occupant, unharmed, waved as we went by. Near Walgreens we spotted a fellow resident sitting on the curb. She climbed aboard and we continued toward Hyde Park Boulevard, with the whirligigs strung along the sides of the bus going like tiny windmills. The bus rolled west on 53rd Street, police barricades keeping traffic off our route. At Nichols Park the horsemen honor guard peeled off south, and paraders hurried into the park.

A vote was taken. We decided we didn't care to dismount for hot dogs. So we headed back to Montgomery Place, satisfied that a patriotic good time had been had been had by all.

Del Bathazar (left) and Mavis Ferguson share a word in the East Room during the Tenth Anniversary "Treasure Tea," August 2001.

5

People to People

We have described some of the ways the residents of Montgomery Place have worked together to make this the kind of place where they wanted to live, and even their efforts to make the world the kind of place they want to leave behind them. None of this would work without the personal relationships that have flourished among the members of this very diverse group.

People who didn't know each other before have become close friends; they have helped each other when they were sick or sad or in trouble. Sometimes they have cheered each other up simply by a greeting in the hall. White residents, African Americans, Asian Americans, Episcopalians, Catholics, Jews, Unitarians, Humanists, and devoted unbelievers have worked together on joint projects, and shared music and plays and jokes. We have mourned together over residents we have lost, and we have been patient together when the Dining Room was out of commission because of floods or redecorating, or the elevators were being temperamental.

This chapter gathers some of the miscellaneous events, encounters, and feelings that form the spirit of this place, and offers a sense of how people who were old at the end of the twentieth century are living together at the beginning of the twenty-first.

The Village Street

In some respects, each hallway is like a village street. We get to know our floor neighbors as we wait for the elevator, and, as we ride up and down, exchange news and gossip speedily between floors. We get to know our neighbors as we rest on one of the benches in the long hall. Sometimes somebody who is feeling fit carries packages to the door of a frailer neighbor. We borrow butter and we borrow milk. We do errands for the woman who has just broken her arm.

Sometimes we have long and surprising conversations on our village streets, as one resident reports:

Conversation with a Neighbor Walking Her Cat in the Hall

ME. (*To the cat.*) Good morning, Calico.

NEIGHBOR. I was listening to the news but she has to have her walk, so here we are in the hall getting our exercise.

ME. I love seeing her out here. It makes me feel as though the hall was a village street.

NEIGHBOR. (*Getting down on her knees to reach under the bench by the elevator.*) Come out, Calico. Come on and walk properly. (*To me.*) Everybody is so nice about her. I really appreciate that. (*Gets up off her knees holding the cat, puts her down in the middle of the hall, aims her in the direction she should walk, and turns to me.*) I'm so distressed at the news about Iraq. You know, I was principal of the American School for Girls in Baghdad for five years, and I identify with those people. (*The cat dashes back into the open door of her apartment.*) Oh, there she goes. Maybe she didn't feel like walking after all.

ME. When were you there?

NEIGHBOR. I'd been there for five years before the July 14, 1958, coup. When King Faisal was shot, the American embassy offered all American citizens free transportation home if they wanted to leave. We had twenty-four hours to decide.

ME. What did you do?

NEIGHBOR. I stayed another two years.

ME. Was it okay?

NEIGHBOR. Nothing serious happened to me in spite of anti-American policy. The Iraqis accepted me. The only unpleasant thing was once a group of school children stopped me on the street and said, "Why are you taking all our money?" I wasn't taking their money. I was working for a very small salary.

(*The cat oozes out the apartment door.*)

Oh, here she is again. I guess we'll walk after all.

(*They head off together down the hall, with Calico sliding catlike along the wall. I go into my apartment two doors down and marvel at this neighbor on our sixth-floor "street."*)

Animals contribute to our community in unexpected ways. Calico the cat helps the sixth floor to feel like a neighborhood. Virginia Bensema, on the eighth floor, describes how her dog Amy functions as a babysitter:

Although I was unsuccessful in finding a job for myself (age discrimination), an unexpected opportunity recently arose for my dog, Amy. I received a call from Betsy Kelly, owner of Cuddles. It developed that Cuddles suffered anxiety attacks when left alone on dark days. The question to me was, "Could Amy take care of Cuddles while I go to the doctor?"

Before I agreed, of course, I had to ask Amy if she had any other plans. She replied, "I don't know Cuddles but, yes, she can come." Then she added, "But she's not eating my food or grabbing my toys." After this she proceeded to the kitchen and gobbled up the food she had scorned the night before. Then she carried her toys one by one into the bathroom.

I met the elevator and grabbed Cuddles and her baggage so Betsy could continue to the doctor. Amy and Cuddles immediately formed a wonderful friendship. The days continued to be foggy and hazy, and it became apparent that Cuddles would be Amy's new best friend.

Our most dramatic dog story is the tale of Precious Blackie, now a resident on the second floor of the Health Pavilion. One bleak November day in 2002 this little black Pomeranian-mix dog was found in our garden, lost, cold, and hungry. She was grateful to be taken in and fed while her rescuers searched for an owner in all the neighboring buildings. She stayed in the office and was walked by volunteers on the staff. No owner was found. It looked as though this very appealing waif had been abandoned.

A collection was taken up to pay her bills, and she visited the vet, who pulled six decayed teeth and said she was an old dog but free of disease and fleas. She was given a bath and came out soft and fluffy. By this time everyone had fallen in love with her. Executive Director Michael Apa, the court of last resort, said she could be a permanent resident.

Precious Blackie now lives in the nursing station on the second floor and talks amiably with the Alzheimer's patients. In dog years, she probably is as old as they are, so they enjoy each other's company. The rest of us also have a chance to talk with her in the Lobby as she goes in and out for her walks.

In addition to our indoor animals, we have a lot of association with the birds we see out our windows. We have made efforts to feed them in the garden (unsuccessful) and efforts to keep them from bashing into windows by pasting silhouettes of hawks on the glass (more successful). Mostly we are acquainted with crows, seagulls, pigeons and geese—the hardy city birds. Several great naturalists live at Montgomery Place, and their articles in the *Montgomery Messenger*, their talks on Friday nights, and their availability to answer questions have helped to make us familiar with the wildlife around us. Thanks to these scientists, when we have ladybugs *inside* our windows or when the occasional butterfly or spider comes through the air conditioning system, we welcome it and feel part of nature. An inhabitant of the fourteenth-floor village street has a special relationship with the crows she has known:

These crows were in residence before I arrived at
Montgomery Place. They were the firm friends of a previous resident who had rewarded them with food for their
frequent fly-bys. The food was placed on the roof by an
employee, who was duly compensated by the resident for
his trips to the roof. The fly-bys continue, very close to
my windows, though the crows are now unrewarded. In
clement weather, when the windows are open, they can
be heard in the late afternoon. They convene in the trees
to discuss the day's affairs before bedtime.

At one time, we on the fourteenth floor heard loud
thumps coming from the roof. One neighbor surmised
the crows had donned heavy boots to march about.

You may conclude that I am anthropomorphic. Not at
all! I just like crows.

Far more important than the birds and animals that keep us
company are our fellow residents. Sometimes a chair in the Lobby
is occupied by a person whose apartment feels empty. He or she
wants to see people going by. There are always people coming and
going in the Lobby, and even when it's empty there is a friendly
person at the desk. Although there are plenty of other places to sit
and do things, nowhere but the Lobby has the same sense of life
and motion. Here one resident meets another:

I was walking through the Lobby, and I saw a resident
sitting there looking very gloomy and unlike her usual
lively self. "What's the trouble?" I asked. She responded
quietly: "I am lonely, very lonely. This happens to me at
different times and it makes me very sad."

On an impulse I told her that I was just going up to
our apartment to play some CDs I was planning to use in
the next music program for which I, as a member of the
Music Committee, was responsible. I knew that she and
some of her friends enjoyed these programs; indeed she
had commented once that she very much liked my
choices. I turned to her and said, "Perhaps you might
like to come and listen to some of the music." She looked

up hesitantly and asked, "Would your wife mind?" "No," I said, "I'm sure she wouldn't mind! Let's go."

At first in the apartment she seemed to feel awkward. The CD I played was a hymn to the moon by Dvořák as sung by Renée Fleming. Soon I noticed that my visitor was lost in the music. Now she seemed relaxed. I told her that in the program I would tell the listeners quite a bit about the composer and talk at some length—as was my habit—about the music. Then to complete the program I would play two other pieces. After a few moments' pause my new friend said clearly and confidently, "I think you could leave out some of the details you were talking about so that you will have plenty of time to give the words of the song, which they will really want to know."

Somewhat taken aback, I nonetheless had to admit that she had made an important point. As she left, smiling, I thought to myself, I helped her and she helped me.

Elizabeth Jones Borst talks about the kind of genial relationship that is the basis for a trusting, supportive friendship:

> The day I moved into Montgomery Place was one of mixed feelings. New surroundings, new people, new customs, and now new neighbors just across the hall, moving in at the same time. Charles and Gloria Greene were new to me and I to them. It did not take long for us to find common ground!
>
> Charles and I both had gregarious personalities. Gloria's thoughtfulness and good judgment curbed our sometimes less restrained impulses. Humor was a trait common to all of us, and conversation and laughter across the hall were continuous. Early on, Charles learned my maiden name was Jones. Since he had not known my husband and me together, he chose to call me "Miss Jones." He knew of my habit of reading the news at breakfast, and if he telephoned at that time he would inquire: "Good morning, Miss Jones! Have you finished memorizing the *Tribune?*"

Hallway Art

There are Christmas and Halloween and Valentine decorations on doors, and interesting doormats in front of some apartments. The corny pictures that lined our halls when Montgomery Place opened have mostly disappeared. Some people have hung their favorite posters or photographs by their own doors. One resident, who has worked much of her life in museums, has framed pictures that needed it, and has helped with hanging them all over the building.

A very impressive event involving art in the hallways occurred when the fourteenth floor was repainted and a new rug put down. Jane Overton, the artist, tells the story:

When I first moved to Montgomery Place, I noticed that the pictures outside some people's doors were distinctly different in character from other pictures in the same hallway. I inquired and learned that, yes, you could put up something you liked by your door. Having more objects than could suitably be accommodated inside our apartment, I hung one of my own pieces at the end of the hall. There seemed to be very few pictures of any kind in our hallway so I thought I might hang a few more pieces without intruding on my neighbors. Then Charles Greene, who lived at the extreme west end of the fourteenth floor, chose one of my pieces to hang beside his door, and a second one to hang directly across from it.

Soon thereafter there was a total redecoration of the fourteenth floor: all pictures of every kind came down, the walls were painted white, and the carpet was changed to a pleasant green-gray. I hesitated to hang anything because I did not want to make holes in those gleaming walls. Charles Greene came by and said nonsense, of course my work should go up, and moreover should be hung the whole length of the hall! I hesitated; Charles did not. He arranged and hung each piece personally.

Then Charles and his across-the-hall neighbor Elizabeth Borst arranged an open house reception for the

"Fourteenth-Floor Exhibit." They sent out invitations, and, when the time came, their apartments were open for socializing. Slides of other pieces of my work were shown in the Recycling Room.

The Game Room at the end of the hall was supplied with wine, sparkling cider, and cookies, and our Activities Director arranged for service. People came all afternoon in small groups so the viewing was always easy, and a circle of chairs in the Game Room encouraged people to stay and chat. I met new friends as well as old ones. All in all, I cannot imagine a more welcoming occasion.

Several other floors have followed suit, with Japanese prints, photographs by a skilled photographer, and artwork from a world traveler and art collector.

The Dining Room

We all need to eat and since we all pay for at least one Dining Room meal a day, most of us come down to the Dining Room to eat it. This makes it a place where people meet and get to know each other. Since seats are not assigned, we sometimes arrange to eat with friends. We call and say: "Will you eat with us tonight? We'll meet you downstairs at 5:00 or 5:30 or 6:00."

Frequently there are guests from outside the building: friends, children, grandchildren, whom we may be invited to join. Sometimes other people's grown-up children who visit frequently become our fast friends. When new people move into Montgomery Place, we do our best to prevent the Dining Room jitters. This is an affliction worse for single people than couples: when you come down to dinner and you don't know whom you're going to eat with. It seems as though everybody else is sitting with old friends, and nobody would want to eat with you, and it would be too embarrassing to ask people to let a stranger join them. If you don't already have acquaintances when you first come, this can be the hardest part of moving in. But take heart! Members of the Welcoming Committee invite you to eat with them. The Dining Room staff will find you a congenial spot or will seat you with other

newcomers. Everybody under-
stands the difficulty, which
doesn't last.

Often we come down and
eat with people we have never
known before even though neither of us is new. People know
enough about each other so that
someone just back from the hospital is probably invited to eat
with somebody who can help cut
up his meat.

So the Dining Room be-
comes a great big tasty social
stew. If you are feeling sad or
puny or just grumpy, you can
always eat by yourself if you
want to, but the most astonish-
ing part of the Dining Room is
the conversation it encourages.

*Colin and Priscilla Higgins
at Tuesday wine and cheese.*

Most of us eat our one-meal-a-day-included-in-the-rent as
dinner, served from 4:00 to 7:00 P.M. After a few uncomfortable
attempts at pre–Montgomery Place dining times, one learns that
arrival time for dinner is expected to be no later than 6:00 P.M.
(Dinner is early so that the waitstaff don't have to go home too
late through a dark city.) One resident recalls a recent week:

> Monday: We eat with a couple we know only slightly.
> The conversation starts with a short review of the new
> menu selection; the decision is made to try the new
> Creole dish, though some concern is expressed that it
> might be too spicy.
>
> Menu decisions made and salad bar excursions com-
> pleted, a careful approach to a discussion of the President's
> latest foreign policy speech is offered. As a shared negative
> view of the matter becomes apparent, a lively discussion of
> the topic follows. Politics are a bit tricky, but if approached
> carefully can be stimulating subject matter.

Tuesday: After wine and cheese with close friends in the lounge, the conversation is made up of a series of anecdotes illustrating the foibles of our fellow man, each of us attempting to top the others' offerings. As usual, we are bested by one friend, whose stories always are the most hilarious of all.

Wednesday: We eat with a new couple who have just come to Montgomery Place. Introductions are made all around. Then the standard newcomer review questions: When did they move in; are they settled yet; where did they live before; are they native Chicagoans? Then it's our turn to answer questions: We've been here seven years; we're from New York originally but we've lived in Hyde Park for fifty years. Then we're on to children—locations and professions. Depending on our respective memories, these facts will provide the base for future encounters, as newcomers turn into acquaintances and, with time, into friends.

Thursday: Eating with two social work friends, the discussion centers on the federal and state neglect of social programs, leading to the problems facing the treatment centers for disturbed and physically disabled children.

Friday: We eat with two single friends. The topic is music: Our local bass vocalist's next concert, this week's Chicago Symphony program. One goes Friday afternoon, we go Thursday night. As is usually the case, there is agreement over the Symphony's offering this week; the first piece was a little restrained, but the second was fine as it was a piece by the conductor's favorite composer.

Saturday: We eat with a couple whose main concern is with the food—tonight's menu, the offerings on the salad bar, the overcooked beans, and the possibility that the cheesecake for dessert may run out before we are served. As fellow members of the Food Committee, we are used to these concerns and enjoy our dinner as usual.

On Sunday we are back with close friends and able to cover politics, grandchildren, and flare-ups of arthritic knees with mutual interest, concern, and sympathy.

The Dining Room also has been a source of exciting adventure and variety in our lives. For years, whenever it rained, a stream of water would flow under the door from the garden, causing the Dining Room staff to pack towels along the base of the door. This made an effective dam and gave a nice, informal homey feel as you came in to eat. How many times did you pack towels across the base of a window or door in your own old house before you moved to Montgomery Place? However, this problem has been fixed, and, even during monsoon rains, we enter the Dining Room with dry feet.

But also we have had a real flood. In 1994 some pipes burst and a deluge during the night left six inches of water on the Dining Room floor. While the Dining Room was being dried out and rehabilitated, we had a glorious time eating in the other public rooms downstairs. A buffet table stretched down the hall, tables were set up everywhere in makeshift dining rooms, and we enjoyed eating in small groups, chatting in the Library or among the exercise machines. The heroic waitstaff had to walk what must have seemed many miles back and forth to the kitchen.

This chance for variety was repeated in 2001, when the Dining Room was being fully redecorated. This time we ate in the "Parkside Lounge" and in the East Room's "Lake Front Café," looking out at the park and the lake. And this time, instead of laying out a buffet, the waitstaff served us as though we were in the Dining Room. Again, they put extra miles on their shoes.

The residents were in on the plans for redecorating the Dining Room. Nobody liked the old chairs, so for some time samples of new ones were available outside the Dining Room. We took turns sitting in them and expressing our views about backs, arms, finish, upholstery, and whether or not to have casters, and, if so, on which legs? It was just like home, with all the family gathered around disagreeing about what color to paint the bathroom. So while we ate in the improvised Dining Room, we waited to see what the new décor would be like.

When the work was finished, one great improvement turned out to be the noise level. The new room is much quieter than the old one, and the (many) hard of hearing among us have an easier time taking part in the table talk. On the other hand, it's not as easy as it used to be to overhear tantalizing fragments of conversation from adjoining tables: "Just a little hole they can pull it out through . . . but if there are so many pretty colors in the ceiling lights because of refraction . . . they'll have to cut me all across the middle like a melon . . . have you noticed? . . . and the *birds* . . . we've tried feeders . . . but for her hundredth . . . we need something besides mixed seed . . . and we're planning a lovely party . . . though the president seems determined to have a war instead. Now, when I was at Los Alamos . . . everybody in my dorm wrote poetry."

You could stand at the door of the Montgomery Place Dining Room and ask a question about anything in the world, from sewing stitches to nuclear physics or Freud, and there would be somebody in the room who could answer it. We haven't reached a mean age of eighty-six for nothing!

Occasionally, spontaneous floor shows occur in the Dining Room; one was reported in the June 2002 issue of the *Montgomery Messenger*.

> Residents at dinner on a recent midsummer evening were startled as our Dining Room was invaded by a wild beast, two noble lovers, a fractured Wall, refulgent Moonshine, and a Prologuizer. Priscilla Higgins (Producer) had assembled and costumed Ann Parks (Prologue), Moonshine (Steve Lewellyn, wearing a silvery disc on his head), Elizabeth Borst (Thisbe), Allen Lang (Pyramus), Bill Perham (Lion, with a captured camel), and Marge Pullman (Wall), all of whom burst into the midst of startled diners and servers with a pandemonium of pummeled pans.
>
> Quincy Jones, Dining Room supervisor, calmed his staff while our company of actors read the Bard's lines in a manner that had to be heard to be believed. This was Shakespeare's *A Midsummer Night's Dream*, excerpted by Producer Higgins for a four-minute performance. The author was not available for comment.

Once in a while the residents of Montgomery Place abandon their American flag-waving and celebrate their inherited ethnicity. Such was true when the Scots invited a bagpipe player to serenade the Dining Room. He appeared, played with vigor—and all the hearing aid batteries in the vicinity were rendered useless.

There was no such disaster when the Welsh—or descendants of the Welsh—celebrated their patron saint's birthday. The only sounds that evening came from wooden spoons whacking aluminum pans to attract the attention of diners. St. David's message could be seen fore and aft on the signs worn by the event participants. The signs, reading "DRUIDS" or "CYMRU AM BYTH," translate into "Welsh Intellectuals" and "Wales Forever." Unfortunately, the Welsh marched rather quickly through the Dining Room, and the messages were illegible or unintelligible to many. One bemused elderly diner asked her ancient companion what the signs said. The friend replied, "Something about fluids, I think!"

On the Bus

Soon after Montgomery Place opened, we acquired our first bus. It has had several successors and some wonderful drivers. The many trips offered each week are a blessing for non-drivers. The bus goes to museums, restaurants, theaters, the public library, and on shopping excursions in Hyde Park and around Chicago. On Sundays our bus drives people to the many churches in the neighborhood. Suggestions for new destinations are welcomed by our Activities Director. Although it is difficult to give up the freedom of driving, when the time comes, the versatility of the Montgomery Place bus keeps us from feeling painfully confined.

There have been several memorable trips, even as far away as to Indiana to see the sandhill cranes during their annual migration. Priscilla Higgins reported on one trip:

Fourteen of us piled into the bus, our winter jackets and binoculars cumbersome on this cold and rainy day in October. Would the cranes fly in the rain? We wondered. No matter. We were off on our long-planned expedition to the landing field where the cranes would refuel before continuing their migration down the Mississippi flyway.

We turned off somewhere in Indiana, onto highways with progressively fewer lanes. Raindrops diminished to mist and talk was of cranes: what kind were they? Maybe the whooping cranes we'd seen in *National Geographic*?

The country roads turned into a country lane, labeled "Jasper-Pulaski Wildlife Refuge." We spotted six birds in a field. They were a dappled gray, had very long necks and legs, and had to be the very sandhill cranes we'd come a long way to see.

We drove to the viewing platform. "Look at them! They're coming in from over there!" And, "There's another group. Aren't they graceful?" "Oh, look at those just coming in over here!" Flock after flock appeared in the northeastern sky, flew down and landed in the bright green field evidently planted with a variety of crane-appealing grain.

"You timed it just right," said a parka, standing with her daughter on the viewing platform. "We've been here for three days, and didn't see a single crane; today you've hit exactly the right time. They're just coming in to eat, and then they'll settle down for the night." The field was filling up, flight after flight gliding in, tootling the primitive cry that sounds like a knotty flute. The birds landed gracefully, folded their long wings, and gathered in rows and circles for dinner after their long journey.

One of our experienced bird-watchers estimated that a cool six thousand cranes were tootling and munching in the field before us, maybe comparing fares and flight delays. The expert defended his estimate: he said he'd counted the birds' legs and divided by two.

We watched until we could hardly distinguish the cranes

 from the clouds. Then we again piled into our nifty jitney bus and headed for the famous Teibel restaurant, where we had a jolly after-crane feast.

This was one of the more spectacular trips undertaken by an adventurous group, but there have been many others: to both Lincoln Park Zoo and Brookfield Zoo, the Garfield Park Conservatory, the Morton Arboretum, and the Chicago Botanic Garden. Those who subscribe to the Chicago Shakespeare Theater can be heard saying, "Alas, poor Yorick" sympathetically to a sick friend in the elevator or "To be or not to be, that is the question" when asked how he is feeling after a trip to the dentist. Regular riders on the Montgomery Place bus become naturally bonded.

Montgomery Place Folkways

An anthropologist among us has noted some resident habits and customs:

> *Sharing Information.* What you discuss with your fellow resident is your own business. When you discuss it is hers or his. Naptime is sacrosanct.
> Incorrect: 2:00 P.M. Call on phone. Count ten rings before hanging up.
> Correct: 2:00 P.M. Write brief note. Slip under door.

Our elevators provide another social setting, in which courtesy and brevity are key.

> *Greetings.* There is a correct and an incorrect answer to the question "How are you?"
> Correct: "Just fine." Or "Pluggin' along."
> Incorrect: "After he saw my X-rays, Dr. Pottinger decided I'm going to have to go in to have nylon stents welded to my medial meniscus in both knees and my right elbow; and here's how he's going to go about it. . . ."

It is also true that we have occasionally had elevators that didn't run. This makes for long waits, and the opportunity to compose verse, as Barbara Fiske discovered:

Uplifting Thoughts

I am an impatient waiter
For the elevator.
My waiting has just begun
Because today there is only one
That will run.

Who is the alleviator
To find us a rejuvenator
For the elevator
And just for fun
Get us one
That will always run?

What administrator
Can deal with the equivocator
And the procrastinator
Who repairs our elevator
And get it done
So it will run?

I am an expostulator,
A vociferator,
Ready to become an excommunicator
Of the perpetrator
Who designed this elevator
Because today there is only one
That will run.

Or, I might migrate
And call myself freight.

Staff

It has not only been relationships with other residents, but also close relationships with members of the staff that have helped to build this community. The waitstaff in the Dining Room become familiar to us. Sometimes, simply by providing occasional thoughtful assistance, these people grease the wheels of our independent living. The person at the Front Desk greets us cheerily by name when we come in from the cold, takes in packages, delivers messages, and performs hundreds of small services during the course of each day. These people become part of our community. We feel like a family.

Because tipping of staff is not allowed, we think of other ways to express our appreciation. The Employees' Christmas Fund is one important way. Money is donated by residents and distributed as a bonus at the holidays.

We also have a children's Christmas party, a tradition that began in 1994, when the residents invited the staff and their families as a way of showing appreciation and affection. Since Christmas means so much to children, it soon became a children's party. Now, thirty to forty children, with a dozen or more parents, show up every year. Residents shop for small presents for the children to be delivered by a willing resident Santa Claus and several of his elves. Entertainment is provided. One year, the resident who plays the piano during the party was touched when a child insisted on giving her his present because he wanted to thank her for her beautiful playing. The food comes from the Montgomery Place kitchen, but everything else is arranged by the people who live here. We love having children in the building!

We rejoice with the staff on other occasions, too. One year there was a great triple baby shower held to celebrate the anticipated arrival of babies of three staff members: the Front Desk receptionist, the Dining Room Manager, and the Executive Director. Residents were informed about the shower and anyone who wished to contribute a baby gift anonymously was invited to do so. At the party in the East Room, three large barrels filled with brightly wrapped packages were presented to the mothers-to-be. The

*Sarah Mack and
Activities Director Dana Witta.*

unwrapping and exclaiming was followed by cake. The baby-wear store in the local shopping center did a land-office business that time!

When a member of the staff leaves, we often feel a real sense of loss, and it's clear how important a part of this community that person has been. In 2002, there was a farewell party for Freddy the bus driver, who left to set up his own landscaping business.

One of Freddy's regular trips was taking people to local churches on Sunday mornings. When asked if he had any special Montgomery Place memories, he laughed and said, "Yes, like having everybody singing when we were driving to church. Mr. Coutts started and everybody, Catholics, Unitarians, Episcopalians, Methodists and Baptists alike, joined in:

> Every time I feel the Spirit
> Moving in my heart, I will pray.
> Yes, every time I feel the Spirit
> Moving in my heart, I will pray."

There are also impromptu expressions of concern over the termination of staff. Spearheaded by one or two residents, collections have been taken up to help an individual cope. One used his fund to set up a private taxi service, a blessing for residents who need a reliable driver to get them places on time.

Volunteers

Communities of course are made up of people, and this stew, Montgomery Place, has people in it from different sources. All of them add to the flavor.

Every year students come to Montgomery Place from the Laboratory Schools of the University of Chicago and from DePaul University to fulfill a school or college requirement to spend time in community service.

The students come with their skills, their interests, and their personalities. The Activities Director assigns each one to specific jobs on the basis of the needs and interests of the residents. Reading aloud is very popular with those on the Health Pavilion floors, as well as with the residents who live in their own apartments. The reading may sometimes be interrupted by a loud announcement of "Can't hear!" and some residents may fall asleep soon after the reading begins, but in most cases the residents are overjoyed to have this experience, especially with a younger person.

Another way the students participate is through individual interviews. The residents at Montgomery Place have had varied and interesting experiences, and they like to talk about them. These informal interviews give the students insights into different life experiences, different times, and different cultures. As one resident said, "He interviewed me, and I interviewed him, and we both had a lovely time."

Another encounter between resident and student took place in the garden. Vinnie Orpen, who had recently moved in, stood looking with some despair at the plot of land that was hers to develop. It was very clear that the ground needed to be broken up before any planting could take place. By good fortune, a volunteer from DePaul University came up to offer the help she needed. Vinnie explained her problem to him and provided the tools necessary to dig up the plot. While he worked, the student began a conversation because he wanted to know something about the life she had led before coming to Montgomery Place. Vinnie described their encounter this way:

A strong young volunteer, a college student from
West Africa, helped me dig up the garden and got most
of the weeds out. Whenever I see the white stones he
carefully placed around the sundial, I remember his telling me that he had always enjoyed working with his father in the family garden and that his dream was to
return home and serve others.

Both were very happy with the working and talking relationship.
It was a good match.

A few people have begun their connection with Montgomery
Place because one of their parents was a resident. One energetic
resident who, for several years bicycled ten or fifteen miles along
the lakefront every morning before breakfast, bequeathed to us
her daughter Carolyn Allen, who volunteers in the dementia unit
of the Health Pavilion, and serves as valued editor and layout person
for our publications, especially the monthly *Montgomery Messenger*.
Carolyn explains:

My mother lived at Montgomery Place for the last
four years of her life and made many good friends here.
After she died, I missed her and I missed everyone I had
met through her. I longed for a reason to come back
regularly, for the opportunity to maintain contact with
the fascinating old people living in this building. My
chance came in the fall of 1997, when I became a volunteer reader in the second-floor dementia unit.

Each Monday morning, from 10:30 to 11:15, I read
fairy tales, folktales, short stories, and poems to an
audience of fifteen or twenty. We always end by singing
"Amazing Grace" (with considerable help from Judy
Collins), and with a group recitation of Edward Lear's
comic poem "The Owl and the Pussycat." The residents are a wonderful audience who really appreciate
the drama and excitement of the stories, and they're
getting quite good at recitation as well. Of all my
regular weekly activities, the time I spend on the
second floor is the one I look forward to most and the

one that invariably gives me the greatest satisfaction. It's a real treat, at least as much for me as it is for the people to whom I read.

The Health Pavilion is an important part of this community. Some of us have been patients there temporarily, some have spent many hours there with spouses or friends, and all of us want both the second and the third floor to be as cheerful and stimulating as possible, since we rely on their existence as a safety net for ourselves. Many residents have contributed their talents to this end. A long time ago, an early volunteer wrote an exhortation for the *Montgomery Messenger*:

> Bored? Talk to yourself? Call the desk to see what is going on? Watch too much TV? Waiting for spring? *Volunteer!* The Health Pavilion needs you to read to patients, sing along with them, play games, help with crafts, engage in one-on-one or small group conversation, read magazine articles, the daily newspaper, or just *listen* as they tell you about their lives and themselves. You will learn so much and at the same time bring happiness into the lives of some who thought it had passed them by. So get up, quit talking to yourself, don't call the desk, turn off the TV, and spring will come. Call the activities director and volunteer. Try it. You might like it!

Encouraged, resident volunteers showed up. Linnea Anderson, an accomplished pianist, wrote: "Just a year ago Elizabeth Borst asked me if I would be willing to play the piano for patients on the third floor. I agreed to do so, and for one year I have considered it one of the happiest of my life's experiences. Although some of the patients don't feel well enough to sing, all of them appreciate music and express it with generous applause. As for me, I've gained many new friends on the third floor."

Not all the volunteer work at Montgomery Place is incoming, however. Children also enjoy reading and being read to, and in the spring of 2003 a hardy band of residents volunteered their skills at the local public school two blocks west of us. A half-dozen old people visited Bret Harte School's kindergarten and first-grade classrooms weekly. A first grader was delighted to be assigned to read to a blind volunteer, who explained hard words as the girl spelled them out. The children discussed versions of "The Billy Goats Gruff": why in two of their books should the story be told differently? One visitor illustrated and read a book she'd written for the class. The children—writers and readers all—were delighted at her gift of a one-of-a-kind picture book, *The Tree Troll.*

At the close of one reading-and-being-read-to session, the teacher proposed that the children give the volunteers a "microwave." Each child lifted a hand and vigorously wiggled the little finger: a microwave of appreciation for shared literacy.

Festivals and Celebrations

Festivals and celebrations enhance the life of a community. They give shape to the year and mark off the seasons; they even give shape to the decade and mark off the years—something very helpful in keeping one's place in time. The Dining Room staff is wonderful at remembering to celebrate special days with special food, and the Activities Director always plans a special event for the Fourth of July. Every month all the birthday people from that month are treated to a delicious luncheon, and holidays, such as Christmas, Chanukkah, and Thanksgiving, are duly celebrated. In between there is red food for Valentine's Day, green soup for St. Patrick's Day, and orange items for Halloween. There are many memorable individual celebrations. People have birthday parties of all sorts with friends and family, and, on major holidays, tables for visiting family are set up all over the first floor. Some people's children and grandchildren are frequent visitors, and we watch babies grow up into school children.

In contrast to the formally decorated Christmas tree in the East Room, a residents' Christmas tree in the Lounge was provided in 1991 for people to decorate as they pleased. It has become a tradition.

That first year, ornaments were unpacked and hung by those who had brought them to their new home, unable to leave behind sentimental bits of Christmases past. These ornaments now decorate green swags over the Lounge doors, as for a number of years the tree itself has had handmade ornaments produced by residents. Under the tutelage of Kathy Berton, the Arts and Crafts Group made three-dimensional stars and other needlepoint ornaments. These can be found over the Activity Room doors.

The following year, a ceramic sculptor was in charge of a group that made clay gingerbread children, toy soldiers, and other figures. Then paper chains and origami in metallic and colorful paper graced our tree.

Ann Parks took on the next decorating project, sixty or more carolers with clay heads and old-fashioned costumes. They are brought out and refurbished each year, to be hung, guessed about, and laughed at. Some are caricatures of residents; all are senior citizens except for a ring of cherubs at the top and two mice at the bottom of the tree.

Making the carolers was a joint project of Arts and Crafts and Needlecrafters members as well as casual drop-ins. Anyone could make a head in clay, paint it, attach it to a pipe cleaner body padded with nylon hosiery strips, and costume it as a caroler with a songbook, a wreath, or packages. There were "specialists" who made these figures or crafted scarves and hats, lace-trimmed petticoats, felt shoes, mittens, kid-gloved hands, shawls, trousers, full skirts, and bonnets.

For New Year's Eve, the residents have taken special initiative in planning what goes on. We couldn't do it without the help of Dana, the Activities Director, who does all the hard work, but we are enthusiastic participants, not just pleased passive guests.

Our New Year's Eve party has become a dance, thanks to the floor bought with the proceeds from our rummage sales. (The first year or two we danced on the East Room carpet—not too easy.) Now we not only have a sizeable dance floor to put down, but we also enjoy a revolving light that makes gala sparkles on the ceiling. At first, Montgomery Place supplied wine and soft drinks, but one resident felt these potables didn't adequately live up to the occasion, so he supplied an extraordinary array of alcoholic beverages. When he died he left us a large supply, enough to last for many New Year's Eves to come.

We dress up in old finery or costumes, and the music is mostly what we remember from the 1930s and 1940s. An eighty- or ninety-year-old couple in their dress clothes dancing and smiling into each other's eyes is a poignant sight. One lively resident dances with the folks in wheelchairs. An expert dances with anyone, or, when a more up-to-date piece comes on, she dances alone and everyone stops to watch.

Out in the hall, a Gypsy is telling fortunes. A croupier at the roulette table is saying, *"Faites vos jeux, 'sieurs et dames. Faites vos jeux,"* [Play your games, ladies and gentlemen. Play your games.], as fortunes in pennies are won and lost. What the "bank" wins goes to the Activities Committee. The television in the Lounge shows New Year's celebrations as they come across the Atlantic, and some people retire with Iceland or Newfoundland or Labrador. Some of us make it to see the ball drop in Times Square, and a very few diehards are still wearing their paper hats at midnight in Chicago.

Tenth Anniversary

A "Treasure Tea" was held in anticipation of the weeklong celebration of Montgomery Place's tenth anniversary in the fall of 2001. Priscilla Higgins reported on it in the *Montgomery Messenger:*

> Seated at the be-skirted reception table in the East Room at "Tea and Treasures" on August 22, Barbara Fiske and Aileen Gordon registered the many treasures Montgomery Place residents brought for the occasion. This preview anticipates exhibiting the treasures in November for the Montgomery Place Tenth Anniversary Celebration. The objects from all over the world and also from many decades were put on display.
>
> There was no doubt about the origin of the miniature "Kvass Keg," bought in Russia, a transportable size of one of the many sizes of kegs of Kvass that peddlers trundled about the Slavic streets. The people there, says Chauncy Harris, lined up in the streets to buy and drink jugs of

Barbara Fiske, Ann Parks, and Aileen Gordon register items for the "Treasure Tea."

room-temperature Kvass, mildly invigorating, but not too tasty, in his opinion.

There was lots of speculation about the parquetry circular game board. Is it what it looked to many, like . . . an early Parcheesi board? There were unmarked "HOME" nests and arrows directing the path around the board. Perhaps the skilled cabinetmaker, who was Joan Swift's great-grandfather, assumed that everybody knew the rules when he fashioned it in 1867. And they probably did, then.

The crowd circulated about the exhibit tables, while Betty Borst played the piano, from the "Whiffenpoof Song" to the stirring Welsh, "Men of Harlech." The crowd examined other fascinating objects on the exhibit tables: "The Shepeard Family History"; photos of a one-year-old, first crying, then smiling; a four-piece oil painting series called "Summer Undressing"; also, five Russian nesting dolls, each one a world

Visitors and residents gather to view the "treasures" on display.

political figure of the fifties, with the largest labeled "Nobel Prize." A sobering note was Kiyo Hashimoto's photos taken at the Japanese Relocation Center where her family and friends, all American citizens, were interned.

On a more cheerful and decorative note, a Native American beaded necklace, lap-quilts made by our Needlecrafters, World War II correspondence, Chinese sculptures, African ebony carvings, and much more. The marketing group put the exhibit on computer, while the rest of us indulged in smoked salmon and cucumber open-faced sandwiches. It was Elegance in the Afternoon, further enhanced by tea served from the Montgomery Place silver tea service, surrounded by large bouquets of flowers.

The anniversary celebration that followed the Treasure Tea and months of planning, ran from November 16 through 19, 2001. The objects displayed at the Treasure Tea were very professionally exhibited in cases lent to us by the Museum of Science and Industry. Ann Parks, a resident with many years of museum work behind her, ensured the artifacts were expertly labeled and beautifully arranged.

Three large maps were displayed in the main hallway: Chicago, the United States, and the World. Residents were asked to put a white pin in the place they were born, a blue pin every-where they had lived for six months or more, and a red pin where they had traveled. The effect was stunning! More of us were born in Chicago than any other single location, but we had been born all over the United States and Europe, and a few in Asia. The most spectacular effect was achieved by the red pins signifying travel. Scarcely a corner of the world was left unvisited by Montgomery Place residents. The maps are now on permanent display for all to admire.

The residents prepared a presentation, giving a brief history of Montgomery Place and its origin in the Church Home. There followed a short slide show with lively description of life here and some of the people who have made it interesting. The presenters read their parts with gusto, and the many weeks of preparation paid off as the audience enjoyed the show and laughed in the right places.

There was, of course, good food and drink, and there were speeches by staff and visiting celebrities. Despite the generous size of the East Room, space was limited, so the whole event was done three times, each presentation for a different constituency.

Two written commemorations arose from the tenth anni-versary. The first was *The Magnificent Messenger*, a 190-page com-pilation of the "best of the best" articles from the first ten years of our homegrown newsletter. Carolyn Allen, the nonresident professional who handles the *Messenger* layout each month, designed the book, and IVY Marketing saw to the binding and cover design. Each resident and every guest at the anniversary celebration were given a book, and extra copies were printed for prospective residents.

The second publication, long in gestation and preparation, filled with memories, the work of a dedicated committee, affec-tionately called *In It Together,* is in your hands.

Death and Children

Resident Joan Swift reflects:

There is one aspect of life in a retirement community that I had not been intellectually or emotionally prepared for, despite our family's experience and a rational understanding of the realities of life: People in "continuing care communities" die. Death is not an isolated or infrequent event from which one can distance oneself.

The new friends (or old) who make living here a pleasure also bring an increased sense of loss when they die. I had not thought about that aspect of it before we came, but as time goes by, it takes on a reality that is missing in the outside world. Some people cannot live comfortably with this aspect of retirement community living. The closeness of our community makes this aspect hard to ignore. We have to make our peace with it.

I have come to balance my sense of loss at a person's death with the potential loss to my life had I never known that person in the first place. If my husband and I were still living in our house or had moved to an apartment building, we would have made very few, if any, new friends. As old friends died or moved away, our social contacts would have decreased appreciably, almost entirely. My husband still goes to work, but his current colleagues are in an entirely different stage of life both professionally and socially. I no longer can get out to the professional meetings I used to enjoy, and there, too, most of the people I knew are no longer active. So coming here, for us, has been a chance to make a large number of new friends—friends who share *this* stage of life with us.

The East Room fills quietly. There are flowers on a stand beside the piano (never *on* our precious piano). A violinist is just tuning up, and a few children are sitting with their parents and grandparents in the front rows.

Each memorial service is different because each life has been different, and when an old person from among us dies we need to celebrate that person as well as mourn him or her. The forms of the services held here differ. There are usually prayers, but not always. The services are generally conducted by Father Bob Petite, our Episcopalian chaplain, who can lead a beautiful and appropriate service for any of the many beliefs or unbeliefs represented in this building. Often friends or members of the family tell us things we never knew about our friend, and we almost always leave the service knowing them better than we did before. Sometimes we wish we'd heard this news earlier.

Under special circumstances a regularly scheduled activity can evolve spontaneously into an impromptu memorial service, as it did in January 2004. Leslie Orear was the presenter of the regular Wednesday-evening music program in the Lounge. As we assembled he told us:

> I planned a light program for the evening. But we have lost two of the tall trees in our forest, and I felt I wanted to pay tribute to Chauncy Harris and Hewson Swift. Chauncy was a font of information. When I needed to know the name of the West African nation just south of the Sahara, he not only answered my question, but also knew the dialect of the indigenous people living there. Hewson could tell us all about our birds and trees, and he taught us to love the ladybugs that infest our building every autumn. He was the high priest of our temple, which is our Steinway piano.

> Mozart's *Requiem,* together with Hovhaness and Scriabin, may seem like a bizarre combination, but you know I have a quirky taste in music, and so be it.

> I am not using the whole *Requiem.* The first selection is stormy: "We are angry! It is not fair! These guys had work to do!" But the voice of reason is then heard: "Calm down." We hear the *Lachrymosa,* and we can cry. In the middle of the *Requiem* we get back to work, repairing the tear in our community and carry on.

> Alan Hovhaness was from Somerville, Massachusetts, but his music reflects his Armenian heritage; it is not

your standard American musical language. His
Symphony No. 2 he called *Mysterious Mountain.* Hewson
Swift was a little like that. Remember he was a microbi-
ologist in search of the building blocks of life.
Hovhaness, in *Mysterious Mountain,* searches for the building blocks of the universe. In his *Prayer to Saint Gregory,*
Hovhaness refers to the priest who in 301 A.D. brought
Christianity to the Armenians. In the high trumpet we
hear confidence in the truth and the authority to pro-
claim it. Then come the bass notes—declaring the need
for a firm foundation.

In the Scriabin I hear a musical description of our
two men. Scriabin wrote some piano music which he
merely called waltzes, but Willard Elliott, the late
bassoonist of the Chicago Symphony Orchestra,
arranged them for a different musical instrumenta-
tion. It is here performed by Chicago Pro Musica. I
think you will get the sense of Chauncy and Hewson in
this music—urbane, witty, and sometimes unexpected.

As the music faded away at the end of the evening, we felt we
could see our friends now gone from us, ambling off into the
distance. And we could go home happy.

Occasionally, friends from the world outside arrange a
celebration for someone while that person is still alive; a woman
who had started professional nursing in the public schools of Chicago and had trained many nurses to follow in her footsteps was
honored one afternoon by many of the people who wanted to tell
her how much she meant to them. We knew her, but many of us
had no idea about the importance of her earlier life.

There was the party for Leslie Orear, who runs the Illinois
Labor History Society and recently had edited a book about
Mother Jones. Undeterred by the inconvenience of blindness
from macular degeneration, he goes to his office downtown
every day on the bus, in order to keep the newsletter of the
Labor History Society going.

Many of his Labor friends gave him a wonderful ninetieth birthday party to express their affection and appreciation. The East

Room resounded with "Happy Birthday," and "Solidarity Forever," and other rousing Labor songs.

Our ties to younger generations are very important to us, and other people's children and grandchildren or nieces and nephews or younger-generation friends form another kind of connection in this place. One resident recalls:

> Yesterday, in the elevator, I met the daughter of a good Montgomery Place friend. I knew the daughter quite well because, although she lives at some distance, she often visits her mother, and we have shared many meals and evenings of talk. I was glad to see her but I hadn't known she was coming now. "I'm here for a sad reason," she said. "Can I walk to your apartment with you?" So we got out of the elevator together at my floor.
>
> She had come to tell her mother that her thirty-eight-year-old son, her mother's favorite grandson, had died suddenly and unexpectedly in a far country a few days before. She wanted my husband and me to come to her mother's apartment that afternoon with a few other Montgomery Place friends. None of us had ever seen this young man, but sitting in our ninety-year-old friend's living room that afternoon, her daughter shared him with us. She spread out pictures, and through tears she told us what he was like. She shared his life with us so that when she went home her mother would have friends who could be more truly with her because they had been let into her grief and shock.
>
> Although we are very closely acquainted with death here in this place, this was different. As we sat around looking at pictures of a strong, handsome, vital young man, our old friend kept saying, "It isn't the young who should die."

Another time, Alice Hayes recognized the son of an old friend eating with his father at the nearest table:

I had a lively conversation with him, catching up on his life and his wife's. I had met them a few years ago when we both were trying to sell self-published books before Christmas. She had written a wonderful children's book and he had illustrated it. Mine was a book of poetry. They were better salesmen than I was. In comparing notes we became good friends and I was interested to hear that his wife had finished law school while continuing to be a cop on the beat!

We sometimes get an envelope under our door containing the next e-mail installment of letters from the West Bank sent by Annie, the daughter of another Montgomery Place friend. We came to know Annie when she was living next door and teaching Arabic in Chicago. Now she is living in Jenin as part of an international presence that moderates Israeli violence. She takes bread to the Palestinian camp or walks Palestinian children to school. She helps with the olive harvest and she lives closely with a family. We feel lucky to share her remarkable e-mails.

These are extensions of our lives that we would never have if we didn't live in a place where our friends' children become our friends and where our own children get to know our new friends. This makes us truly a family and Montgomery truly a home, as Alice Hayes recounts.

Coming Home

Just after Labor Day we moved back to the city from our log cabin in the country, after a wonderful sequence of visits from children, grandchildren, and one great-grandchild. Twenty of them had come, two by two, like the ark! It was a fabulous present for my eightieth birthday.

Coming back to Montgomery Place is like coming home after a long voyage, back to another kind of family. There are so many welcomes! People keep saying they're glad we're back. We feel enfolded in friends. We are back

where it doesn't matter if you forget a good friend's
name because she probably can't remember yours either.
Back to where you can discuss the world you care about
even if you can't remember the name of the British
Prime Minister or the head of the U.N.

Where "whatchamacallum" and "whatshisname" and
"who-is-it" litter the Dining Room conversation, where we
help each other remember:

"I think it begins with an R."

"Not quite rugby. Ragweed?"

"No, but that's close. . . ."

Where people are neighbors, the hall is like a village
street, and you can borrow milk from a neighbor or
make a sandwich for a friend who forgets to eat. People
pick up bread at the store for each other or leave flowers
when someone's sick.

When we came back, there were plump red tomatoes
from a Montgomery Place garden on a table in the front
hall. "Help yourself," said the note on the basket. Yesterday we found two little sweet tomatoes hanging on our
doorknob.

People make close friends; newly formed couples care
for each other and keep each other company. New arrivals
are welcomed by their neighbors. Although everybody
doesn't know everybody else, there is a strong feeling of
concern for each other and of being part of a community.

When someone dies there is genuine mourning for that
person, sometimes very intense. In a place like this, where
the mean age of residents is about eight-five, people do die,
and yet many people are willing to make close friends, even
knowing that the friendship can't last for very long. It's hard
to get used to the gaps in our community left by deaths, but
interesting new people keep appearing and taking over the
functions left behind. Their abilities and interests are still
welcomed and used.

To be needed in one's old age is a real blessing, and
to be surrounded by friends when you are old is a wonderful thing. We are glad to be back!

Section III:
The Lives We've Led

6

The Early Years

Among the rapidly rising numbers of retirement communities today, each presents itself as providing the same basic amenities of secure and comfortable living that have become standard in the industry, while proclaiming its uniqueness as an institution. In fact, each community is unique.

Each is a reflection of its location, of the auspices under which it is managed, and of the mission it is designed to serve. Most importantly, it is a reflection of the individuals who make up its population. Each individual who reaches the age to join such a community brings with him or her a lifetime of experiences. It is the residents' unique characteristics and experiences that determine the essential character of a given community. The story of the first ten years of Montgomery Place demonstrates the roles its residents have played in building the particular kind of community it is today.

The majority of our Montgomery Place pioneers were born between 1910 and 1925. A smaller but still active group was born between 1900 and 1909, a still smaller number between 1926 and 1930. As a group we have experienced, directly or indirectly, the major events of the twentieth century. Some of us remember the First World War, all of us the second. Almost all of us were touched by the Great Depression and all of us have benefitted from the scientific advances that have helped us achieve our present advanced ages.

The stories, sketches, and vignettes that make up this section are the work of residents of Montgomery Place. Most of the stories here were contributed in response to a request from the committee writing this book. The request was a general one, covering all aspects of individual lives and major historical events of our times; the topics included represent the choices of the authors themselves. Additional material was selected from earlier resident submissions to our monthly newsletter, the *Montgomery Messenger*, and from interviews and oral histories provided by residents. Together, they give a kaleidoscopic picture of the residents who make up Montgomery Place.

Early Memories

The world we live in today is very different from the one most of us knew as children. It was a simpler place in many ways. There was time to enjoy the "Marshall Street Moon"; there were fewer choices to be made, fewer competing demands on one's time.

While the early years of the twentieth century included many events that shaped the world we would inherit from our parents, our conscious memories tend to reflect our interests and concerns at the time: We were children and our world was a domestic one, centered around family, home, and school.

There was no television and there were no electronic games. Play was a do-it-yourself activity. Communities were smaller and more closely knit. Playmates were the children in the neighborhood; "play dates," Little League, and other adult-organized activities were not required.

Marshall Street Moon

I was born in a manufacturing town about fifty miles south of Fort Wayne, Indiana. There was much natural gas available in the area, and work for all. My glassblower father blew Blue Ribbon prescription bottles.

In 1913, when I was five years old, my parents built a house at 325 East Marshall Street. The sidewalks were cement with curbs, but the street was gravel; if you fell off your bike, you got well skinned. We enjoyed what we called the "Marshall Street Moon" as we sat on the steps in the evening, making figures out of clouds and playing games with stones, while our relatives visited. The lots on Marshall Street were about fifty feet wide and one hundred fifty long, and we could play in ours and the one next door as well as a vacant lot which had a lovely tree to climb and all kinds of wildflowers. Many games of croquet were played in summertime, and in the winter we played rook. We were forbidden to go out of these lots.

This left my mother able to be of help to other people. She could always be counted on for a crochet pattern, to solve a sewing problem, or for help if you had a sick child or a new baby. Of course the doctor brought the baby in his black bag; then the next day Mother was there to give the child its first bath.

When World War I was declared over, the paper boys were on the street at an early hour, shouting "*Extra!*" All schools and companies were closed. A neighbor had a hay wagon, and a crowd piled on and rode around town, yelling, pounding on saucepans, and blowing whistles. After doing the neighborhood, we went downtown, where the greatest crowd was gathered in the square. We finally left the wagon and walked around, greeting friends and talking. My six-year-old sister found change on the sidewalk amounting to $1.89 (probably dropped by some happy drunk!). With this money she was able to buy Christmas presents for all her relatives at Mr. Woolworth's red-front store.

Aileen Gordon

Things Change

Clothes have certainly changed. When I was three, I wore an undershirt on top of which was a cotton vest which buttoned up the middle of the back with yellow buttons, each with two large holes, and with buttons of the same type around the waist to which garters were attached, two on each side, to hold up long, white cotton stockings. On top of this went underpants, then nicely ironed bloomers, which matched a nicely ironed dress.

Very early one beautiful spring morning I woke up when it was fresh and damp and the cattails had fallen off the trees to cover the terrace. I wanted to go outdoors so I got dressed for the first time by myself by putting on my vest or "pantywaist" backwards, with the buttons up the front rather than the back.

When I was four, my allowance was five cents a week. My mother was advised to avoid the severe Chicago winter because of a sinus infection, so we went to France. She had planned to take a course at the University of Grenoble, but on arriving in Paris discovered that Grenoble was known as "the pee pot of France" because it was cold and damp and rained so much in the winter, so we went to Grasse. My allowance was now one franc a week. I think perhaps the exchange rate helped to make France attractive to Americans in the twenties.

In Grasse, I could look out the window and watch every week to see a caravan of Gypsies settle across the road to sell bundles of firewood, and in the evening a lamplighter came by to light the gas street lamps with a taper. I went to a convent school and, like all the French children, wore a black apron to keep my clothes clean. After school we were each given a chunk of bread and a chunk of chocolate to eat as we walked home, supervised by a nun, along steep, slippery cobblestone streets with water running along the gutters.

I visited Grasse recently and there were no children in black aprons, no Gypsies, no lamplighters or gas lamps, and the cobblestones of smaller streets were neatly covered with flat paving stones, but one could still hear the water trickling in the gutters underneath.

Jane Overton

Living in Two Worlds

As a child I spent my summers in the country and my winters in the city. My official home was with my parents in New York City, amid apartment buildings and crowded sidewalks. In the summer, I lived with a farm family, walked barefoot on dirt roads and grassy fields.

It seemed I had the best of two worlds. Winter on the farm was cold and windy, with deep snow covering the fields, making life hard. School was difficult to reach and limited in scope.

Summer in the city was hot, with little relief from the glare of the sidewalks and stifling nights. There was no air-conditioning in those days; the best you could do to cool off was to open all the windows and hope a breeze would bring a little relief. Fire escapes were used as sleeping quarters for some. Winter meant school and structured days; summer was free time to do with as one wished.

Between the two, I learned the basic facts of life. City life was diversity—different people, different colors, different lifestyles, different voices, different ways. In the country, everyone I met spoke with the same down-east accent, wore the same kind of work clothes, sturdy boots, had tanned faces, work-worn hands. In the city, everyone hurried; in the country, people worked hard and steadily, but there was no rush; there was time to stop and chat, to compare observations on the weather, the crops, and "that man in Washington."

It was a small family farm with three cows, one horse, chickens, an apple orchard, and several fields dedicated to a variety of crops—hay, corn, potatoes, lettuce, carrots, beets. Wild raspberry and blueberry bushes around the edges supplied the family with fruit for pies and jam. While as a summer visitor I was not required to take on heavy chores, I was expected to help out with the everyday jobs like picking the lettuce and carrots for supper, or collecting the day's eggs from the chicken house.

One chore we children were expected to take on was the care of the pony and the horse we rode. Stabled in the big barn attached to the house, our steeds required grooming, food, and water, and, most demanding, their stables cleaned out daily. A hole in the barn floor provided for convenient waste removal but was something of a hazard for a young person not watching where she was going, as I found to my dismay one time—but only once—as I swept myself backwards down the hole onto the manure pile in the basement.

The barn was a favorite place to play on a rainy day, especially after the hay had been freshly cut and stored in the haylofts filling the back walls. Once the lofts were filled, we would climb up to a suitable height and *jump,* arms extended, out into space—to land slipping and tumbling in the fresh hay. As with so many things in life, jumping in the hay had its downside, especially for a little girl with hay fever. After a few jumps I would retreat with weepy eyes and dripping nose only to return the next day to live dangerously again.

My favorite activity, after riding the horse and jumping in the hay, was climbing the apple trees in the orchard. It was an "old" orchard, not carefully tended, so its trees had been allowed to grow as they pleased, with intertwining branches and good places to sit, hidden from the earthlings below, to contemplate important matters of the universe.

I learned a great deal in those summers on the farm, not only where our daily food comes from—our vegetables, milk, eggs, and chicken dinners—the problem of potato beetles; what a dry summer can do to a corn crop; and why farmers don't like crows, but also why those fiercely independent farmers didn't like the Democrats, so staunchly supported by my liberal-thinking city father. It was an important lesson in politics and economics.

Joan Swift

An Indiana Boyhood

When I was three years old, we moved to Wayne County, Indiana, to Aunt Lydia's eighty-acre farm on Lost Mile Road, with its comfortable house that had been built in 1867. It was a typical family farm of the time, with horses, cows, pigs, and lots of chickens. It also had a large fertile garden, a long grape arbor, and lots of fruit trees. Of course, in 1920, this home and farm had no electricity. I vividly remember the cold sheets in the upstairs bedroom, where the only heat came from the flue of the downstairs stove, which radiated for a few feet from its source, but not as far as the bed.

Drinking water came from a pump on the porch connected to a deep well. Water for washing came from a cistern that collected water from the roof. The bath was taken in front of the wood fire in a large copper bathtub filled with water heated on the stove and mixed with the "right amount" of cold water. Bathing was limited to once a week—Saturday night. Toilet facilities were located about eighty or ninety feet to the south of the house, a rather forbidding trip in the dead of winter or in the dark of night. Of course, there was always the "thunder mug," [chamber pot] and the great outdoors that was not quite as far away.

When I was seven and my sister was sweet sixteen, we moved into Hagerstown, Indiana, and my father became superintendent of schools. We lived in a very nice home, traditionally the superintendent's home, not far from the very fine, modern (for those days) high school. Halloween was a great time in Hagerstown, and I don't think a single Halloween went by without the superintendent of schools' outdoor toilet being tipped over and the windows of his house being thoroughly soaped. Unfortunately, as a family member of the victim, I had to help repair all this damage.

Hagerstown was full of everyday small-town activity that was naturally very interesting to a small boy. The fishmonger came with his horse-drawn carriage every Thursday or Friday, and my parents bought fresh fish, usually pickerel, or oysters from him. Two doors down was a house I was sure was inhabited by witches. The yard was all grown up and old ladies who were seldom seen in the neighborhood were the only residents.

There was a gully in front of the house that I enjoyed playing in after warm summer rains, making little dams and waterfalls. Not far from our home was a small creek. From the bridge across that creek I pulled my first fish. It was a catfish with antennae protruding, and I was very frightened because my friends told me it would sting. Nevertheless, I did manage to get it home and we had it for dinner.

Robert Wissler

Gaslight in the Bronx

We had heat in our apartment but no electricity. Light came from gas jets, each sheathed in a thin mantle that glowed in the flame. My parents kept quarters at hand to pay for the gaslight. Once or twice an evening, Father would drop a quarter into the meter and then we'd get light for a period—I don't remember for how long; I was only four years old.

Helen Rice

The Coaster Wagon

I remember one special Christmas when I was preschool age. We came downstairs to a lovely tree lighted with candles. (There were buckets of water around for safety's sake, of course.) There, under the tree, was a real coaster wagon, with side pieces that could transform it into a small farm wagon. The wagon lasted for years and was used by all three small children in the Coppock family, but I don't remember it coming with us when we moved to Chicago in 1922. There were no sidewalks where we lived in Nebraska, so it must have worn out quickly.

Grace Coppock Bibler

Mumble-the-Peg

Mumble-the-peg was a game popular in 1916, when I was ten years old. Each boy twirled his pocketknife from various positions, starting with a slide from the scalp, with the knife facing backward. This contest of skill consisted of making the knife stick in the ground so that at least three finger-breadths could fit below it, parallel with the greensward. This was in the heyday of Boy Scouting, when pocketknives were standard equipment.

The loser of a game of mumble-the-peg had to pull out a wooden stake from the grass with his teeth. The grass tickled his nose. The lawn we used was in front of the six-flat at 4219 South Ellis Avenue, where I lived. The lawn smelled luxurious from regular janitorial watering. By 2001 that building was the only one standing in a several-block area.

Max Sonderby

My Scooter

At age eleven, in pre-Hitler Germany, I entered an essay contest for children, sponsored by our town's newspaper. The title was "What Children Like Best and What They Want to Be."

I addressed only the first part, stating that I liked most of all *reading*, particularly adventure stories. Next I liked playing my violin, but just the songs *I* wanted to play, or to compose my own, not those my teacher assigned, which were strictly classical. Thirdly,

when the weather was nice, I liked to ride my scooter. I mentioned
doing this with my girlfriend and that both of us had bells and
directional signals on our scooters. Most of all, I stated, I enjoyed
that "everyone had to get out of our way." The newspaper used this
last phrase to head the story, and it was published!

Renate Vambery

Water Magic

I had not known it could be so cold in summer.
I'd had small dealings with the predawn day.
I woke to life most days about a sun-warmed seven,
as if school still kept—vacation time or not.

But here at camp there was an extra swim for those
who could, who would, brave crawling out of blankets
into the daunting dawn, and I, a mini-mermaid,
was drawn to water like a frog.

Tooth-chattering dawn could be some warmed
by leaping down the hill above the dock stretched
grey, silent, empty, from the shore, waiting
for campers in their bright bathing suits to come.

Hugged by a towel, the cold damp suit not dry
from swim to swim, the hops from stone to boulder
kept one's mind off shivering and on the joy
of being first to break the silent surface of the lake.

Towel dropped, I'd run the length of dock to dive
into pure liquid pleasure, sauced by the shock
of cold, only to meet with more surprise on coming up for breath
to find the water warmer than the air. Magic in that!

Water magic, which could turn the silver lake
to cobalt blue by ten o'clock and chop the mirror surface up
with sharp-edged wavelets, would make the late morning
swim a cool delight to spite the heat of coming noon.

Ann Parks

From Horses to Horseless Buggies

Many of the technological advances we enjoy today were "works in progress" during our childhoods. Automobiles were still a novelty and a challenge to their operators. Horse-drawn vehicles still brought the milk, the ice, and provided the most reliable transportation.

Utah Sleigh Rides

Toward the end of the horse-and-buggy era, about 1915, we were living in a small rural town at the foot of the beautiful Wasatch Mountains of Utah. The town's elevation was around 5,000 feet, so there was a lot of snow in the wintertime. One of my happiest memories is of the sleigh rides we took on all kinds of errands in the family buggy.

My father owned a coal black riding horse, which was also a good buggy horse. There was plenty of room on the floor of the buggy for us four children to snuggle up under a buffalo robe or blankets to keep warm, aided by hot bricks, properly wrapped, provided by our mother.

When the snow came, my father removed the wheels from the buggy and attached four specially made runners. These runners were crafted to fit on the same axles that held the wheels, and made a perfect sleigh-buggy. I don't know where my father got those runners, and I don't remember seeing another buggy like that.

Ben Meeker

The Milkman and His Horse

In the summer at my grandmother's, I remember Mr. Bergsma, the farmer, sliding great flat white enamel pans of milk through the window from the back porch onto a counter in the pantry. There they sat, waiting for the cream to rise to the top and be skimmed off for cream and cottage cheese. Curling strings of sticky flypaper hanging down kept the flies out of the milk.

They gave me the milk still warm, and I was expected to think it was a treat; but the little pieces of fat floating on the surface made me gag and beg for the "milkman's milk" I had in the city. This made everybody laugh. "Where do you think milk comes from, anyway?" they said.

It was only in the city that the milkman and his horse brought me proper milk to drink. The horse waited patiently outside our apartment building, his face in his nose bag, munching, while the milkman brought butter, eggs, cream, and cheese, and left them outside our back door, taking away the empty bottles. When he finished with our building, he'd climb into the back of the milk wagon, and the horse would go on all by himself while the driver refilled his carrying rack.

From our front windows I could see that wonderful horse stop again, halfway down the block, and with his bottles rattling, the milkman hopping out the back of the wagon. The horse would go on munching his breakfast.

Alice Hayes

When Stanley Ran Out of Steam

When I was four or five years old, I lived in Denver. A family friend had bought a Stanley Steamer touring car, and invited us on an outing. We drove on the dirt road to Colorado Springs without event, then headed up into the mountains for the trip back to Denver. We came into a mountain hailstorm, so we stopped and put up the isinglass curtains. We went on, ever higher. The car slowed down and then wouldn't go any more. At the higher elevation, the steam engine just wouldn't boil water!

Leslie Orear

Getting an Electric Charge

Whenever our family—aunts, uncles, and cousins—met to celebrate some special holiday, it involved travel, from the east side of Chicago to a western suburb, or vice versa. If the trip was from west to east, much advance planning was essential because of the eccentricities of my great-uncle's car—an Electric!

This was a boxlike car with windows all around but entered from one side only. The interior had well-upholstered, bench-like seats . . . and no steering wheel! A short upholstered stick was available from two locations and this steered and accelerated the car. The "fuel" was electricity, which meant a long period "on the charge" before departure. This charge would power the Electric to the destination, but would not take it home again. Halfway to the gathering, my resourceful great-uncle found a garage on Washington Boulevard which could replenish the lost power, thus, on most occasions, assuring a round trip.

Nevertheless, the greeting when the Electric arrived was always, "Good! You didn't run down!"

Elizabeth Jones Borst

Diamond Lake, Michigan, 1911

I spent the summer of 1911 in my grandmother's cottage on Diamond Lake, near Cassopolis, Michigan, 110 miles from Chicago, the next stop after South Bend on the Grand Trunk Railroad as it continues on to Canada.

In 1911, air-conditioning was unheard of. Going to Michigan or Wisconsin was a way to escape the heat of Chicago's summers. My grandmother's household left in June and stayed until October. Her apartment was "closed." Furniture was draped, rugs rolled up, trunks packed, services canceled. Railway Express was called to ship the trunks; Emery Livery was called to take us to the Grand Trunk station.

Two aunts went with us. Their husbands came later for weekends. Another aunt and uncle with their two teenaged sons had a cottage across the road from my grandmother. They returned to Chicago right after Labor Day. My uncle and cousins went on the train, and my aunt left a few days later in their seven-passenger Pierce-Arrow limousine. She sat in the front seat next to the chauffeur.

In 1911 motorcars did not have trunks. There was a toolbox on the running board. The back seat of the limousine was piled with so many boxes that there was hardly room for me—a five-year-old kid. On the floor was a stack of spare tires. From where I sat on the right side, I could barely see the chauffeur's head.

In 1911 there were no paved roads, only gravel-covered, very narrow roads. The farm fence posts were almost close enough to touch as we drove by. The chauffeur stopped the car at a farmhouse and asked the lady of the house if my aunt might use her "outside facility." (This is a reversal of the movie, *Driving Miss Daisy*. The chauffeur is white in my story, and it is the lady who needs the accommodation.)

Catherine German

Coyote Hunting in the Model T

Father had recently purchased a Model T Ford touring car. He enjoyed it very much. He liked to put the top down, place the two big Airedale dogs in the back seat and take off over the prairie. Occasionally he took me along on a coyote hunt.

Father would drive at a maximum speed across the large expanse of prairie pasture until he saw coyotes in the distance. Then he would drive toward them with breakneck speed. Eventually the pursuit would reach a point close enough that he could release the dogs. Father would cry, "*Coyote! Coyote!*" and the dogs would bound from the Ford and go in hot pursuit of their quarry. Usually, the dogs would catch a coyote, but Father reasoned that, even if the coyotes weren't caught, the chase might scare them away. For me, it was an exciting ride across the prairie pasture. Such chases took place during the day, when I was normally at school; only when there was a holiday could I go.

Grandfather went on an occasional chase and found it exhilarating. Father's new Ford captivated Grandfather, and he resolved to join the motorcar owners.

Grandfather went to Kansas City and purchased a lovely four-cylinder Buick touring car. Some basic driving instructions were included with the sale of the car. Then Grandfather drove about two hundred miles over primitive roads back home to southeastern Kansas. It was a heroic trip. Grandfather was proud of his new acquisition and called to ask my father and mother to have a ride. Father was delighted; Mother was skeptical, for she preferred her horse and buggy. It was decided that I should go for the ride. (My sisters were much too young.) Off we went north to the Altamont–Mound Valley road, which was wider and better kept than our road. We headed toward Mound Valley, where Uncle Guy and Aunt Lenora lived.

They had to see the new car and give their approval. Grandfather loved speed, so he accelerated up to twenty-five miles per
hour. The ride was rough and the wind blew the ladies' veils
streaming backward; I huddled in fear between Mother and
Grandmother in the back seat.

Grandmother screamed desperately, "Papa! Papa! You are
going much too fast! Slow down, please!" It was rough and noisy,
and Grandfather never heard or else ignored the plea. Aunt
Lenora and Uncle Guy gave their approval. We finally returned
to our farm, shaken but alive, and glad to end the adventure.

John Rust

Sleds and Cars in New England

We coasted on sleds down a suburban street that had a
coating of a couple of inches of snow and ice. Fortunately for us,
the snowplows didn't plow closely. We sailed down a hill into an
intersection, the visibility being quite limited both by the corner
houses and by the hill on the next street. Why did our parents
let us do this? Why didn't a sled and a car ever collide? I think
the answer must be that there were very few cars out on the
slippery snow-ice, and they moved very slowly.

One morning we awoke to find several inches of new snow on
the ground, so my brother and I volunteered to put the chains on
the rear wheels of the car. When we finished, it was too late for us
to walk to school, and our mother didn't need the car after all, so
we washed up and then drove to school—a special treat for us.

A few years earlier, the family had a car with isinglass windows, which came off on warm and dry days but offered a little
protection against the cold. I'll never forget my surprise and
pleasure at seeing my father drive up one day in a car with
regular glass windows and a heater. Of course, this was a used
car. We couldn't afford a new one. But it was clearly a step up.
The change was from a Franklin to a Nash.

Some fifteen years later, my wife Barbara and I bought our first
car, a Crosley. It was a midget car with no heater, no gas gauge, and
a hand-operated windshield wiper. Total cost was under $400.

Donald Fiske

Childhood Illness

Most of us remember the common diseases of childhood—measles, mumps, whooping cough, and chicken pox, which emptied classrooms on a regular basis in the spring. We remember, too, the more serious diphtheria, typhoid fever, smallpox, and scarlet fever, which put the whole family into quarantine and might have serious aftereffects; all were feared, but perhaps the most frightening menace was "infantile paralysis," poliomyelitis. It was both a killer and a crippler, and its threat dictated the summer plans of many families and decimated attendance at normally popular summer attractions such as swimming pools, circuses, and other public gatherings. Illnesses that were life threatening in our childhood are no longer factors in our children's lives: Some have been eradicated almost completely; others have been controlled by vaccination and still others by antibiotics unknown in our childhoods.

The Green Girl

Hallucinations! I know about hallucinations. I learned at an early age. I had just begun mid-semester of first grade when a late-winter epidemic of measles raged through the school. Not the three-day, but the at-least-three-weeks variety. It must have cleared out the entire first grade of those without older brothers or sisters to bring it home to them when they were preschoolers.

Being the first child in my family to go to school, it was I who brought the measles home to my baby sister. Her inherited immunity must have just lapsed—in any case, measles could be fatal and the doctor stood by her crib shaking his head. Then perhaps thinking she needed a jump-start to get her going again, he picked her up by the heels and beat her back to life as if she were newborn. She survived and is busy to this day.

I knew nothing of this at the time. I was lying in my own junior bed, too sick to do more than restlessly move my aching head. Later, I could listen for children's voices. The neighborhood children came home for lunch and, if I was awake, I could hear the tantalizing sound of what I was missing. There were children in every house on our block, and I seldom lacked for companionship. But now I was very much alone. No one could come to play even if I had not been too sick to sit up. No one seemed to ever come in to see if I was awake (or so it remains in my memory), although I know I was tenderly cared for even with the desperately ill baby needing constant attention.

At first I slept and woke, or half-woke, to fall asleep again. The blind was kept down, creating permanent night, as light was supposed to be harmful to measley eyes. But once I half-woke to see the blind only three-quarters of the way to the sill, and in the window space it allowed me, I could see a bit of the pear tree outside just coming into bloom. There, standing on a leafy swing, was a little girl in green and white, just learning how to pump standing up. She was holding on tightly and seemed almost to have the knack—when the wind blew—but she didn't quite get the hang of it.

I had already learned to pump standing up and I wanted to tell her to lean back, pulling with her hands while pushing with her feet, but she seemed not to understand and kept on with her futile swaying. Then a grown-up came in and adjusted the blind to the windowsill. I tried to tell about the girl who needed a little help, just a little, but the grown-up smoothed my pillow and offered me a sip of water through a straw, soothingly murmuring "hallucinations," and then tiptoed out, leaving me to fall asleep again.

Ann Parks

Radioland

When I was thirteen I came down with measles, as did half my freshman class in high school that year. By then I had had tonsillitis, chicken pox, whooping cough, and an appendectomy. Measles seemed easy enough, once the fever went down and the rash began to subside, but then came the bad news. The darkened room I had been comfortable with during the fevery days was to be a feature of the next two weeks—two weeks in a dark room, no reading, to prevent damage to my eyes. (I had a strict doctor and a mother who took his directions seriously). No reading! I read in every spare moment I could find during the day.

Normally, being sick meant being able to stay home and read all day. My family had no radio—"Nothing worth listening to!" according to my father. But the situation was desperate. A bad-tempered, convalescent teenager pulling out all the stops, I persuaded the family to let me use my hoarded allowance to pay for a radio, and I entered a new world, filled with excitement and adventure. I hung out with Jack Armstrong, the All American Boy; I followed Little Orphan Annie and her dog named Sandy; I explored the Yukon with Sergeant Preston; I flew with Sky King; and I knew who that masked man was on the horse named Silver. Who needed books?

Two weeks later the shades were opened, and I was released to return to school and my usual pastime of reading. I still needed books, it seemed, but on sick days or vacation time I rejoined my friends Jack, Annie (and Sandy), and the Lone Ranger in Radioland.

Joan Swift

Overcoming Polio

In 1921, to celebrate my father's birthday on August 8 and my ninth birthday on August 3, we had a family picnic outing to Lake Ontario. Unfortunately, the place selected for the party was at a lake later found to have been badly contaminated. My older sister Margaret, younger brother Stanley, and I all came down with poliomyelitis. There was round-the-clock nursing care for Margaret and Stanley. Margaret nearly died. Stanley was badly lamed on the left side. I didn't complain and no one even knew I was sick. The doctor came and went and never looked at me; I had long since learned during a sickly childhood that the best way to deal with illness was to act as if it didn't exist. I had decided my motto in life was "I walk alone."

Most of the two weeks while the others were sick, I spent alone in the playroom and on the second-floor porch off the playroom. When the polio scare decreased, it was September and hay fever time, and my condition still was not noticed. It was late September when school began, and the hay fever was gone, and Margaret and Stanley were no longer so desperately ill, before it was discovered I could barely walk the short distance to school. Stanley could not walk at all. Gladys always needed special care with her very labored breathing from asthma. Mother was pregnant with the twins, and that left little for attention to me.

I returned to school in early October, and the teacher was one of my favorites, but my classmates were awful. Apparently, people felt I might contaminate their children because I was lame. Most recess periods I sat alone on a bench in the schoolyard. My parents did not allow me to cross Sherbourne Street to walk with my classmates; I had to walk along the east side of the street.

One day in the summer of 1922, when the twins were six months old, Mother was pushing them in a carriage to Yonge and Bloor. As always, I had a hard time keeping up. When we were across from Toronto's Home for Incurable Children on Bloor Street by Jarvis, Mother scolded me: "If you do not stop limping and hobbling, I am going to turn you in there and leave you." I was horrified, and afraid she meant it.

It was the late 1920s when our cousin Walter Rawlinson realized how crippled Stanley was from the polio, and that I was affected, too. Walter was in the Canadian Cavalry and was sure that horseback riding was the prescription for Stanley and me. Obviously, I couldn't go riding with the Cavalry, which was exclusively for men. But Walter could take Stanley, so he got intensive training under Walter's guidance. Stanley had had several operations to split muscles on the inner half of his left leg to be moved around to serve on the outer half. The combination of the operations and the training was effective. Stanley learned to ride, and he learned to walk again, although one leg was shorter than the other and he always walked with a very pronounced rolling gait.

I was sent to a riding school and taught to ride English saddle, which emphasizes balance and rhythm. I was determined to walk without a limp, and I dedicated years to developing the muscles of my "good leg" to compensate for the complete loss of calf muscle in my "polio leg." Stanley and I went riding daily for years in North York near the summer cottage. Because of Gladys's many allergies, we could not have our own horses or take the rental ones near the house. We always had to take off our riding clothes outdoors and leave them there until their next use.

Later, I taught myself to ride a bicycle to strengthen my legs. After I retired, I rode every day along the bike paths on Chicago's lakefront. I started early, about 5:30 a.m., to avoid the hordes of cyclists and runners who come out as the day goes on. Usually I rode between 55th Street and McCormick Place at 31st Street, but sometimes I rode as far as Fullerton Avenue; that was a twenty-four-mile round trip and could take as long as four hours. During my riding season, April to October, I regularly logged between 2,000 and 3,000 miles a year.

Beverley Allen

Quarantine!

I was nine, in the fifth grade, when I came home from school one day and said to my mother, "My friend Margaret has scarlet fever." My mother groaned. "You'll get it!" she said, wringing her hands, "and your father and I won't be able to go on vacation." She was right. I always caught everything. So at the end of the incubation period, I dutifully came down with a fever and a sore throat.

My parents canceled their trip, my brother was sent to stay with our grandmother, a large red sign saying "Scarlet Fever" was put on the door of our apartment, and a patient nurse and I were sealed into two rooms of the apartment. Food was passed in through the door of the nurse's room, and for twenty-eight days we were prisoners.

Nobody could come in except the doctor. Although my parents talked to me occasionally through the door, Dr. Biggler was my only 3-D contact with the world. At first I was sick enough so that I didn't care, but as I got better I got very bored. There was no television in those days. I didn't even have a radio, I guess because, if they'd let me have one, then when I recovered, it would have had to be burned along with everything I had used when I was sick. What couldn't be burned would be washed in Lysol.

To entertain myself, I invented a fantasy about living in a tent in the wilderness where I had everything I needed, even a sort of furry suit I sewed out of soft terrycloth, which my mother procured at my request. (If you sit up under your top sheet, it makes a tent in which you can be quite self-sufficient.) My other occupation was reading the newspaper. The Lindbergh baby had just been kid-napped and I followed this real-life mystery story cold-bloodedly with avid interest. I could hardly wait for the next installment. I remember being sternly reproved by the nurse for the pleasure I took in seeing what would happen next.

Otherwise, the monotony was only relieved by visits from Doctor Biggler. He was young and handsome and came often, as doctors did in those days, and I looked forward to his visits. Once the nurse found me biting my toenails and said she would tell Dr. Biggler. I cried. Finally, when the twenty-eight days were past, I missed him and wrote him a letter:

> *Dear Dr. Biggler,*
> *I love you. I love you. I love you. I love you. I love you. I love*
> *you. I love you. I love you. I love you. I love you. I love you. I*
> *love you. I love you . . .* [for a whole page]
> *love, Alice*

I didn't know how to send my letter so I showed it to my mother. She had two friends for lunch that day and asked me to read the letter to them, which, believing it to be a good and honest letter, I did, and they laughed. Oh, my cruel mother! I don't know whether she sent it to him; I never got an answer. But soon I was back at school and finished with my first romance and my humiliation.

Alice Hayes

Minding Our Manners

Adult intervention in other areas was a basic fact of life: manners were important; codes of behavior, prescribed by the adults in one's life, were strict and well enforced. Dress was a matter of strict protocol, not always easy to follow.

Pantywaist Buttons and Long Stockings

I remember how arduous a task it was as a little girl to get dressed by myself during the winter months. We lived in a two-story house, which, I'm sure, was adequately heated. But not for me! Thus I searched for a warm place to dress—especially to put on my long white stockings. I found my spot in the bathroom, sitting on the floor next to a heated pipe.

First the long underwear legs had to be pulled down and folded over at the ankles. Then—carefully—the long white stockings were put on, one leg at a time, over the foot, past the neatly folded underwear leg, over the knee and slowly elevated to meet the garters which were, in turn, fastened to the pantywaist.

It was the pantywaist that, most often, was a source of embarrassment. All other under things could be concealed and could be depended upon to remain so. But the pantywaist had buttons, which were a source of ignominy. They were unique and easily identifiable. They would invariably detach themselves from the pantywaist at an unfortunate moment and cheerily roll across the floor.

All little girls hated pantywaist buttons!

Elizabeth Jones Borst

A Girls' School in the 1920s

When I see the girls from our neighborhood parochial school, I remember the uniforms we wore at the girls' boarding school I went to for four years in Marin County, California. We, too, wore pleated plaid skirts in shades of blue. With them we wore white cotton blouses and blue-gray cardigans. In the spring and fall we wore blue-check gingham dresses. In all seasons we wore brown cotton stockings held up with garter belts and white cotton bloomers, which were required to extend to just above the knee.

We had gym uniforms, too—black bloomers, white middies, black stockings, and white sneakers. When we discovered holes in our black stockings, we blackened our knees with india ink to hide the holes. And we whitened our sneakers with chalk dust from the blackboard erasers. We had track pants for the broad jump, high jump, javelin, and shot put (I once won third place in shot putting). The track pants were shorts lined with elasticized pants, but when newspaper photographers came, we had to wear our gym bloomers.

Every spring the headmistress had us parade by her in our
uniform bathing suits (one-piece black cotton knit with a blue
or red stripe around the skirt) to be sure we had not outgrown
them during the winter. After one such parade, my mother
received a note: "It is time for Barbara to wear a brassiere."

Barbara Fiske

Alvar Bournique's Dancing School

From late fall until early spring, every other Thursday afternoon from four to five was devoted to learning ballroom dancing and ballroom etiquette. Classes were limited to children in
the sixth to eighth grades, then later to high school years.
Special dress was required. For girls, it was "best" dresses, just
below the knee, with ribbed-silk white stockings and Mary Jane
shoes, which were patent leather one-strap pumps with a moiré
bow on the toe. All this, plus long white gloves. Boys wore long
trousers or trousers to the knee, white shirt, tie, jacket, and gray
cotton gloves.

Mr. Bournique, slightly built and extremely graceful,
always wore a morning coat. He taught us all the steps appropriate to ballroom dancing—the waltz, the two-step, a deco-
rous tango—as well as proper manners related to inviting a
partner to dance: a low bow from the boy and a curtsey of
acceptance from the girl.

Music was provided by a pianist, who was always ready with
the tune requested by Mr. Bournique and always played at the
correct tempo. Between dances, the students sat at the edge of
the dance floor conversing—even laughing—together. One area
provided chairs for the parents, who talked in low tones.

Often Mr. Bournique conferred the highest honor on one
of the girls by asking her to be his partner for the demonstration of a dance step. For the girl this would be a red-letter
day, since it signified she was "a good dancer." The other
"honor" for a girl was being chosen early for each dance by a
male partner. Since there were always one or two fewer boys
than girls, the ultimate embarrassment came when two girls
had to dance together!

I loved all this. I went joyfully to each Thursday-afternoon session. My good friend Martha remembers the same classes with horror, saying, "I was *never* chosen!" It was not just being chosen that gave pleasure. It was by whom!

I remember only one departure from decorum at dancing school. The son of the city's chief of police was a regular, if reluctant, student. One day he brought a small packet of sneezing powder to class, and, at what he deemed an appropriate moment, he opened the packet and blew the powder into the air. Many of the students and Mr. Bournique himself were seized with paroxysms of sneezing. At subsequent class sessions there was one less male student in our midst!

Elizabeth Jones Borst

School Days

School was a universal reality in our young lives, although our school experiences themselves differed widely. Eagerly anticipated or dreaded, for some it was an exciting adventure, for others a routine to be endured.

The early decades of the twentieth century were a time of educational experimentation in America. A popular conviction regarding the importance of fresh air gave us the "Open Air" classes. The schools based on the theories of John Dewey were among the "progressive" schools of the day.

A Schoolgirl in Stuttgart

When I was four-and-a-half years old, my mother took me to enroll in kindergarten, which was not part of the public schools at that time. The director, "Aunt Mathilda," said she had "*Keinen Platz*" ("no place") for me. Thinking she meant that there was no chair available, I said, "Then I can stand." The director decided to let the eager little girl stay.

I was impatient to go to public school like my sister, Ruth. When I was old enough, my mother took me for the first day. All the six-year-old girls had to sit quietly for a whole hour with both hands placed on the desk while the teacher was telling us about "learning." When we were allowed to leave, I told my mother that I didn't think I liked school: this after having looked forward to going to school for three years.

Renate Vambery

Education at Hayes Elementary

I was born in Chicago in 1912; my family lived on the near west side, one block north of Lake Street, near Robey Street (now Damen Avenue). When I was a youngster, my mother would pack a picnic lunch and take my two older brothers and me on a trip to Municipal Pier, which is now Navy Pier. We took the Robey Street trolley to Grand Avenue, then the Grand Avenue car to the pier, where the streetcar went half the length of the pier before making a U-turn and returning to the street.

My school, Hayes Elementary on Leavitt Street, was a four-story red brick building with a circular fire escape at the front. The girls' schoolyard was on the south side of the building, and the boys' was on the north. There were manual training classes for the boys. The girls took cooking and sewing, and had to make their own graduation dresses. However, Hayes did not have facilities for these classes, so the girls went to Emerson School for sewing and to Brown School for cooking. Children today don't get the kind of education I had in the 1920s.

Dorothy Coleman

Early Schooling

In 1916, at a time when the Great War was being fought in Europe, my best friend and I were entering kindergarten at Rosedale Elementary School in Toronto, Canada. My first memory of school now seems like a bizarre dream. It may not have happened as I remember it, yet the experience has remained vivid in my memory. My best friend and I were chosen to participate by carrying the two flags—the [British] Union Jack and the Canadian flag—into the assembly hall. Two little boys, barely able to support the flags, we proudly strutted along as the chosen leaders of the kindergarten. I still have a glow of pride as I remember it.

Three other experiences stand out from my elementary school years. In second grade, a composition I had written on rabbits was read to the class by an approving teacher. It was a work of pure fiction, unsupported by any facts. I was especially pleased by the part that told how the parent rabbits took care of their little ones—lots of little ones—so that they never got in harm's way. But one did, and he surely got a scolding. I was convinced that I would become a great writer when I grew up.

The second memory comes from fifth grade. There was a boy who was incessantly insolent to the teacher, Miss Price. One day, quite unexpectedly, she moved to her desk, took out a black box, slowly removed the cover, and lifted out a long leather strap. She walked the boy to the cloakroom. Our desks faced the wall behind which our coats were hung. In frozen silence, we heard her as she took three quick steps—and then the sound as the strap hit the boy's outstretched hands. We could feel it as we heard the second and third blows. Not a sound out of the boy. We began to admire him as a plucky lad. It was not until the fifth blow that he let out a howl and sobbed, "I'm sorry! I'll be good!" The drama was concluded. The lesson was learned. Or was it?

The third memory comes from eighth grade. We were seated at desks in rows, and where we sat was determined by our monthly grades. It was a terrible struggle to stay in first place, and I didn't always succeed. At that age I never questioned the importance attached to being first, or how those who were never in first place, or even second, must have felt about the obvious ranking. But I must admit that my rank in class enabled me after eight years in grammar school to be admitted to the University of Toronto Schools (U.T.S.), an all-boys high school with an excellent reputation. My mother had always hoped that I would be admitted there. Maybe because I argued so much, she thought I would grow up to be a lawyer.

U.T.S. boasted an outstanding faculty and a carefully selected student body. It was a high school known for the number of students who received scholarships to the university. I assumed that, in an environment such as U.T.S., the students would be eager to learn, but, just as in my elementary school, self-discipline did not come automatically.

As an idealistic teacher at U.T.S., Mr. Phillips assumed that interest in the material world would assure an orderly class. He tried to engage our interest and seemed to care about us, but some of the boys thought that he would be an easy target. The first weeks were a maelstrom of chalk throwing and an avalanche of back talk, all for the purpose of testing Mr. Phillips. At some point he must have gone to one of the veteran faculty to talk about his troubles. When, in his next class, one boy after another tried the old tricks, Mr. Phillips walked down the aisle and slapped one culprit and then another. After that, order prevailed, and teaching and learning began to take place. At that time, I was too young and too naïve to question the method. Perhaps I had been too pleased at seeing the bad boys punished.

The geometry teacher, Johnny Workman, proctored tests by putting his feet up on his desk as he read the newspaper. Occasionally he would walk down the aisle to answer questions. What we were amazed at and what made us feel secure was that he clearly trusted us. It was Johnny Workman who, when I returned to school after my mother's death, walked quietly over to my desk, where I was struggling over a test, messed my hair in a casual manner, and said that I would have another chance to take the test the next week. The memory of that understanding touch has stayed with me all my life.

Another teacher, irritated by something I had said in class, snapped, "Ellison, the trouble with you is you are an iconoclast!" Not knowing what the word meant, I assumed the worst. But when I looked it up in the dictionary, I felt proud.

Jack Ellison

School in the Open Air Room

I attended the university laboratory school in Ann Arbor, Michigan. I was in Miss Mary McDermott's very unusual "Open Air Room." We had floor-to-ceiling windows that were open all year. We had a nap in the afternoon on a plain canvas cot, with a blanket we pulled over us. We wore our warm clothes all day, with heavy lined boots and heavy wool socks. In winter, we wore ski-style suits. We never got sick.

Starting at age seven, we swam from seven to eight o'clock every morning, then we went to have breakfast at the lab school. Our hair would freeze in sheets as we walked from the college gym building across the street to the grade school. But we never caught cold.

My parents, coming from Mississippi and Louisiana, thought this was a wonderful experience, and they never heard of anybody dying or even being ill from doing this.

Growing up in the Open Air Room, we learned everything about birds, wild animals, plants, and trees. This education was very useful to me years later, when we lived in Flossmoor, Illinois, and I was able to identify many of the animals and plants in our backyard and the area leading down to Butterfield Creek.

Catherine Watkins

Progressive Education in the Twenties

When I was five years old, we moved into an apartment across the street from Chicago's Lincoln Park Zoo, and I began first grade at the Francis Parker School. Parker was a still-young progressive school founded in 1901 by Colonel Francis W. Parker, a friend and colleague of John Dewey, whose Laboratory Schools were also young and feisty. I understood from the beginning that I was part of a wonderful experiment, and, long before I was out of elementary school, I knew and understood that a school is an embryonic democracy where children learn by doing, and that school is not a preparation for life, but life itself. Sometimes in daily all-school morning exercises we all said the school word: "RE-SPON-SIBILITY" very loudly in unison, and the school motto: "Everything to help and nothing to hinder!"

These morning exercises were the great original show-and-tells. I remember first-grade Indians on the stage, second-grade nomads, third-grade pioneers, and, once, a fourth-grade Achilles and his soldiers wearing their homemade helmets and shields, reciting their original Homeric poem. As each verse ended, they waved their spears fiercely and chanted, "We're the Host of the Myrmidons!" For me this was an unforgettable experience.

Sometimes we had grown-up speakers. I remember Memorial Days when very old Civil War soldiers came and sat on the stage while somebody told us about the Civil War and the freeing of the slaves. By the time I was in sixth grade, only one inconceivably old man was left, and I was shocked to realize that all the others were probably dead.

On Armistice Day (now Veteran's Day) the principal, Miss Cook, told us about peace and how the "war to end all wars" had ended on the eleventh minute of the eleventh hour of the eleventh month, in 1918. At exactly 11:11, we all stood up and faced east, and thought about how lucky we were to live in a time when there would be no more wars.

Miss Hattie Walker was my teacher in first grade. I sat at a double desk with a girl named Patsy and I learned to read. The first words on the blackboard were *wind* and *seed*; "Wind blows seed" was my very first whole sentence. From that lively beginning we went on to *milk*, a comforting word for a first grader, and pretty soon I was able to read my first book. I brought it proudly home: *The Merry Little Grig*, it was called. I'd never heard of a "grig" (as you probably haven't either), so I read it as *girl* through most of the story, until my mother told me my mistake. But even she didn't know what a grig was.

At the Parker School in the elementary grades we had a "Central Subject" and in first grade we began by learning about "Tree Boys." Miss Walker drew a picture on the blackboard of two trees with a boy, discreetly wearing some sort of animal skin, leaping spread-eagled like a monkey between them. We went to the Field Museum of Natural History and saw the life-sized dioramas of Neanderthal and Cro-Magnon men where the little Neanderthal boy wasn't wearing anything at all and the Neanderthal mother was feeding her baby milk—a word we could proudly read.

I guess our Central Subject must have been "Evolution," because after Tree Boys and Prehistoric Man, we went on to Indians and Eskimos. We could wear Indian suits to school and we built an igloo out of cubic paper boxes. I think the big advantage of all this was that we learned early to identify with other kinds of people. We were proud to be Indians, and although our conception of how

Indians lived may have been extremely sketchy, it was very positive and very different from life at home.

Then there was Poetry. Mr. Merrill, the drama teacher in the high school, had grown up in New England, so to our small Midwestern ears he sounded very English and exotic. He came down to the first grade and read us poems. He read Shakespeare, Tennyson, Sandburg, Vachel Lindsay, and lots of others. I don't think any of them were written for children, but when the words were hard, he explained them, and he gave us small black two-ring notebooks to hold mimeographed copies of the poems he read.

In second grade, where the Central Subject was "The Early Herdsmen," Mr. Merrill read to us again. When he read a story about a person called "Abraham," I remember waiting eagerly for the punch line, when Abraham would turn out to be Abraham Lincoln, but it didn't happen and, because I was sick a lot in second grade, it was years before I understood who Abraham and the early herdsmen were. My religious education was confined to Bible stories my grandmother read to me and my cousins to try to make up for our non-churchgoing parents.

In the heart of the city we had chickens in back of the school. We took turns feeding them and collecting the eggs and taking an egg home for our supper. There was a little garden in one corner of the playground, and I can remember collecting seeds from the morning glories that grew on the fence around the jungle gym and helping to plant the seeds the next spring.

Later, in fourth grade, we were Greeks in Periclean Athens. We made chitons trimmed with stencils of Greek key designs or waves, and we wore them to school. We wrote plays and poems about Athens in the fourth century B.C. I wrote one about Leonidas, who died heroically at the pass of Thermopylae keeping the Persians out of Greece and how Phidipedes ran from Marathon to Athens with the news and then dropped dead. I learned how the Delphic Oracle told the Athenians to "take to their wooden walls," so they built ships and defeated bad Xerxes at the battle of Salamis while he watched from the opposite shore and wept. We learned how people practiced for the Olympic games and oiled each other and scraped the oil off with strigils. We studied the Parthenon and Phidias's sculpture and democracy in Athens. We were Greeks!

It never occurred to me that as a girl in ancient Athens I couldn't have worn a chiton or fought the Persians or voted or scraped oil off another athlete with a strigil. It wasn't until seventh grade, when the girls had to have cooking while the boys had shop, and sewing while the boys had printing, that the disadvantages of being a girl fully dawned on me.

On cold mornings we came into the front hall of the school, where there was a roaring fire in the big fireplace, with two benches beside it where you could warm up if you needed to. I loved that school. Progressive education, which was such a novelty in the twenties, is mostly familiar now, but the feeling of being part of a great experiment is gone forever.

Alice Hayes

Teachers Ought to Know

Miss Rafter told us to spell "faw."
I thought of "saw" and "paw" and "caw"
The nearest I could get was "fall."
She jumped on me. "That's not at all
The word I said. You're very bad
At spelling." I was pretty mad.

I closed up tight. I didn't dare
To tell her that she was unfair.
I didn't know a word called "faw,"
What did it mean? I could write "saw,"
But I heard "f," not "s," and so
I ask you, how was I to know?

Now I understand that she
Does not know where the "R's" should be,
And so they fly away from "far"
In speaking and you find they are
Attached to make "idear" in talk
But never written so in chalk.

Last year I knew just how to spell,
I think I did it very well.
But we were living in Montclaire
And first grade teachers there were fair.
Besides they all knew how to say
The word "far" in a writing way.

But talk is turned around this year
Miss Rafter's talk is really queer.
You see, there's just no way of telling
What she says when you do spelling,
Surely teachers ought to know
Just where "R's" should and shouldn't go!

Jean Bowman Anderson

Lessons Out of School

Growing Up in Chicago

I remember playing softball and other games in the street
from about 1910 to 1918. We used the curbs for first and
third bases. Second base and home plate were in the middle
of the street. There were no cars. The only disturbance would
be the iceman or the mailman coming through with a horse-
drawn wagon.

My elementary school was two blocks away from my home,
but when I went to high school I had to ride the streetcar. Often
I would have to hang onto the bar while standing on the outside
step because the streetcars were so crowded.

My behavior was guided by my father's admonitions and
the threat of his four-inch razor strop, which kept me in line.
My weekly allowance was ten cents, which I didn't get to
spend. My father led me to a piggy bank to deposit the dime,
and then, when the piggy bank was full, we went with it to the
big bank.

Alex Coutts

Long Hours for Little Pay

When I was a teenager, I would board the streetcar at 54th Street; the streetcar ran on rails down the middle of Halsted Street. I'd get off at 111th, about 3000 West, then walk through a forest alongside a cemetery to 107th, and to the Ridge Country Golf Club. I would have an apple that I brought from home as my lunch.

On most days I would get to caddy a golf cart for eighteen holes. At the end, I would be paid seventy-five cents, most times with no tip. I walked back to 111th to take the streetcar home. A good part of the day was gone. After spending six cents on streetcar fares, I'd earned sixty-nine cents to give to my mother.

Clement Carroll

Life Lessons

In the late 1920s I began my journey toward the future, my adventure of self-discovery. My journey began when we moved to West Philadelphia, 437 Napa Street. The ambience of the neighborhood was Irish, German, Czech, Hungarian, African, and, to a lesser degree, Mexican. The elementary school we attended, Morton McMichael, was about ten blocks from where I lived.

It was a job becoming acclimated to the area. Almost daily I was chased home after school by a group of white boys. When I came in sight of our house, I would be running, crying, and hollering to my mother so she could let me in. One day she was standing in the doorway waiting for me. She saw the gang chasing me. I cried out to her, "Let me in!" She wouldn't let me in. I circled the block and this time she opened the door. She threatened me with a beating herself if I allowed anybody to chase me home again. Believe me, that was all the encouragement I needed. From that time on, for about a week, I fought my way home daily. I became the "baddest" kid in town. She never had to whip me or escort me again.

During the cold months, my home away from home was the main branch of the Philadelphia Public Library. Here was fairy-land—books and more books—and the story hour on Saturday mornings. My world was full of magic, mystery, and music.

I liked being alone, being by myself. I loved reading books of adventure, philosophy, and Bible stories. They were my friends and companions. I was especially fond of readings in philosophy. Plato and Spinoza were my favorites. Plato enabled me to form friendships—platonic love—with girls, and Spinoza provided me with a context—Idealism—for thought and behavior. They taught me I could be friends with girls and boys without having to prove anything.

We always had RCA Victor classical records at home. On Saturday afternoons, I listened to the *Texaco Opera Series* and my favorites were the Italian masters: Giacomo Puccini and Giuseppe Verdi. Those Saturdays I went sailing, flying on wings of lyrical sounds, a completely disembodied spirit among the stars. Mom never had to worry about me on weekends.

Phillip Harley

Gertrude Stein at Hull House

One unforgettable Friday in the late winter of 1933, when I was eleven and my best friend Nancy was ten, we decided to walk to Hull House to visit her grandparents who lived there. From 2200 North, where our school was, we walked west to Halsted Street, turned south and aimed for 800 South Halsted, where we knew Hull House was: thirty blocks. Still winter. Late afternoon. In the growing dark, two little girls through the heart of what was called "Skid Row."

It was farther than we had thought, but whenever we got discouraged we stopped and asked the men leaning against a doorpost or sitting on a curb where Hull House was and they would smile at us and say, "You're on the right track. Keep going. It's not too far." So finally we arrived and, uninvited as we were, received a warm welcome by Granpapa, who invited us to dinner in the Residents' Dining Room. We had just time to take off our coats. Nobody thought to telephone our parents.

There were two or three long tables in the dining room, and pretty soon we noticed the back of somebody very strange sitting at the next table. I guessed she was a woman though I wasn't sure; her hair was cut like a man's, she wore a man's shirt and over it a gray woolen vest. Eventually Jane Addams stood up at the head of her table and made a short speech, and Granpapa (Robert Morss Lovett) stood up and made another. I was probably still eating my dessert, because I don't remember anything they said. But when the person with hair cut like a man's rose and began reading, my attention was riveted:

> Pigeons on the grass
> Pigeons on the grass, Alas!

Gertrude Stein was in town for the opening of *Four Saints in Three Acts*. We had stumbled on one of Jane Addams' literary lions!

Alice Hayes

Meeting Diego Rivera

I first saw the artist Diego Rivera at the Detroit Art Institute in 1926, when I was ten years old. My family dropped me off to watch him painting murals, commissioned by Henry Ford, depicting the automobile industry. My parents had another engagement and said they'd be back for me in an hour, and, while they were gone, I should go watch this 300-pound man painting on the walls from the top of a strong stepladder. He had boys handing up paint and brushes to him. I thought, what if this enormous man falls off?

I couldn't believe what I was seeing. Even as a child, I was aware that the murals showed all the people working in the automobile plants as if they were slaves. Diego Rivera came down from his ladder, with much help from the young men, to speak to me.

He said, "What are you doing here, little girl?"

I said my parents thought it would be very interesting for me to watch him work because he was so great.

He said, "Do you like this?"

I said, "Yes, but those automobile workers have to work awfully hard."

He said, "Yes!"

When Mr. Ford first saw Rivera's work, he was just horrified.

Three years later, in 1929 when I was thirteen years old, I met the painter again and he remembered me. My father went to Mexico for six months to establish an educational system of teachers' colleges for the Batista government. We lived in a beautiful home in the city and were invited to Ambassador Morrow's every Sunday for dinner. Ambassador Morrow, who had a superior education and the great wealth of the Eastern upper class, had commissioned Diego Rivera to paint murals on the walls of Cortez's palace in Cuernevaca. Here in Mexico, Rivera's work was exactly the same as in Detroit. It showed that the Indians were all treated like slaves by the rich whites, even though the Indians were 96 percent of the population.

Rivera was a Communist in his leanings. Yet he had two great millionaires sponsoring his murals in which he showed how terrible it was that people were being used as slaves: in the Detroit auto industry and by the Europeans in Mexico.

Catherine Watkins

Franklin Roosevelt Arrives

In 1928 my family was invited to stay at the Onondaga Country Club in Fayetteville, outside Syracuse, New York. We arrived about suppertime and were told that Franklin Roosevelt would be there to give a campaign speech. He was running for governor of New York. In those days, his inability to walk was carefully hidden from the public. Newspapers never mentioned it. My brother Billy and I watched with great interest as the Pierce-Arrow touring car drove over the golf course and the putting green, so that no one could see Mr. Roosevelt being carried to the podium.

My mother had told me never to walk in ordinary shoes on a golf course, and certainly not on a putting green. The touring car left deep tracks. No one seemed to notice or to care. I was shocked!

Elise Cade

Happiness, Early and Late

One of my husband's favorite questions to ask new acquaintances is "Did you have a happy childhood?" My answer would be "On the whole, yes."

I grew up in a small Mississippi town in the Great Depression. My father lost his job and we lost our home. He ended up chopping weeds on the highway for the WPA. To earn a dollar a day, my mother stood up the whole day as a salesperson in a local discount store; at night she embroidered baby clothes and, with the help of my older brother, sold a special bread from New Orleans, called Bond Bread, to local customers. My brother added to our income by delivering papers at three in the morning. The only assistance I could give at the age of twelve was to cook the main meal on days my mother worked.

Despite this hard time, I remember being happy about many events in my childhood. At an early age, these included delighting in licking the bowl with the leavings of the cake batter my mother had mixed and being allowed to taste the delicious ice cream from the blade of the hand-cranked maker my father had turned.

My father was one of a family of fourteen children (not Catholic, just sexy Methodists, as they used to say) and I later enjoyed the large family reunions at my grandparents' farm in the country, as well as smaller reunions of my mother's family in the big city—New Orleans.

Most memorable of all were the many happy holiday celebrations. My mother believed in not missing a one. For example, on birthdays each person chose the kind of cake he or she wanted. Mine was three-layered, one pink, one chocolate, and one yellow; my brother's was chocolate and white marble pound cake; my father's a yellow cake with white frosting dotted with walnut halves.

I cherish other special memories. First was attending Mardi Gras in New Orleans. Mississippi did not celebrate the occasion, and school officials were displeased when my mother took my brother and me out of school for the day. But she insisted that the whole experience was as educational as a day in school. So early on a February morning we three boarded an Illinois Central "excursion train" (the fare was $1 round trip) and went to the big city, where, at my German grandparents' home, we children put on our costumes (mine was either a Gypsy's or an Indian maiden's, my brother's a cowboy's or policeman's). When my cousins and their families arrived, we all walked a few blocks to the large boulevard, Carrollton Avenue, near my grandparents' home. There we pushed through crowds of people to get as near the curb as possible and waited for the parade. The decorated floats seemed magical to us but what we delighted in most were the beads, trinkets, and gold-wrapped chocolate coins that were thrown into the crowd. My uncle lifted the younger of us to his shoulders so we could more easily catch the favors. After the last float was gone, we headed back to the house with our treasures. There, we sat down to a meal of delicious crab gumbo, avocado salad (the avocados were called "alligator pears" then), and mouth-watering homemade doughnuts—not with round holes, but square and rectangular—deep fried and dusted with powdered sugar by my grandmother. Evening came all too soon and we returned to the station to take the excursion train home, tired but happy.

Another pleasant memory was my friendship with a Syrian girl in my class when we were adolescents. I considered her rich because her father managed the movie theater and owned an interest in a local restaurant. On Saturday afternoons I would meet Yvonne at the movie, and we would enter without having to pay the dime admission charge. This meant I could buy a candy bar and popcorn with my intended fare. After the movie, we would walk to the restaurant and order a free meal. This was a special treat since my family could never afford to go to a restaurant. My friend, on the other hand, loved to spend Friday nights with my family. Early Saturday morning before it was too hot, we took our tennis racquets and went to the school courts for several games of tennis. I don't remember either of us being very skilled at the game, but we had great fun. Then, starving from our workout, we came back home, where my mother prepared as many pancakes as we could eat, with bacon and maple syrup. (Yvonne insisted the pancakes were far superior to all others she had ever eaten.) We shared these heartening experiences until my father finally got a good job in another city and we moved away.

Happy memories, a happy childhood.

Ruth Kolb

7

The Great Depression

For the older members of our generation, the good times of the Roaring Twenties may bring memories of flappers, jazz, speakeasies, and the high jinks we read about or see depicted in the movies. For many of us, however, the stock market crash of 1929 may have been the first encroachment of the outside world upon our personal lives. For most of us, the 1930s, with the shadow of the Great Depression hanging over them, colored our teen and early adult years.

Although it was our parents, for the most part, who had to cope with the effects of the Depression, the anxiety and uncertainties of the period affected each of us to some extent. For those whose families suffered major losses—of jobs, of life savings in bank failures, of homes to mortgage foreclosures—life changed abruptly. For those whose families were less drastically affected, the economies adopted may have passed almost unnoticed by the younger members: less expensive cuts of meat or no meat at all, fewer new clothes, more hand-me-downs, fewer treats.

Even for those fortunate enough to have avoided the direct effects of the stock market crash itself or the loss of the family income, the images remain: families evicted from their apartments sitting dazedly with their piles of furniture around them, shantytowns built of cardboard and discarded lumber, hungry people lining up in bread lines and soup kitchens, well-dressed men in fedora hats selling apples on street corners. Franklin

Roosevelt's election to the presidency and the programs he put into effect almost immediately (in his "first hundred days") made a major difference in many lives, as federal relief funds became available, the Works Progress Administration (W.P.A.) provided jobs, and the threat of bank failures was removed.

Many of the social programs that have changed the nature of today's retirement years were initiated during FDR's tenure in office, Social Security being perhaps the most far reaching in its effects today.

Gramah's Stock Market

In the early twentieth century, ladies of culture and refinement shunned beauty parlors. The beautician came to them. She washed their tresses in the sink or the tub, and used rags or paper to curl their hair. It was a long, drawn-out process. Gramah displayed unusual ability as a hairdresser, and it was something she really enjoyed.

Her first customer, and someone she later adored, was Mrs. P. D. Armour, wife of the famous stockyards man.

Gramah said to me, "Imagine! The first question Mrs. Armour asked was, 'By what name shall I call you?' I answered, 'I would like to be called "Davenport."' Compared to plain 'Mary' it sounded so much more respectful!" Receiving respect from an employer was very important to someone who had been born in slavery.

Gramah slowly added more names to her list of customers, and it soon sounded like a "Who's Who" of Chicago. In addition to Mrs. Armour, there were Mrs. Swift, Mrs. Libby, the wives of famous architect Ferdinand Peck and District Attorney Perry Hull, Mrs. Peacock, Mrs. Marshall Field, Mrs. Bishop Chaney, and Mrs. Potter Palmer, whom Gramah emulated by always wearing a velvet ribbon around her neck.

I went with Gramah to the beautiful homes of some of these important women. They would have a room with animal-skin rugs on the floor, and nothing else in the huge room but books, from the top to the bottom. There was a ladder that went all the way across, and I could get on the ladder to push myself along.

They'd say, "Well, Mary, what do you want to read?" They had books for children; they had books for anything. I would tell them what type of book I wanted, and then I'd lie on the floor with my head on a bear or a leopard or a lion and read all day while Gramah worked.

Mrs. P. D. Armour was crazy about Gramah. One day she gave her a little piece of paper and said, "Now, Davenport, don't you tell *anybody*, not even your husband, about this. Someday it's going to turn into a whole lot of greenbacks."

After that, Gramah said, for her birthday, or for George Washington's Birthday, or for any reason at all, she got these pieces of paper. Around 1930 she told me, "Do you know, Mary, I got so many that the box I had to hold 'em was just *filled*. And then I put 'em in the top of my trunk."

I said, "Well, what did you do with them?"

Gramah said, "Why, they never did turn green. I burned them up."

They had been stocks, and she thought they would turn into dollars!

I wouldn't hurt Gramah for the world, so I said, "I don't blame you. You should have burned them up, 'cause they weren't anything." I couldn't tell her what the pieces of paper really were, so she died not knowing that she had burned up thousands and thousands of dollars.

Mary Brock

My Middle-Class Depression

My family didn't, so far as I knew, suffer from the Depression. I was a child when it began. My father, who had been a poor boy once, had worked his way up to a comfortable middle-class income by 1929. He was a civic-minded lawyer who loved birds and animals and his family, and was passionately interested in education. We had a house, a cook, a maid, a car; my brother and I went to private schools, and every night for supper, eating with our parents, we had meat, potatoes, and a vegetable (usually peas) and junket or custard and one cookie for dessert. My mother was an artist who didn't know how to cook. For Sunday dinner, after we had walked in the park instead of going to church, we had a roast and ice cream, or went to my grandmother's, where we also had a roast, always with jelly, and a unique kind of ice cream containing nuts, pineapple, and marshmallows. An uncle and aunts and cousins were there, too. My grandmother's table always had an empty place set "for Lord Chesterfield," who was invisible but present "to mind the children's manners," and often commented in the voice of my grandmother. During Prohibition there was never any alcohol of any kind in the house and nobody smoked.

But I did catch glimpses of the real world. Occasionally a sad old man would come down the alley to the back door of our house begging for food, and the cook would sit him down at the kitchen table and give him something to eat. I could see that he was hungry even though my father insisted that nobody in the United States ever starved.

There were woods at the back of my grandmother's summer house in the country, and beside these woods was a railroad track with freight cars trundling north loaded with coal or back to Chicago with lumber and milk. Hobos rode the empty freight cars, and when a train stopped beside our woods it was easy to get off. There were often little encampments of men in this back woodlot beside the tracks. My father, who was sympathetic to the campers, would go down to make sure they were being careful with fires and tidy with trash. We children were not allowed to go down to the woods when the hobos were there, so they remained shadowy hearsay figures in my mind: small consequences of the Depression at the edge of my consciousness.

Then there were school friends. One friend's family ate in their crowded kitchen because their dining room and front room were rented out to two old ladies. My friend slept in the bed with her mother, and her brother slept with her father in two beds in one room. "Birth control," said my father, but it was also a lack of space. Both her parents were teachers, and they used the small table in the kitchen for correcting papers after the children were in bed. Both my other best friends lived in bigger families in somewhat dingy apartments. In one house I learned to eat turnips and spaghetti with garlic, whereas we never even had onions in our house. But it's only in looking back that I realize what a hard time those families were having. I certainly never thought of these people as poor.

My most intense Depression experience was at Hull House, where my very best friend's grandparents lived in the attic. Her grandfather had been a distinguished English professor; after he retired, he lost all his money. Jane Addams invited him and his large, motherly, always-knitting wife to come and live at Hull House, where he was the master of ceremonies for her literary salon. The attic where they lived was dark and vast. Granpapa had a gigantic flat-topped desk in the middle of the room where he wrote things, and Nancy and I, who were always welcome, slept in a tiny room at the side. We slept in an old sloping double bed, taking turns falling out on the low side. The street-cars rattled by outside our window. Nobody ever told us to do anything; they only invited us: "Would you like to come down with us and eat supper? Would you like to join a dancing class? Some children are giving a play, would you like to see it?" It was my idea of paradise!

Alice Hayes

Hooverville on the Hudson River

I grew up in New York City and graduated from high school in 1938. In the mid-1930s, signs of the Depression were every-where, in the panhandlers in the streets and the idlers in the park, who often spent the night stretched out on the benches. My father had an academic job and so we did not worry, but the effects on many others could scarcely be ignored. We were told not to give out money to the needy, because it often went for liquor, but instead were given meal cards to hand out, which provided a bowl of soup and cup of coffee at a local food counter. A poem I wrote for our high school magazine began:

> The wooden benches in the park loom large,
> The buildings reel beneath a drunken sky,
> And dark and hungry streets outline the marge
> Between this thieving world and dark infinity.

They are excluded from the hopes of men,
Fraught with despair, bereft of dignity.
Good lord, are they but cattle in a pen
Of streets and windowed cliffs, shut in to die?

One pastime for the unemployed was selling apples on street
corners. Often the fruit was hand polished and arranged on top
of wooden crates. The price was five cents. A joke of the times:
"Did you hear about the man who ate an unemployed apple?"
"His stomach hasn't worked since."

For a number of years we lived in an apartment on Riverside
Drive, overlooking the Hudson. Between the drive and the river
was a wide park, bordered on one side by a high stone wall,
where one could watch the rats coming and going among the
crevices. Below the park, the land dropped off steeply to the
railroad tracks, where trains came in from points north on their
way to Grand Central Station. Between the tracks and the river
was a strip of wasteland, where, for a couple of years, a
shantytown of a few dozen packing-crate sheds provided homes
to the unemployed.

My school, which had a loose association with Teacher's
College and Columbia University, took students on tours to
various points in and around New York. Among other places, we
visited the National Biscuit Company factory downtown, the
Sunoco refinery across the Hudson, and the "Hooverville" along
the river. There we talked with a few of the men about their
lives, how they lost their jobs and searched for new ones, and
their need for food and warmth. One man had found a fish tail
discarded from a local restaurant, mostly bone but with a bit of
meat still on it, and he told us how he was going to make himself
fish soup for dinner. Others had bits of bread and fruit
scrounged from garbage.

We didn't stay long, but I remember thinking that some of
the temporary residents along the river were friendly and
pleased to talk with us, and were not all the antisocial misfits we
might have imagined. At night, we could sometimes see their
flickering campfires from our apartment. After our trip, this
Hooverville, with its hunger and suffering, seemed somehow a

more friendly place. Later years saw the railroad tracks enclosed
and the new West Side Drive built over them beside the river.
Riverside Park became beautified, although it still was never the
safest place to walk at night. Our own small Hooverville is long
gone but it remains in my memory as a reminder of the hard-
ships of the Depression even within sight of some of New York's
upscale apartments.

Hewson Swift

Oklahoma Windfall

I graduated from college in the spring of 1932. The Great
Depression was in full sway. Unemployment was at the highest in
the history of the country. Long lines of men looking for work
appeared on the sidewalks of every community. President
Roosevelt had hired a man named Harry Hopkins to develop
the Federal Emergency Relief Administration, a program of
financial aid for families in need. Offices were springing up
throughout the country. At that time, I was enrolled in some
graduate classes, including one in sociology, at the University of
Oklahoma. One day the professor of this class said, "I would like
to know more about this new program. Is there a student here
who would volunteer to visit the office and bring back a report
to the class?" I raised my hand and said I would be glad to do so.
The next day, armed with the name of the director and address
of the office, I embarked on this mission. The director proved to
be a friendly, outgoing woman who said she would gladly give
me an account of the program.

We spent an hour or so during which she gave me a full
report on the organization and purpose of this new program. At
the end of the interview, I thanked her for granting me the time
and giving me so much information. As I was about to leave, she
said, "Do you have a car?" I said, "Yes, I have an old roadster in
running order." Then she said, "I am just completing my staff,
and have an opening for a man. The position is that of case-
worker, and entails visiting the homes of applicants and helping
make decisions about their eligibility." I told her that I was going
to school on borrowed money and was living in the home of a

faculty friend where I earned board and room by helping take care of two small children. I said the job offer sounded exciting, but I would like to talk to my friend and would return the next day with my answer. As you can imagine, my friend thought it a great idea, and so I returned with an acceptance.

That was an exciting day; I walked around in a daze realizing that I had a totally unexpected job during the Depression, in a time of terrible drought in the West and Southwest. The area around Norman, where the university was located, was like a desert. All the wheat and other crops had died, grasslands were brown, and dust storms pervaded the atmosphere. Thousands of cattle were dying, and teams that farmers relied upon were perishing. And here I had luckily found a job.

After five years of very interesting and rewarding jobs in the Oklahoma state welfare services, I advanced to the role of Regional Supervisor with headquarters in Tulsa, Oklahoma. My district included the cities of Okmulgee and Muskogee. Okmulgee is where the Oklahoma State Prison is located, and from time to time I had business there, perhaps regarding some prisoner's parole plans or some emergency in the family of an inmate. One day I was late in leaving the prison and headed for Muskogee. It had been raining all afternoon but I had not thought it unusual. Both towns were in a hilly part of Oklahoma where the roads are mostly black-top and wind through forests of black-jack oak and other woods. I knew the roads well in that part of the state, and was just going at a rather slow rate downhill, when the car ran into deep water and the motor stopped dead.

I was barely able to get out of the car and was in waist-deep water. I scrambled back up the hill and made it just as I heard my car begin to roll down the rocky streambed. It was found the next day with the top crushed, a door missing, the hood cover and rear trunk cover gone. It looked like a tin can all beaten up. I had been caught in the midst of a flash flood, as were several other drivers that night.

I was able to find an insurance agent in Muskogee, who said the car was a total wreck. It was the only new car I had owned and had cost around $800. The insurance company agreed to pay about $750.

I began to think what to do with that fund and, with advice from family friends, decided to invest it in getting a master's degree in social service. Some years earlier I had visited an uncle in Chicago who had a great admiration for the University of Chicago. He took me out to visit the campus, and I thought, I wish I could go there. So I resigned my job in Oklahoma, applied for admission to the School of Social Service Administration, was admitted, and began an entirely new career. I guess the flood was good luck!

Ben Meeker

Enmeshed in the Chicago Machine

In 1935 the country was deep in the Depression. My own family was fairly fortunate. My mother was teaching and, of course, she was paid in scrip rather than in cash. My father was a commissioner with the Board of Health, as he was until his death in 1936. I was attending the University of Chicago's School of Social Work. We lived at Vista Homes, one of the tallest courtyard buildings in Chicago, overlooking Jackson Park near the entrance to the Midway Plaisance.

The discipline of social service was without much status in those days, but it had one great attribute: it was going to provide jobs for everyone going through the school. Many of us were placed in public agencies; federal funds were not forthcoming for private agencies at that time. I worked for the Chicago Relief Administration at 63rd Street and Cottage Grove Avenue in an old bank building. The original banking floor was the waiting room, and it was jammed no matter what time of day you went in there. You were face to face with stark poverty.

I had no trepidation about going into what might be considered an "alien society," to work in a field that was completely foreign to me. I think with better sense I might have had some concern. I was imbued with the idea that people needed help, and I was terribly impressed with my ability to give it to them. When I think of the armor that I went into battle with at the age of twenty-three, never for a moment questioning my own ability to function, it's incredible. My ego was as strong as it could be, but perhaps my brain wasn't in perfect working order.

I did not get my master's degree at the U. of C. because, at the end of a year-and-a-half of graduate study, we were all much in demand. I was so gung-ho over the whole business of helping that I didn't want to start at the level of my fieldwork assignment, the family level in the Chicago Relief Administration. Instead I wanted to go where social workers feared to go and had no wish to function: I chose to apply for a position in the Venereal Disease Clinic at Police Headquarters, 11th and State streets. When I announced this at home, I also announced simultaneously—and there was quite a sigh of relief over this—that in order to get the job I had to have a political appointment. The appointment would come through Ben Lindheimer, the Democratic Ward Committeeman of the Fifth Ward.

The record of voting in Vista Homes in those days—and to this day, I regret to say—was absolutely 100 percent Republican. I had voted once, and I had voted Republican, too, but I could conveniently change my politics to get this job and "serve humanity." So I went to Ben Lindheimer and he instructed me in what must be done to get a political appointment, that is, you had to go out and ring doorbells. You had to bring in the vote. I said I would gladly do this. He said, "All right, you start in Vista Homes. We don't have a foothold there."

A foothold! They had *no* hold!

To the utter astonishment of all my parents' neighbors, I began ringing the doorbells in Vista Homes and talking up the Democratic Party, which was without *any* status in that whole building. I worked! I worked like a demon. And I was subject to the whims of the precinct captain, who was a small man, physically, mentally, and morally. He would call me at all hours of the day and night. My father would say, "If you want a political appointment, that's what you do. Go ahead!"

I should have recognized the gleam in his eye at that point.

When voting day came, Vista Homes was not carried by the Democratic Party. As far as I know, no inroads were even made. But I had worked and functioned well. Finally I got the much sought-after letter from Ben Lindheimer, recommending me for the job as social worker at the Venereal Disease Clinic. Then came a shock.

Mr. Lindheimer said, "Of course, this letter does not get you that job. You are subject to being approved by one of the commissioners of the city; that will be on the basis of your accomplishment and your training. But, of course, there'll be no difficulty there, Miss Jones."

So I gladly sent my letter of application, with the covering letter of recommendation from Mr. Lindheimer, to this commissioner, whose name I didn't particularly notice. I waited and I waited. And in the course of ten days a letter came back—not to me, but to Mr. Lindheimer, of course, whose appointment this was.

Mr. Lindheimer called me and said, "I want you to come into my office. I have an answer." Gaily I tripped down to 55th Street and sat in Mr. Lindheimer's august presence. He read the letter to me. It said:

Dear Mr. Lindheimer:

Thank you for suggesting the name of Miss Elizabeth Ann Jones to act as Social Worker in the Venereal Disease Clinic of this city. We recognize that her training would make her a valuable participant in this program. However, it is our judgment that because she lacks experience and is of a very youthful age, we cannot accept her as the appointee.

Hugh O. Jones, M.D.

My father!

And that was the end of my political aspirations, other than voting. I have voted meticulously, but have never again sought a political appointment.

Elizabeth Jones Borst

Chestnut Ridge—My Introduction to the War on Poverty

Though I did not know it at the time, the two summers I worked at a children's camp in West Virginia served as a fitting introduction to the work in which I was to spend a major portion of my professional career. I was a graduate student in psychology, on my way, I thought, to a career as a research psychologist. It was near the end of the Depression and the beginning of the country's entrance into World War II. The first year I worked as a counselor; the second I served as program director. My newly acquired husband served as camp naturalist, chief splinter remover, boil lancer, and dispenser of iodine and Band-Aids.

Our staff consisted of five counselors, college students from the North, and two home economics majors from the University of West Virginia. The Presbyterian youth minister from the university, under whose auspices the camp was sponsored, provided the administrative oversight. The camp was in the process of being built—but still in the first stages. There was one stone building, which served as the mess hall and recreation center on rainy days; it consisted of a single big room with benches and long tables for serving meals. Tents provided sleeping quarters, orange crates served for bureaus. An old-fashioned privy and outside shower provided the . . . amenities. An outdoor stove and pump under a tent covering provided hot water for washing one's clothes—a task that fell to campers and counselors alike.

The children were delivered to us at the welfare office in Morgantown. One by one, they were picked up at their mountain cabins by the social worker and brought into town to join other boys and girls at the office, en route to a three-week stay at Chestnut Ridge Camp, fourteen miles out of town. Each child carried a small bag of clothing and a shiny new toothbrush supplied by the social worker—a requirement of the camp and rarely available in their homes. Some wore conspicuously new shoes, another requirement of the camp, where rattlesnakes were frequent visitors to the fields and roads.

The children stood quietly, for the most part, in tight family groups or alone, heads lowered, peering shyly, often sullenly, through their bangs at the adults so suddenly thrust into their lives. Some of the bigger boys strutted about arrogantly, proclaiming by their manner their refusal to be intimidated by this intrusion into their sovereignty.

The social worker checked over her list: twenty names, twenty children. The back of the camp truck was opened, and the children urged to climb in—the bigger children helping their little brothers or sisters to climb up, the little ones clutching their bags—their last tie to home—anxiously; the camp counselor rounding up the boys on the edge of the group, whose pretense of indifference to the proceedings required them to refuse to hurry. The counselor climbed in back behind the last camper and the truck took off for camp.

The trip to camp up the heavily wooded mountain road was accomplished without mishap—or enthusiasm on the part of the children, who sat quietly holding their bags and staring straight ahead, some frightened, some resigned, some sullen, some curious.

At the camp, the counselors, smiling, hearty in their greetings, helped the children out of the truck and, lists in hand, called out the names of those assigned to their care. Initial chaos was gradually dispelled as child after child was identified, and the "Gwendellyn Ruth" on the list was found to be "Gwinny," and "George Washington Smith" discovered, by the process of elimination, to answer to "Bud."

Chestnut Ridge Camp, sponsored by the Presbyterian Church of Morgantown, provided three weeks of camp life, nutritious meals, and stimulating activities for these children. The children lived in scattered homes near the sites of abandoned mines in those West Virginia mountains. Most of them lived with a single mother or grandmother, the families with an able-bodied father, capable of work in the mines, having moved on to where active mines provided employment. These were the children orphaned by mining accidents or black lung disease; they subsisted on welfare checks. The social workers chose the children from their caseloads on the basis of greatest physical need—from those families whose welfare benefits had run out and for whom food for even one meal a day was uncertain.

Underfed and undernourished as these children were, feeding them posed as many problems as one encountered with well-fed, overindulged middle-class children. Each new dish was met with suspicion; variety was the last thing they wanted. Beans with a flavoring of bacon grease, bread, and generic meat stew twice a day, with more bread for breakfast disappeared rapidly— salads, soups, fresh vegetables were scorned. Since the food we had to feed them was courtesy of the federal surplus foods program, this sometimes presented a problem. Our home economics majors conquered our biggest problem—three pounds of surplus soybean soup mix. Used as prescribed, it made a dark gray, unappetizing soup, however rich in vitamins. Baked into a grayish brown bread, it went down enthusiastically—vitamins and all. The children knew about bread—a staple in their diets.

At the end of three weeks, the process was repeated in reverse. The children were lined up, names read off, and children and their bags bundled into the back of the truck. There was a difference in the ride down the mountain, though. Led by a counselor, the children sang the songs they had learned around the campfire at night. Most of the children were anxious to get home, but it was with mixed emotions that they left counselors they had bonded with, friends they had made, new experiences they had enjoyed. Their cheeks were rosier, and their faces and bodies fuller after three weeks of good food.

On this trip the children were not returned to the Welfare Office but taken, one by one, to their own homes. With maps and directions from the older campers, the driver followed bumpy dirt roads through the woods, up hills, down into valleys, until a small wooden shack would be hailed by its camper as home. Each home was different, yet similar in some way to all the rest. Some had porches, some had cleared space around them, some were neat, some surrounded by rubbish—but all were small, rickety, sad. Often a small child in the yard would sight the truck first and run for the mother in the house. She would appear and quietly greet her returning offspring. There was little running and hugging, the returning child often settling quietly behind his mother's skirts or greeting, more enthusiastically, a tail-wagging dog or an excited sibling. As the truck drove away, children waving from the back, the reunited family could be seen, often still standing quietly watching the truck disappear down the road, some engaged in more enthusiastic discussion now that the strangers had gone, some turning away quickly to disappear into the house.

It is hard to know what those three weeks meant to the children taken so abruptly from their homes and then returned

equally abruptly to the same isolation, meager diet, limited
options. Had the opportunity to live a different kind of life, to
try new things, to make friends with strangers from a different
world made them a little less suspicious of the new and different? Did it matter? It's hard to know.

For those of us who had volunteered to serve as counselors,
it was a valuable learning experience, a glimpse into another
world: a world that we city folk had only read about in the
papers when mine accidents occurred, when John L. Lewis
roared about conditions in the mines, when the mine workers
went on strike, but had never seen up close. We learned a little
about what poverty looks like and how much more is needed to
make a difference than three weeks of good food and well-
meant intentions.

Twenty-three years later, I joined Lyndon Johnson's War on
Poverty—with a larger army and a larger arsenal of weapons:
education, social services, nutrition, medical and dental services,
employment and training opportunities, and a commitment to
community involvement. But that is another story.

Joan Swift

A Bolt of Lightning

It's strange that a single bolt of lightning from the sky in August
1933 would be such a life-changing event. It was late summer and it
was threshing time in rural Rock County, Wisconsin. Threshing was
a cooperative affair, involving two dozen farmers who were bound
together in a "run" and who had purchased a separator, a large
machine that sifts grain from straw. Bundles were shocked and
waiting to be run through the separator.

In August, it was the Masterson farm's turn to thresh. Men
and women were busy planning the event. The men decided
how many teams and wagons were needed to haul the bundles
to the separator and the number of pitchers needed to pitch the
bundles onto the wagon. Some bundles were more slippery than
others, depending on the species of grain being threshed.
Wheat and rye, being non-bearded, were the slipperiest; barley
and oats were the easiest to handle. The women also had work

to do: They had to reorganize their homes to set tables for two dozen very hungry men. In fact, it has been said for many years that if a man is a big eater, he "eats like a thresher-man." The women made bread, pies, cakes, huge roasts, and all the trimmings. This was all done on wood- or coal-burning kitchen ranges. Threshing was dirty, dusty work, and every farm had to set up an area where two dozen men could clean up before going in to eat on the ladies' clean tablecloths.

The day was cloudy and overcast. Rain and threshing do not go together, so the Masterson men were watching the skies for the threatened rain. My brother Nick, a farmer from a nearby town, was on hand to fill in if needed. He was a skilled farmer, and could do any one of the dozen jobs needed on threshing day. Nick and I were standing on the house porch, facing the farmyard and watching the dark, overcast sky. A fifteen-by-thirty International Harvester Tractor was pulling the separator on County Trunk Road A to our farm. It was decision-making time.

The help—the teams and grain wagons, pitchers, and, yes, a water boy who offered cool, clean water from a clay gallon jug— all had to be called in if threshing was to take place.

As Nick and I watched the skies, we were momentarily stunned by a super-loud sizzle sound accompanied by a huge flash and a great clap of thunder. Our horse and cattle barn had been hit by lightning, and huge balls of fire shot off in all directions from the center strike that had opened a great hole in the barn roof.

Nick yelled, "The horses!" and sprinted to the one barn about a hundred yards away. I remembered the two calves that we were going to show at the Rock County 4-H Fair were still in the storage barn. I ran there.

The barn was full of hay in two large mows with a driveway between them. The calves were in the driveway. I opened the sliding door and picked up the first calf. (We later estimated this calf to weigh about 200 pounds.) I carried it away from the burning barn. By the time I got back for the second calf, the hay in both mows was burning from top to bottom and down both sides. The calf was stunned and offered no resistance, so I carried it to safety.

Then I ran to help Nick with the horses. I remembered being told that horses will not leave a burning barn, because their barn means safety, comfort, and food. The horses were in the lower level of the barn. To get there, I needed to go through a narrow mesh gate in a four-strand barbed wire fence that stood between the burning barn and a storage barn about a hundred feet further away. When I touched this gate, I received a substantial electric shock. It was not enough to stop me, and I helped Nick get our two teams out. We had to cover the eyes of one horse to get it out of the barn. By that time, more help was there, and I remember them dragging a thirteen-year-old child away from the barn.

The barn was a total loss, partly because the fire trucks from Janesville would not fight a fire until the property owner guaranteed their fee. It took valuable minutes to find one of my parents so that someone could okay the charge. The fire truck did save the second barn, and we later pushed the insurance company to change the rules so that the fee was always guaranteed for any property in our county.

The fire was a blow to our family. This was 1933, four years after the 1929 crash. Our insurance was inadequate, so we had to mortgage the farm in order to replace the burned barn. We rebuilt the barn, but the strain was too much for my father, who developed heart problems and died early in 1935. As for me, I think this incident was the basis for my decision not to become a farmer.

Willard Masterson

How I Became a Labor Organizer

In 1931, I found work at the Chicago stockyards in the Armour and Company meat packing plant. The pay was 32½ cents an hour. I was the helper to the tractor drivers on the cured meat shipping floor. I made up little "trains" of trucks, each truck filled with about 900 pounds of hams, cured bellies, and other products to be pulled by the tractors to the refrigerator cars waiting at the loading docks below.

What an exciting place that plant was! Over 5,000 men and women doing countless operations in a maze of buildings spread over many acres. The processes were fascinating, the skills amazing, the statistics impressive. The kill chain ran at the rate of 600 hogs per hour, and there was a second chain of the same capacity that operated during the busy winter months. It was a new and different world for a middle-class kid, fresh from college, and how hard that work was! How bone weary you could be at the end of a ten- or twelve-hour day. Or, when work was slack, how frustrating it was to be sent home after only a couple of hours. It would be a short paycheck at the end of the week, and maybe a pink slip and a layoff card. If that happened, it could mean days or weeks of haunting the employment office at 7:00 a.m., hoping to be called back to your old job, or maybe getting a day's work unloading a car of salt. You had to be present, for there was no union, and there was no requirement that you be called back from layoff when work picked up again.

Beyond the uncertainties, there were the indignities. There were the screaming, cursing foremen to endure. There was that bit we called "working for the church," when the boss told you to punch out and keep working a bit longer just to help him out of a tight spot. On holidays, like Christmas and New Year's Day, you didn't have to work, but you didn't get paid either. Vacations were one week after five years of unbroken service. It was just one week, no matter how many years of service you might have put in. But there weren't many who ever qualified. Any layoff of sixty days would break your service record. You might be re-hired, but as a new employee!

In 1937, John L. Lewis and the Coal Miners Union launched a great union organizing drive in the mass-production industries under the Congress of Industrial Organizations (CIO). The CIO was formed because the American Federation of Labor (AFL) refused to accept the industrial (as opposed to craft) union concept. Yet the industrial union was the only thing that made sense in a great industry like automobile, steel, or meatpacking.

Like many others, I became a volunteer organizer in my plant. So when the CIO formed the Packinghouse Workers Organizing Committee in October of 1937, we already had a network of union supporters in practically every one of the Chicago plants. Much the same thing had happened in other packing centers. Then began the battle to oust the company unions that had been put in place after World War I. We had to convince a majority of the workers that the power of the mighty meatpacking companies could be curbed by the power of the people if the workers were united.

That was not an easy task, for workers feared the company and mistrusted one another. Poles and Lithuanians had scant regard for each other, and the industry was full of both. Black workers were reviled as the strikebreakers of previous years. In turn, black workers mistrusted whites, remembering the bloody race riots of 1919. And the Mexicans, how could you know what was on their minds when they didn't even speak English? But we got the job done, although the first contracts were not signed with the big packers, Armour and Swift, until 1941, and even later in the case of Wilson and Company.

Fear of the company was countered by confidence in Roosevelt's New Deal and its National Labor Relations Board. The Board had the power to punish companies for unfair labor practices, such as discharge for union activity, and in those days long ago, the Board really did its job.

Mistrust of one another and mistrust of the union were countered by a rigorous policy of race and nationality (and gender) inclusiveness within the local and national leadership. Every level of leadership had to be balanced. The source of power was held in the local union. Grievances were settled right on the shop floor. Workers learned the meaning and power of solidarity, as they stopped production and gathered around some shaken foreman or superintendent to communicate their discontents.

And the fruits of those very first contracts? After fifty years, I don't really remember how big the pay raise was, but I do know that the company began to give paid holidays, and they agreed to call people back from layoffs, according to seniority, by telegram to their homes!

"Power to the People!"

Leslie Orear, President
Illinois Labor History Society

Local 100, Beef Boners and Sausage Makers, 1934

I grew up four miles out from Tuskegee, Alabama. When I was in my teens, my brother-in-law said, "Come and work with me, I'll give you this plot of land. Whatever you raise is yours; that's your pay for the year." So I plowed and did everything like I did at home. At the end of the year, when I took my cotton to the gin, I had a whole bale of cotton—500 pounds. They took the seeds out of the cotton, and you could sell the seeds and you could sell the whole cotton after that.

My sister Nettie said to me, "What are you going to do with your money?" I said, "I think I'm going to buy myself a nice suit." She said, "Buy yourself a suit and a ticket to Chicago." And so I did what she said. I sold my cotton and I bought myself a nice suit, shoes and everything. And I was silly enough in those days to put on the best I had to ride on the train. People don't do that now; they just wear any kind of mix-match and everything else.

My uncle in Chicago was working in a basement where they picked chickens. Upstairs on the first floor they had about twenty beef boners. I was hired as a laborer. We washed the meat barrels and steamed them out. I would put plastic liners in the barrels, and the beef boners would put the meat in the barrels. I had to roll those barrels away, out into the next room, 370 pounds of meat. All the beef was refrigerated. You had to have extra heavy clothing. I had to load the meat and put it in the truck, and they'd roll the barrels into the rails taking the meat into the plant, the forequarters on one line and the hindquarters on the other. And then I had to take them on the band saw and cut them into pieces to put on the table so the butchers could bone them.

This one Polish fellow at work saw me trying to learn, and said, "John, I'm going to show you how to do this job." He was just so cool; he showed me how to handle a knife, and I learned to produce pretty good. I learned how to handle a knife, how to bone. You had to clean your bones and trim the meat right, of course. I wasn't the very best, but I could make the good money.

They didn't have to watch you work; all they did was watch your bones to see did you clean them. Of all the bones that come out of the piece of cattle that you boned, there was one bone that you counted, and you had a barrel to put your count bones in. The rest of them went on a conveyor down to drop in the truck. But this count bone, you'd better have saved it or otherwise you wouldn't get credit–didn't matter if you boned ten, if you didn't have the count bones to show for it. They had rib bones, they had chuck bones, the hindquarters had a certain bone, and so everybody had a count bone.

It was cold in there. You had to have gloves, because you couldn't work with bare hands. You'd wear a mesh steel glove on your left hand, in case the knife might slip or something. You'd put a cotton glove on, then the metal one over it. That would protect you from getting stabbed with the knife by accident. But one day I had some meat on the table and my knife in my cutting hand. I hit my elbow against a piece of meat that I had piled up. My knife fell out of my hand and I tried to grab it, but it flipped over real quick, and sliced through my finger just like that. So that's why my finger's missing, although it was the only accident I ever had. Of course, I had to take off work because I couldn't use my other hand. I got compensation because I was injured. Then I went back and I got along fine.

On payday, after we got through working, we got our check. There was a tavern a couple of doors away, Schenk Brothers, right on the corner of Fulton and Peoria. We'd go in and have a drink, the three of us, the two Polish guys and me. Each of us would buy a drink and then we'd go home, because we had to work the next day. We didn't get drunk; we just had a shot. Cash our checks, you know? Only once a week.

Back in 1934 nobody wanted to be Union steward. They came around trying to organize at a Polish hall, not a Union hall, just a Polish hall. The fellows trying to organize were Polish. I was the only one that went up there from my company. When I got to the meeting, they said, "Well, if he's stupid enough to come up here. . . ." There wasn't any other colored; they didn't have nothing but Polish people and white people. So they said, "That monkey coming up here by himself, he must have some kind of nerve, or something." They didn't know if I was a spy for the company or what. In order to test me out, they told me, "Look, nobody else was here from Rothschild, you go sign them up, so the Union can represent you fellows at Rothschild, get you better working conditions, money, and all that."

And you know? I got those rascals to sign up. They were Polish and German. I was the only black fellow there, see? Because I was still a laborer at that time, you know, the rest of them all handled the knives.

When I got them signed up, the Union people said, "You don't have to pay no dues." And that was my pay for being the Union steward. After a while, after the Union grew and got a little stronger, I got a job as a field agent, to go around and visit the different plants. We were Local 100, Beef Boners and Sausage Makers.

The young guys didn't want nothing to go out of their pay for pensions. And so I told all the old guys, "Look, you'd better come out to the Union meeting tonight. We're going to be asking the companies to pay more money into the pension fund, so that when we retire, we'll have it." The young guys said, "Damn that! I want my money now! I might be in East Hell when I get sixty-nine years old." But the old guys got the pension in the contract.

I retired from boning and was a full-time Union representative. My job was mostly trying to help people get a fair shake from the employer. We had to go to maybe three or four plants in one day. Oscar Meyer became one of my plants. I'd go there and spend the whole day twice a week, on Mondays and Fridays. The rest of the time I went to other plants.

Well, I retired from Local 100 in 1981 at sixty-five years old. Actually, I haven't done a lick of work since. I'm eighty-six now. I do work for the church for free, Monumental Baptist, down between Langley and Cottage Grove.

John Lassiter

A Yank at Oxford and in London 1934-1937

In 1933, after I graduated from college without a job, I was extremely fortunate to be awarded a Rhodes Scholarship for study at Oxford University in England for three years. Up to that time, my experience had been largely limited to living in a relatively homogeneous small town at the foot of the Wasatch Mountains in Utah.

Oxford gave me the opportunity to widen my horizons through contact with a diverse international group of students, serious study focused on the geography of Europe, and living abroad and traveling widely.

Oxford University is made up of residential colleges in which students live together. Each college provides student quarters, dining halls, sports facilities, common rooms, chapel, and tutorials. One of my closest friends was from the Gold Coast (now Ghana). We traveled together in Nazi Germany, where we were followed by crowds of children, shouting, "Look, a black man!" I asked him if he were embarrassed and he replied no, that in his home village, the children would be just as surprised to see a white man and just as openly expressive. With fellow students from India and Southern Rhodesia (now Zimbabwe), which were part of the British Commonwealth, I engaged in many lively conversations. A student from Newfoundland explained to me the economic problems of this then-British colony, whose self-governing status had been suspended during the Depression. There were also refugee students from Germany. British students taught me to hear my own broad American accent in the word *water*, and I became for a time partly bilingual in British and American English.

The academic program at Oxford included tutorials, in which students were required each week to write an essay on an assigned topic and to discuss it in an individual conference with a tutor. The discipline of doing this every week greatly increased my critical faculties and was excellent training in studying, thinking, and writing. I received special permission to spend the third year of the Rhodes Scholarship in study at the London School of Economics. In London I treasured the opportunity to see Shakespeare's plays at the Old Vic Theatre and to enjoy other cultural features of the great metropolis.

The scholarship also enabled me to travel widely in Europe and to live during vacations with French and German families to improve my language skills. Many of the trips were on a second-hand bicycle, including one in the mountainous Basque country athwart the western Pyrenees separating France and Spain. Travels in Czechoslovakia and Yugoslavia helped me understand the complex ethnic structure of these countries. I came to value tourist guidebooks, especially Baedeker and Michelin, as informative sources on art museums and other cultural institutions.

The discussions, study, and travel in Europe helped me better to appreciate the cultural diversity of countries, of national differences in history and attitudes, of the ethnic complexity of many countries, all of which have continued to play a central role in our evolving world.

Chauncy Harris

European Unrest

For those of our residents who were living in Germany through the post–World War I years and the 1930s, conditions were especially difficult. Depression, followed by the advent of the Nazi regime and the persecution of the Jews led many Germans to emigrate in search of more favorable living conditions. Many came to the United States at that time.

Quaker-Essen *after World War I*

My hometown, Darmstadt, Germany, had a large medical factory, Merck, and toward the end of the First World War we were bombed. I was taken to see the damage. This was an entirely new experience. I saw a living room that had lost a wall. Probably this attack was talked about, but not in front of a child. That is why all I remember is somebody's living room with a missing wall.

When the war ended I was a child of seven or eight; Germany was in a desperate state. Across the Channel, English

Quaker women, Germany's former enemies, collected food and arranged to get into Germany to feed the children. Just imagine: The war was barely over, but the Quakers thought of the hungry German children and arranged the major job of feeding them. I was one of the lucky ones to get a hot lunch every day. The food, called "*Quaker-Essen,*" was very good and we loved it. The Quakers must have stayed for a while because I remember them so well. It must have been difficult for our parents to let us eat what the English brought, but I do not think any of us were asked not to eat the English food.

Anne Langenbach

German Inflation

I was born a few months before World War I and grew up in Germany between the two world wars. Being well protected as a child, I was unaware of the serious depression and political unrest following the war.

Around 1919 there was a general strike in Berlin. This biggest and most modern German city was immobilized: no gas for stores or lamps, no electricity, and most importantly no running water for drinking or toilets. I remember with great pleasure walking with my grandmother to the nearest remaining water pump to fetch bottles of water. I was surprised that she didn't think it was much fun.

Another sensation: my other grandmother came to visit and brought something I had never seen, an orange! Only much later did I realize that the grownups suffered due to food shortages and galloping inflation. Every day my mother went with my father to pick up his salary for the day in order to quickly buy things before the money became worthless.

Of course, as a teenager in the late 1920s, I was well aware of the troubles that were brewing, which led to my reluctant departure from Germany in 1933. Worries about my family and friends overshadowed the next four years, until my parents and young brother were able to join me in France for the immigration to America.

Elizabeth Jacob

Art Class, 1932, Stuttgart, Germany

I sat in my assigned chair in art class and looked at my painting of a stained-glass window. It was colorful: red, green, blue, and yellow sections, outlined in black, the way I had seen such windows in churches and cathedrals, with Christ on the cross in the center. The cross was wood brown, Christ's body, flesh colored. I had carefully detailed the nails piercing the palms of Christ's hands and feet, with dark red blood oozing out. I felt proud of the painting, on which I had spent so much time and effort. I expected to be praised for it and, maybe, get an A.

I was waiting for our art instructor, Professor S., to stand by my chair after looking at three or four other students' works and critiquing them. Professor S. wore his gray lab coat and looked stern and uncompromising with his reddish beard and balding head. He put down the painting of the student to my left and moved, slowly and deliberately, toward me. I felt the blood rush to my head and my heart pound as the professor came close. It was the same feeling I had whenever he critiqued our paintings. I was afraid of him, as were most of my classmates. But I didn't want him to know.

He was standing in front of me now and picked up my painting. I looked at him, still feeling proud of my production, but also apprehensive. He looked at the painting and then at me. His face turned red, and I sensed trouble. I hoped for a positive comment, but instead heard a stream of curse words that turned into loud yelling: "Who do you think you are?" he screamed. "As a Jew, you have no right to paint Christ on the cross!"

I felt deeply embarrassed, hot and cold, unable to say anything. What did I do wrong? Was it really a crime for me to paint Christ? Had I deceived myself when I thought I'd done a good job? But Professor S. was not finished with me, not yet. He flew into such an uncontrollable rage that he reached back to his desk, picked up the inkwell and threw it across the room, the contents emptying over a cabinet and onto the floor.

The heads of my classmates turned toward me. A constant stream of insults was hurled at me. Everyone seemed temporarily in a state of shock. I felt immobilized, as did, apparently, my class-mates. I was also terrified, because I realized that no one would or could come to my rescue. These were dangerous times.

Professor S. moved on to the next student. There was dead silence in the classroom. At the end of the hour, I picked up my materials and walked quietly and alone out of the classroom.

Renate Vambery

My European Education, My American Life

I was born in Berlin in 1902, and was the youngest of three children. My older sister, Charlotte, became a dermatologist like our father. My brother, Herman Karl, also followed the family tradition into medicine, becoming a pharmacologist and physi-ologist.

In the German school system, when I was growing up, reli-gion was a required subject. Each student and family had to choose whether to undertake religious instruction from the Jewish, Catholic, or Evangelical (Protestant) curriculum. When I asked my parents which course to take, they said, "Which teacher do you like best?" I made my choice, and that's why I was instructed in the Protestant faith, rather than the Jewish.

Hitler came to power in 1933. My husband, Dr. Helmut Paul George Seckel, a Protestant, was dismissed from his position at Cologne for the offense of having a Jewish wife: me. In 1935, after a few months in Berlin, we left for England, where we had relatives, then came to New York. My husband worked there for a few months in association with Presbyterian Hospital.

In New York City one day we visited the roof garden of our hotel and looked up to see a sight to make any German proud: the 775-foot-long airship the *Hindenburg*, was circling the city. The tail fins of the great ship bore the swastika. Most Americans did not yet know how hateful that symbol was to us, and was to become to the whole world. On May 6, 1937, on the train to Chicago, the conductor came through our car and said, "I have a sad story to tell. The *Hindenburg* has crashed and burned."

Margaret Seckel

Nazis Looking for Guns

After Hitler and the Nazis came to power in 1933, an aunt of my mother's in Texas signed an affidavit that would allow my family to emigrate to the United States. However, we wanted to stay. We considered ourselves Germans of Jewish faith and thought that Hitler's policies would "blow over."

In 1936 an agricultural training school was founded in Gross-Breesen, near Breslau in East Germany, now in Poland. Its purpose was to prepare young Jewish people for farming careers overseas. I worked there as a secretary and a group leader for girls.

The most frightening experience of my life occurred in November 1938. A German diplomat in Paris was assassinated. The Nazis claimed that a Jew did this. The following day, they burned synagogues, destroyed shops, broke windows, and put people into concentration camps. This is now remembered each year in November as *Kristallnacht*, "the Night of Broken Glass."

The Gestapo came to our farm school in Gross-Breesen. They took the director of the school and the agricultural instructor and all young men over eighteen years of age to Buchenwald concentration camp, from which they returned after four weeks. But at the time, we didn't know if we would ever see them again. The only adults left after this roundup were the agricultural instructor's wife and myself. I was twenty-four years old.

The storm troopers broke dishes and windows, smashed tables and broke the grand piano, which was one of our prize possessions. We had played it and listened to classical music every night. The Nazis claimed that we had guns hidden, and demanded that we turn them over. They put a pistol to my forehead and told me that if I didn't produce the guns they would shoot me. But I could not produce guns because there were none at the school. Finally, when everything was smashed, the Nazis left.

I then decided that I had better make plans for getting out of Germany.

Ruth Hadra

An American in Germany

In 1932 we went to Germany to climb in the Bavarian Alps, where my grandmother had a favorite guide with whom she had climbed many seasons. We stayed with some friends of hers who had originally lived in Berlin, but had lost their money in the inflation after World War I and so had moved to their summer home near Garmisch to take in paying guests. There were about twenty guests, largely distinguished people and aristocratic types from Germany and England. When we were there, this included Catherine Cornell and Madame Stokowski, who had brought two Jewish students from the Juilliard School. Our host had very strong feelings about the political situation, as well as a weak heart, so any conversation about politics was banned. We practiced climbing regularly, and, at the end of the summer, went up one of the more difficult faces of the Zugspitze with a guide.

It was a beautiful summer, and we encountered nothing unpleasant of any sort except for on one day. The brother of our hostess had designed a new set for Bayreuth, and it was to be used for the opening night, when Hitler was to be there. In this aristocratic environment, children were hardly noticed or included, but we could not avoid sensing the extreme tension that arose until a message came through with the news that everything was all right.

I went back to Germany in the 1980s and found a whole new generation of people to whom events associated with World War II seemed to be no more than ancient history.

Jane Overton

8

World War II

One Hell of a War

This is the tale of one Richard J. S.,
A lawyer of outstanding fame,
Who left all his cases and family's bright faces
To take up the soldiering game.

In spite of his homework with family at night
And his toil in the courts in the day,
His draft board refused to say, "You're excused,"
But sent him that notice, 1A.

He arrived for his scheduled induction exam
And was told by the docs, "You can't win."
They counted his toes, his eyes, ears, and nose,
And announced, "Private Stevens, you're in."

So he kissed his dear wife and his kiddies goodbye.
He kissed his stenographer, too.
In fact in his leaving there was little of grieving,
For he kissed every girl that he knew.

They sent him to Sheridan Fort by the lake.
Gave him tests, shots, and gear by the pecks,
Dressed him up in a suit, khaki colored, but cute,
And showed him some movies on sex.

When the weekend came round he was still at the fort,
So they gave him an overnight pass.
He streaked right for his flat, kiddies, wife, and all that
And got one last piece of advice.

But his stay there was short; he went back to the fort
And was shipped to a far distant camp.
There he sweated by day and at night froze away
And was cold, tired, hungry, and damp.

But this diligent twit didn't know when to quit
So on Sunday, a day meant for rest,
He threw his slight frame around the obstacle game,
And, alas, his bones crunched at the test.

Now they've got him out flat on a hospital mat
Where life is but one endless bore.
So all he can say in poetical way is:
This sure is one hell of a war.

R. J. Stevens

World War I was our parents' war; World War II was ours. Although it would be two years after Germany invaded Poland before America was officially proclaimed to be at war, our lives were already affected: War news dominated the daily papers; movies and the newsreels brought the war in Europe to us in vivid images. And while the full horror of the Holocaust was yet to be disclosed, refugees from Germany brought firsthand accounts of the persecution of the Jews.

The possibility of America's involvement in the war threw a shadow over plans for the future just as our generation reached the life-planning stage. With educations underway or just completed, it was time to get on with our personal lives. Instead, our young men found themselves players in a gigantic lottery—the draft—under the direction of the Selective Service Administration. Many did not wait for their numbers to be called up, but volunteered for their choice of service. Others waited it out until they received their letter of greeting from Uncle Sam. Eventually, all men of the appropriate ages were sorted out, from 1A to 4F; other categories further defined one's role in the impending war effort.

The bombing of Pearl Harbor was a provocation too large to counter with lesser measures, and President Roosevelt declared war on Japan. The declaration of war on Germany was accepted as inevitable.

While most of the opposition to America's entrance into the war was dispelled by the attack on Pearl Harbor, a number of individuals refused to join the military as a matter of principle, religious or political. Civilian Public Service (CPS) Camps were set up for conscientious objectors, whose refusal to fight was based on religious grounds. Jail terms were meted out to those who refused to register or whose draft boards were unimpressed by their pacifist convictions.

The war touched every aspect of our lives: Gasoline was rationed and one thought carefully before taking that Sunday drive in the country or to a market across town; sugar was saved for special baking projects, and butter was spread extremely thin. Meat shortages made the butcher a person to treat with deference in case a supply of bacon reached his shop.

It was a wartime we all shared, but each of us experienced it differently. For some it was an exciting adventure, for others days of drudgery and boredom; for some a time of waiting, for others a time of hardship or danger.

Remembering December 7, 1941

It was a quiet Sunday afternoon, the children were napping, the symphony played on the radio, and I welcomed the free time to write Christmas cards at the kitchen table. The announcement of the attack on Pearl Harbor interrupted the symphony, and our world changed.

From our back porch high on the third floor, there was a clear view across the Midway to the International House [for foreign students attending the University of Chicago]. During the day after Pearl Harbor, the student residence was visited by government officials—we called them G-men—and Japanese students were removed and driven away.

A few months later the university converted the nearby tennis courts to temporary housing for the naval recruits in training at the university. Some of their classes ended late, and in spite of the dark they would march in formation on the sometimes-crowded streets. Our concern prompted my husband to protest to the university and to write a letter to the *Chicago Tribune*, captioning his appeal "Lanterns for Marching Men." It worked! The recruits were given small flashlights. The flashlights provided protection from the passing cars.

Elizabeth Jones Borst

Socks at Pearl Harbor

Bill Cade and I were married in June of 1940 and, after a three-month honeymoon touring the United States, we sailed to Honolulu on the S.S. *Matsonia*, Bill to be an instructor in civil engineering and I to teach nursery school. We found a small but comfortable house in Manoa Valley, a short walk from the University of Hawaii. Life was happy and uncomplicated.

Early in the fall of 1941, residents of Hawaii were advised to store soap and canned meat, making room in the warehouses for more supplies—a possible clue to things to come, which most of us failed to recognize.

The morning of December 7, 1941, we were still in bed when we heard low-flying planes and sounds of explosion—most unusual for a Sunday. I said to Bill, "How could you tell if this were the real thing?" He answered, "You couldn't."

Bill climbed up into the storage space above the refrigerator and began dropping down pieces of equipment: a belt, cap, shirt, trousers—too wide and too short; they were his father's. An ROTC officer at Michigan State, Bill had recently been promoted to first lieutenant, so my task was to scrape the gold off the bars to show the silver underneath. That accomplished, he left.

Later that evening, he came home on a motorcycle with a sidecar and no headlights. The island was completely blacked out.

"Do you know how to load a shotgun?"

"Certainly not."

Well, we struggled, but alas, I was seven months pregnant and trying to break open a gun in front of my *opu* (stomach) was impossible. He gave up and left again.

Several days later he called saying that his ROTC troops had been on guard duty for forty-eight hours with no relief.

"Bring the soap that's in the closet and go buy all the socks you can find. Use our grocery money."

I did so: argyles, stripes, plaids, bright colors—twenty-eight dollars' worth of socks from a small store nearby. I took them to the other side of the island, to a school where the boys were stationed. When I got to the gate, a young Japanese student of Bill's, complete with a rifle with a bayonet on the end, pointed directly at me and wanted to know what I was doing there. I said that I wanted to see Lt. Cade. He queried, "Who are you? His mother?"

I didn't see Bill. The supplies were unloaded and I drove home. As soon as I got inside, the phone rang. "Take the socks back," Bill said. "The Army has just issued supplies."

About six weeks later, a ship brought mail for civilians, and we received a large cardboard carton from Bill's family in Michigan. Christmas at last! What could it be? Nothing less than a case of Spam!

Elise Cade

My Peripatetic War

I left Huntsville by train to New York via Chicago. On December 7, 1941, I boarded a bus to Fort Monmouth, arriving in late afternoon and went to the PX. All present were listening to a radio broadcast, and I joined the group. An old (about forty) master sergeant asked, "Are you a group of recruits for OCS [Officers Training Corps]?"

"Yes," we answered.

He said, "Pearl Harbor has been hit. We will be at war in the morning, and all of you will be in the Army for the duration."

He was so right. The next ninety days were tough, both physically and mentally. A few days before I was commissioned, I was called before a full colonel. My fellow cadets told me it was a bad omen, that it was the way they reduce numbers before commission. They were wrong. The colonel asked me many questions about my civilian work and what I knew about pole and tower work, and about power lines. I was selected to go to a special Ranger school to learn explosives. The school was short, but it was pure hell. Every day started with a three-mile run. Subject one: do's and don'ts in the use of primacord, a deadly explosive placed inside a flexible cord. We figured out that we were being trained for a behind-the-lines drop in a coming invasion.

Our class was awaiting overseas shipment, when again I was ordered to the colonel's office. He questioned me further about my telephone experience as a civilian, and then said I would be going to a group known as the Plant Engineering Agency (PEA) with headquarters in Philadelphia. Boy, what a bomb he dropped! I searched high and low, but couldn't find a word about said agency. I learned later that PEA was a secret civilian/ military organization that was responsible for construction and maintenance of high-tech communications.

So I got on the first available bus and went to Philadelphia. After one week there, I moved on to Presque Isle, Maine. My assignment was temporary duty for the base commanding officer of Crystal Two, located on Upper Frobisher Bay on Baffin Island [Canada]. I found that I would be responsible for the construction and installation of a telephone system for the air base. The weather in the winter was cold. Sixty degrees below zero was common, as we were above the Arctic Circle. Winter was twenty-four hours of darkness with bone-chilling cold.

Thank God for my civilian stint with AT&T. I contacted Otto "Red" Cameran, who had been my big boss, and asked for a set of books to set up a complete phone system. He responded, and I started a school on telephone work with the GIs sent to me as staff. The men were good and willing, but lacked experience. We worked with gusto and it was a great system. However, the earth was permafrost, frozen to a depth of twenty feet—it never thawed, even in the short summer.

Baffin Island has huge deposits of iron ore underground and therefore radio transmission was nil. PEA thought about the problem, and then I was asked to build a milelong antenna five feet off ground level. Transformers and power units were furnished, and the antenna worked.

Later I was contacted and told that a member of my home office would meet me in New York to give me my summer uniforms. I was moving again, this time going to a hot project in a warm area. In Bermuda, I was to help build and install a radio Teletype system between the U.S.A. and Africa. Bermuda was the first leg. The job was an A1 priority, and we were to learn why: Fighter aircraft heading for Europe were equipped with extra gas tanks and flew with a modified mother bomber ship. These planes were getting iced up and were going down. The RTTY system would furnish navigation aid to planes so they could fly over warm air. My job was again antennae; this time the design was rhomboid. Because this job was A1, we worked seven days a week, dawn to darkness. All crews did great work, and on test day we had scads of Air Force brass in attendance. Then an Air Force major sat down on the Teletype machine and made contact with the U.S.A. — Success!

After D day, our organization did not break up, as they were transferring men to the Japanese war. I was given the opportunity for release. I took it and was home in April 1946.

Willard Masterson

Camp Following

On December 7, 1941, my husband and I had been married for five months. I was nineteen and Ned was twenty-two. We were living in a tiny apartment in Madison, Wisconsin, where I was a junior at the university; Ned was attempting to be a writer in a rented room where he went every day to think. I cooked hamburgers and frozen peas and boiled potatoes nearly every night for dinner, having no interest in cooking and no knowledge whatsoever of how to do it. In the evenings Ned practiced the flute, I did my homework, and then he read *War and Peace* aloud. We acquired a stray kitten, which we named Anna Pavlovna.

On that fateful Sunday we were listening to the New York Philharmonic on the radio and Anna was playing with a piece of string on the floor. Just as the concert stopped and the announcer told of the attack on Pearl Harbor, Anna swallowed the string, leaving a small piece hanging out of her mouth. I was horrified. Only after I had grabbed the end of the string and pulled it slowly out, did I notice what the announcer was saying on the radio. It seemed less important than the predicament of the cat.

By the time my husband was drafted we had a baby, the first I had ever held. When her father went off to basic training, the baby and I became camp followers. The feeling of being totally responsible for this valuable child in a strange place where I knew nobody, and where Ned could only come home for the night at the whim of his sergeant, was terrifying.

Every day I washed diapers, made supper, fed the baby, and waited. Sometimes Ned came home and sometimes not. Once he came home saying that the sergeant had told him to have his hair cut before he came back at six in the morning, so I got out the scissors and cut. When I was through, there were little round bald spots all over his head, but the Army wasn't after beauty.

After basic training, because he knew French and a little Italian, Ned was sent to Columbus, Ohio, to learn German. Susan and I followed and settled in two rooms on the second floor of a ramshackle frame house. Our downstairs neighbor was a crazy woman who spent a lot of time hiding behind the bush beside her front door and peering down the side street at the corner grocery store. She told me that the proprietor of the store was her lover, so I assumed that she hid behind the bush in her pink satin dressing gown in order to check on possible rivals going into the store. On some mornings, the iceman brought her a hundred-pound block of ice but, afraid of his intentions, she wouldn't let him in; so he left the chunk of ice on her doorstep. All morning I could hear her dragging and chopping and grunting as she heaved chunks of ice into her icebox.

I was very lonesome, but of course Susan was company. She learned to walk, and jump up and down on the bed and talk. I put up three jars of pears and set them on the windowsill, not to eat, but for reassuring decor. During the day I rarely had a chance to speak to an adult so I relied heavily on a radio soap opera called *The Guiding Light* for companionship.

One day I actually met and talked with another woman. As we companionably walked our buggies, she told me about her husband's failures in sex, failures of possible successes I hadn't known existed. I tried hard to find her again, but even though I looked for days she never turned up.

Once Ned and I invited another soldier to come for Thanksgiving dinner. By now I had learned to cook a few things, and I actually roasted my first turkey. My husband and the other soldier seemed to appreciate it, along with the sweet potatoes and pie. It wasn't until the next day that I found out they had already had a sumptuous Thanksgiving dinner provided by the Army an hour before mine. There are more ways than one of being a hero!

The soldiers were being taught German by a pretty, plump young woman who had grown up in Berlin. They fell for her like tenpins. She even caused one young man to hang himself in his dormitory room. Finally, though, she settled on one person and married him secretly, thus closing off the options of the others. The couple was married in a big empty church where some of the soldiers went on Sundays to hear a person called "Sleepy Lagoon" sing Baptist hymns. Ned and I were the only witnesses to the ceremony.

And once I remember a woman with a German accent standing in the doorway of our room and telling me that she had just recovered from pneumonia, and that she and her sister and stepmother had crossed over the mountains from France into Spain with a guide paid to help them. It was dark and cold, and they were exhausted. The guide kept telling them to be very quiet, and then, as they struggled up the mountain, her sister and her stepmother got into a terrible screaming fight. Suddenly, for the first time I was connected to the actual war. I don't know where this woman came from and I never saw her again, but now I wish I had known enough to do something kind and comforting instead of just helplessly letting her leave.

Then one day the crazy lady downstairs came to the bottom of the narrow stairs to our rooms and called, "*Fire!*" I grabbed Susan and the fire extinguisher and rushed down. At the bottom, outside, a trash barrel was modestly burning. I put the baby down in her buggy and, frightened and confused, I proceeded

to squirt the fire extinguisher full blast into my own face. Luckily
I wasn't blinded, only very embarrassed. The fire in the barrel
went out of its own accord and I climbed back upstairs with the
baby under my arm. After this I was not only lonesome but I was
steeped in anxiety; I was more skeptical than ever of my ability
to protect my daughter from danger.

The program in German finished just as the war in Europe
ended. Now that the army had taught Ned German, they sent
him to a Chinese Signal Corps company in Missouri. By the time
Susan and I joined him in Carthage, Missouri, he was learning to
be a high-speed radio operator.

It was summer and hot, but Carthage was wonderful. The
people across the street, who had a peach orchard, were friendly,
and their children came over and played with Susan. On Saturday
nights we all walked into town together to the concert on the
bandstand by the county courthouse. Even when Ned couldn't
come home, I didn't feel entirely alone in the world. It was so hot
that sometimes we slept on the front porch, where it was cool and
miraculously mosquito free, although after a long day of listening
to Morse code, Ned sometimes had trouble sleeping because of the
messages sent to him by the crickets and the katydids.

He had to get the bus from Carthage every morning at 4:30
in order to be back at camp on time. I would get up and cook
him breakfast while it was still dark, and the flame of the gas
burner made a cozy flicker in the kitchen. Then, since we lived
about two miles from the bus station, I would hop into the car in
my very thin summer nightie and, leaving Susan asleep, I would
drive him to the bus.

There was a diner beside the bus station, and at this hour it was
full of soldiers eating eggs and drinking coffee. One morning just
as it was beginning to get light, we crept up to the bus stop: chug
chug chug, and realized that we'd run out of gas. The bus was just
coming around the corner. Ned had to catch it or he'd be late and
never allowed to come home again. He kissed me goodbye, gave
me a dime and left. There I was, at five in the morning, transpar-
ently dressed, my baby asleep alone in a house two miles away, and
no gas station anywhere near. I knew there was one taxi in Carthage
so I got out of the car, went into the diner, and walked majestically

down its whole length in my nightgown, past all the soldiers eating eggs, to the telephone at the far end. Using the dime Ned had given me, I woke up the Carthage taxi driver, told him my predicament, and, looking neither to the left nor to the right, I marched back down the length of the diner and out to wait in my car. I have to say that the soldiers at the counter were 100 percent gentlemen. Not one snicker, giggle, or snort did I hear during this whole performance. They just buried their noses shyly in their coffee cups and looked the other way.

I had been in a waiting mode ever since Ned had been in the Army; however, along about Thanksgiving the ax fell, and it became clear that soon he would go to a staging area to be sent overseas. The time of being a camp follower was over. Susan and I went home, and a long period of serious waiting set in.

Alice Hayes

My Enemy Alien Camera

In December 1941, I was a student of occupational therapy at Hastings State Hospital in Ingleside, Nebraska. On Pearl Harbor Day, I suddenly became an "enemy alien." I had arrived in the United States in 1937 and was not yet eligible for citizenship. Enemy aliens had to turn in weapons, shortwave radios, and cameras. I had a German camera, not the best or most expensive, but I was no longer allowed to possess it.

Ingleside was a small town; I went to the closest sheriff's office to hand in my camera. The sheriff was a big man, at least 6 feet tall and 200 pounds. When I handed him my camera, he asked, "What for?" I had to explain to him that I was an enemy alien and no longer allowed to own a camera. Apparently he had not been informed of this.

He accepted the camera and kept it for me until I became a citizen in August 1943. By then I was living and working in Chicago. I wrote to the sheriff and gave my certificate number. Upon receiving this information, the sheriff returned my camera in the same condition he had accepted it approximately a year and a half earlier. He also sent a letter of congratulations with it.

Renate Vambery

Oh So Secret—At Home and Abroad

My military career was varied and chaotic: I was initially trained as an airplane engine mechanic in the Air Force, but when I arrived at a maintenance depot in Utah, I found myself the chaplain's assistant and the editor of the post newspaper.

After about a year there, I was suddenly assigned to a company of men to be shipped to the Pacific theater. At the time, I was in the post hospital with an ear infection, but the medic certified me as ready for action. So I boarded the train to Pittsburg, California, on San Francisco Bay, where we would board a ship. On arrival at Pittsburg, however, we were all subjected to a rigorous medical exam, and I was pulled out of the departing company. The Army wasn't going to put an infected soldier on a crowded troop ship. These last minute pull-outs were frequent, and, for about a month, I belonged to a strange assembly of men and women (the latter mostly nurses) of all ranks. We would meet for drill every morning, with our bags of gear and clothes all packed, and the officers in charge would announce who was now reassigned to an outfit leaving that day—no delays for sending a man back to get his clothes. The rest of us took the ferry to San Francisco to enjoy the town.

I knew this paradise would not last, and through a Harvard friend who could certify that I had studied meteorology, I was sent to McClellan Field in Sacramento, to be part of the Weather Squadron. This was my introduction to special status. The Air Force rules were that the weather people reported directly to Washington, not to the local commander, and even though I was still a private, I was accordingly a special sort of private.

Throughout my stay in the OSS [Office of Strategic Services], from September 1943 to November 1945, I was a part of the Research and Analysis division. We had no role in undercover or covert operations. A large part of our work was exhausting public and private sources of information regarding specific current or anticipated needs. A current need might be the establishment of priorities for sabotage through undercover operations, or for aerial bombing targets. Anticipated needs might be ways to help a military government administered by the victorious Allies, and ways to deal with a disordered and devastated Central Europe. In Washington, for no reason other than "somebody-has-to-do-it," I became an expert of sorts in telecommunications, particularly the telephone systems of Germany and Italy.

In the late summer of 1944, those of us in uniform who had been working together in Washington were formally organized as a military unit. I received a commission as a second lieutenant in the Army, and, with that gift of prestige, was formally in charge of fifteen or twenty Army personnel going abroad. Before the orders to travel were issued, however, we had a brief period of evaluation and training. We were ordered individually to show up at an abandoned schoolhouse near Georgetown, in Army fatigues, without any personnel identification, and with an assumed name—I was "Bradford." We were not to reveal our true names, our rank, or whether we were in the Army or the Navy. The process was organized so that none of us went through it with anyone we previously had known or worked with. The disguise was not perfect: Although fatigue uniforms were, well, uniform, somebody forgot about shoes. Army shoes differed from Navy shoes, and in both services enlisted men's shoes differed from officer's shoes!

Part of what we went through was psychological testing. We were to construct and adopt a phony identity and personal history. The training included a series of events in which four or five of us were put in a room, under the observation of the testing staff, and given an impossible or nearly impossible task. The one I remember is a room with a ping-pong table, a large piece of canvas, a couple of two-by-four boards, several glass-headed pushpins, and several large clamps. We had twenty minutes to construct a tent. We rapidly learned that nothing fit. The clamps were pretty big, but just a little too small to attach the two-by-fours to the edge of the table, and too small to attach 2 two-by-fours together. I have forgotten whether we gave up before our allotted time or whether we made some fragile but plausible tent. What I do remember was that we took the whole thing very seriously. After the war, when I read a little about the whole system of evaluation, I recognized that the observers were watching to see who, in a room full of strangers faced with a ridiculous assignment, would lead, and whether the others would accept his leadership. The leader was not modest little me!

At the end of all this, the evaluation team made recommendations to me, as the ranking Army officer of the group, as to who seemed satisfactory and who not. The evaluation team did not have authority to approve or disapprove anyone for overseas service, but could only make evaluations and recommendations.

Just as I received orders to go abroad, I was given a commission as second lieutenant. In Washington this would have been nice but not necessary; in the milieu of wartime Europe, it made a big difference. We flew to England via Prestwick Airport in Scotland, and ended up at an OSS station in the Mayfair district of London. There was confusion there. The local officer in charge did not expect us and did not know what to do with us. He was principally involved in briefing undercover agents to be parachuted into occupied parts of France, a highly secret activity, and it was clear that he found us to be a pain in the neck. The confusion was straightened out, and we were flown to Paris in August 1944, about two weeks after the liberation of the city.

Here we were intelligence maids-of-all-work, undertaking frequently unrelated tasks, operating out of a still-extant office complex at 79 Champs Elysées, and quartered in what would in peacetime be regarded as a good but not luxurious hotel (I refer to the precise French system of classifying hotels), which was then, of course, without heat or hot water. But most of the time I was sent out of Paris on assorted unrelated missions.

During the Spanish Civil War, which had placed Franco in power, thousands of antifascist refugees fled over the Pyrenees into France and were interned throughout WWII in camps near Toulouse. Despite some French efforts to restrain them, various groups would go over the passes into Spain and commit minor sabotage operations, then slip back to Toulouse. Charles de Gaulle's government forbade all this, but lacked effective control over parts of France this far from Paris. Eisenhower's headquarters worried that Spanish forces might respond with an invasion of southwest France. Information available in Paris was conflicting and vague. I was sent with a jeep driver to the Spanish border, where I went on every road or track a jeep could handle to see what I could see, and talked to some of the actors. I concluded that nothing was going on that should worry anyone; all responsible leaders fully recognized that provoking Spain into retributory actions would be a serious detriment to the Allied cause, and such leaders were using their influence to keep any talk about attacks on Spain confined to talk. This was perhaps an example of the opportunistic, errand-boy nature of our role: Ideally all sorts of data would be available to leadership in Paris—but everyone was overworked, so why not send Overton?

When the war was nearly over and Western forces occupied the parts of Germany and Eastern Europe that were to be turned over to the Russians, raiding and looting parties were mounted. The objective was to get for the West—or prevent the Soviets from acquiring—various goodies. The happy surrender of the German rocket scientists was a very high priority in this. I was sent to Jena to see if we could acquire the huge Justus-Perthes map collection. This was the largest such library of maps in the world, surpassing anything comparable anywhere. Unfortunately, moving any significant portion of the collection would have taken dozens of trucks on dozens of trips, and all I had was a jeep, so I couldn't take them.

George Overton

OSS Testing

During World War II, the Office of Strategic Services needed help identifying and assessing candidates suitable for confidential government work. Henry Murray, head of the Harvard Psychological Clinic, got together a team of psychologists with a few psychiatrists. Within a week or two we had a program with about twenty different tests and procedures, and were ready to meet our first batch of candidates trucked out from Washington—mostly men in fatigues and an occasional woman. Over the next twenty months, to the end of the war, we greeted sixteen to twenty candidates at four-day intervals, three groups each two weeks, with two full days off for the staff out of fourteen days. Altogether, we assessed 2,371 people at Station S. Everyone came anonymously, identified only by a nickname awarded back in Washington. Sooner or later we had personnel of every rank, from privates to generals.

My wife, Barbara, who had worked with Henry Murray at the Harvard Clinic, met the challenge of typing the assessment reports on each candidate—single-space texts with nine carbon copies and not a single typo, not a single erasure permitted. That work had to be done after the staff conference ended in mid-evening and after the drafters of the reports had smoothed out their rough worksheets. Another part of her job was taking down, over the phone, security reports from the FBI, Naval Intelligence, and so forth, including how many liquor bottles were found in a candidate's garbage.

Barbara and I were at Station S from its founding in December 1943 to its termination on August 23, 1945. Station S was an estate in Fairfax, Virginia. We were given a house on the grounds, formerly the gardener's cottage. OSS allowed a rumor to start in the local village that we were studying soldiers returned from the front. Since these soldiers were clearly in good physical health, it was obvious that they must be in poor mental health, so the locals kept their distance from the estate.

In the assessment situation we interviewed each candidate under "clear" conditions. They were told that this interview was the one and only time when we would expect them to drop their cover story and be quite candid. All the rest of the time at the station they were expected to use their cover story to answer any questions from staff or fellow candidates. Their ability to maintain their cover stories was one of the things on which they were rated.

Many of the procedures that confronted the candidates were situation tests, in which an individual or a small group was told to accomplish a task within a specified short time, or "as fast as you can." Psychologists had used the Discussion Situation Test for some time before World War II. A group of candidates in fatigues was told, "In the next forty minutes, we would like you to discuss this question: 'What are the major post-war problems facing the United States, and, if you have time, along what lines do you think they should be solved?' This is to be a group discussion. Allow each person to express his opinion. Just before the end of the period we should like one of you to give us the conclusions of the group."

As you can imagine, this test gave us some evidence pertinent to rating the central traits: Effective Intelligence, Social Relations, Energy and Initiative, and Leadership. At the end, they were asked to indicate on secret ballots which candidates they had found to be most persuasive and also which one they would wish to have as their chairman at an assumed future discussion.

In sharp contrast was the Construction Test. I must confess this test was the one the staff enjoyed most as we watched the ingenuity of our two "helpers." We did feel some sympathy for the utter frustration each candidate must have felt. The candidate was instructed not to do any of the work. The helpers were told to obey all commands from the candidate. One of the helpers was slovenly and slow moving; the other was much more active and took the lead in their verbal onslaught on the candidate. The record shows that no candidate ever successfully completed the task in the allotted ten minutes with two helpers, though it was obvious that one person working alone could complete the task within the allotted time.

At the end of that test, the staff member who had been giving the instructions walked off with the candidate. Establishing friendly rapport, the staff member asked the candidate what he thought of the whole test. This interview was thought of as therapeutic, and it was, by helping the candidate adjust to the unpleasant experience as quickly as possible.

There were scores of other tests. There were tests designed for people who would be doing intelligence work, and tests for people doing "black propaganda," that is, writing propaganda pieces with the source concealed. Some were tailored to the specific task for which the candidate was being considered. For instance, a candidate for the position of instructor might be given some "time pencils," which are simple delayed-action fuses. He received considerable material, both printed and diagrammatic, about the pencils and was told that he would have fifteen minutes to deliver a demonstration lecture the next day on the design and use of such pencils.

The assessment work had to be extended to Station W, a one-day version of Station S, in Washington, and to a West Coast station. Overseas operations were located in Ceylon, China, and India. In countries where the assessment staff did not speak the language, assessment was very difficult. In one Chinese program, a large number of candidates had to be reduced to a smaller number; so only a selected few were asked to return the following day. The next morning, the group of candidates did not look familiar to the assessment staff. It turned out that none of those who had been asked to return did so. Their chief had decided that those who were asked to return must be the choice people for his elite force, and so he had kept them instead of sending them in for more testing. Such were the problems when channels of communication were bad.

Donald Fiske

Britain in the Blitz

In the summer of 1944, I left boarding school, and I planned to attend Westfield College in the fall. I spent holidays at Oatlands Park Hotel in Weybridge, Surrey, about twenty miles southwest of London, where my parents lived during the war. It had a golf course, two tennis courts, a swimming pool, and Saturday evening dances. The guests were of many nationalities.

When the Nazis invaded Norway, members of the royal court left by sea and took a number of diplomats with them. Several stayed in our hotel. The second-in-command of the Czechoslovakian brigade also spent much time there, which was great because my brother Paul was his aide-de-camp. Life was never dull when Paul was around.

Among the guests was a Dutch family, the Olifiers, whose daughter Karen was very pretty. One of the fighter pilots from the nearby airfield evidently thought so, too. He came to our Saturday dances, and he also buzzed the hotel when he flew over us, just to say hello to her. The trouble was that one couldn't be sure that it wasn't an enemy plane up to no good. It was during the Battle of Britain, and there was a lot of activity in the air.

At that time, a number of women together rented the basement ballroom at the Grosvenor Hotel for Sunday afternoon dances. Each had a large table to which she invited girls and officers. I was one of the lucky ones to be asked. On one occasion, when both my brother Paul and my future husband, Mike Rowbon, were there, we heard sirens, but what with the noise of the band and all of us, we paid no attention to the raid. When the dance was over and we came out, we saw fires everywhere. The Nazis were trying to burn down London. As Paul and I drove back to Weybridge, we saw fire engines, ambulances, and fires everywhere.

Meanwhile, Mike walked down to Piccadilly. He saw a fire in the belfry of the small, well-known St. James Church. Fire engines had more pressing engagements than this. So he went in and tried to put the fire out. He couldn't, but he did pick up a piece of a bomb as a souvenir and I still have it.

Later, after I had my bachelor's degree and joined the women's army, the ATS, I was posted to the Czechoslovakian Ministry of Defense, which was in the Rothschild Palace at Hyde Park Corrals, in the heart of London's West End. My ATS colonel, a nice, motherly woman, arranged for me to be attached to a nearby ATS unit in Eaton Place. They were quartered in two large houses. The other ranks slept in large rooms that had been turned into dormitories. The servants' quarters on top floors served as single rooms for the officers.

The first time I arrived ready to report to the commanding officer, it was after 6:00 P.M. and none of the officers was around. The rest of the officers' corps, about eight of them, returned in a due course from the Antelope, where they usually went at six o'clock for a drink. They were older than I, around twenty-five to thirty-five, although the oldest must have approached fifty. (She had gray hair.) She also was the niece of the Queen, but they were all well connected, and our mess was a busy place with many visitors.

I have particular reason to remember one officer in the Horse Guards. Toward the end of the war, the Nazis sent unmanned rockets over London. They made a droning noise and were called "doodlebugs." When the noise stopped, it meant the engine had cut out and the thing was coming down. We were at dinner with the abovementioned officer when the air-raid sirens went off, which they did so often that one hardly paid attention. At this point I heard a loud doodlebug quite close. When it cut out, I dived under the table, to the amusement of everyone else. They knew that the Horse Guard chap had practiced and practiced until he could sound just like a doodlebug. I didn't mind being teased, but I did mind the run in my hard-to-come-by stockings.

There was a place in London called the Café de Paris, with a dance floor in the middle and open space on the side. My brother Erik was there when a bomb landed in the middle of the dance floor, causing many casualties. Fortunately Erik was not sitting at a table when it happened and was not injured, but, as a brand-new doctor and the only one there, he did what he could to help. The event was written up in the newspapers and the "unknown doctor" was mentioned.

I married Michael Rowbon on September 30, 1944, at St. George's Church in Hanover Square in London. The V2 rockets were coming over at the time, but none tried to crash my wedding.

Mila Meeker

My Moment in Teheran

During World War II, I was stationed in Teheran, Iran. It seemed as remote to me as Timbuktu until I discovered the American Presbyterian Mission there. Lo and behold, the head of the mission turned out to be the brother of one of my aunt's best friends in my hometown of Erie, Pennsylvania, and the principal of its school the brother of one of my former Sunday school teachers. I spent some of my free time with them, and soon began to use their excellent library, learning more about that strange country where I was so surprised to find myself. I decided to use their many books on Iran and the Middle East to write a brief history of Iran for myself. High-ranking officers decided to publish it for our GIs stationed there. It was a surprising success, and gave me a reputation in the Army as an expert on the country.

Consequently, in November 1943 when the famous Teheran Conference of Roosevelt, Churchill, and Stalin was held, I was called in as a minor consultant to President Roosevelt regarding the agreement to respect the political independence of Iran after the war. It was the high point of my life.

It began strangely. I had just come off guard duty at the American Embassy when a car carrying a major drove up to get me, only a sergeant, and take me at once to the Russian Embassy, where the conference was being held. I was flabbergasted, and so was everyone else. I was told that I could not even finish shaving in my steel helmet.

At the Russian Embassy, we were waved through ring after ring of Russian soldiers as if I were a celebrity. After we arrived, I was hurrying up the drive when the major restrained me and pointed. Just ahead of us was a military figure with a circle of five stars on his shoulders. It was George C. Marshall, Chief of Staff of the U.S. Army. Military etiquette would not permit us to pass him. So I slowed down.

Arriving at the main building of the embassy, I walked in, but did not know what to do. I stopped in the vestibule until someone came out of the inner sanctum and asked if the sergeant had arrived. Since I was the only person there under the rank of general, I stepped forward and was taken into a conference room, where I met President Roosevelt's son-in-law, Colonel John G. Boettiger. He asked me a lot of questions, which fortunately I was able to answer. He asked me for maps. I knew where to get these in our headquarters and brought them back to him quickly for more consultation.

At the conclusion of the conference, I was summoned back in case there were any loose ends. As I waited in the Russian Embassy again, the "Big Three" came out of the inner sanctum to leave. I was so excited to see Stalin about ten feet from me that I did not notice anyone else until I was brushed by something. I turned my head and found that I was literally rubbing shoulders with Winston Churchill while someone helped him into his overcoat.

President Roosevelt was in his wheelchair. At the top of the improvised ramp over the steps down to the ground level of the porte-cochère, the Secret Service men asked the president if he wanted to go down forward or backward.

FDR hesitated a moment before replying, "Take me down backward, please."

As they did so, he turned his head over his left shoulder to see where he was going, and kept his hands on the guide wheels of the wheelchair as though he were doing the whole thing himself.

When they reached the president's car, I expected him to take one step from his chair into the car. But no, they lifted him bodily, like a huge infant, into the back seat. He did not take a single step. When I reported this in a letter home, the Army censor called me in and told me that I could not write that, and must delete it.

So of course I did. But I could tell it after the war.

Wallace Rusterholtz

POW

Like most of the men I knew, I signed up right after Pearl Harbor. Although I'd never been in a plane, I wanted to be a pilot and chose the Army Air Corps. I was taking business courses at the University of Chicago. The AAF let me stay in school until my call-up in March 1943. I was eager, but the examining physician said I had an overbite—a malocclusion. I was rejected. Fortunately I knew a major, a fellow Beta Theta Pi. I wrote to him, telling him that I wanted to fight the Japanese, not bite them. He pulled some strings and got me into the Corps of Cadets, U.S. Army Air Corps.

My fellow recruits, Midwesterners, made up the first class of 1944, Class 44-A. It took us nine months to become pilots: primary, intermediate, and advanced training all over Texas. When I got to Salt Lake City, I joined my crew as copilot. There were ten of us in our B-17 Flying Fortress. The pilot, copilot, bombardier, navigator, and engineer were up front; in back were the radio operator, two waist gunners, a tail gunner, and the man with the meanest assignment of all, the ball-turret gunner, who did his fighting from a glass jar hung from the bomber's belly.

We flew to New Jersey. From there we sailed on the cruise ship *Mauritania*. It was a rough crossing and there were many seasick fliers. In England we joined the 351st Bomb Group of the Eighth Air Force. After five missions, our B-17 had gotten so shot up we had to transfer to another plane. We were to be rotated home after thirty missions—just recently raised from twenty-five. The sixth mission was our last.

Our target was Leipzig, and we hit it. Just starting home, we were hit. It could have been fire from Luftwaffe planes or flak from the ground, or both. "Tell everybody to get out," the pilot said. Two engines were kaput, the other two were smoking. We sank down from 20,000 feet to 8,000, our formation far beyond us. I hit the alarm, grabbed and strapped on my chute. Those of us in front went out the nose-hatch, others out the tail-hatch, the waist-gunner out his hatch.

Floating down was beautiful, peaceful. I saw fingers of silver light. Chaff, I thought, the aluminum-foil confetti that planes dumped to disrupt enemy radar. There were no planes above me, though. Those silver spears were bullets. I drew the risers of my parachute tight in to speed my descent.

I landed hard in the vegetable garden of a little farm. The farmer, wearing Lederhosen, was not little. He was over six feet tall, and shouting "Terrorflieger! For you da var ist over!" I did not take that as a welcome.

The uniformed men who came to gather us up were unfriendly boys and old men. They forced me to exit between two lines of these home-guard troops, and some of them hit me, again and again. They dislocated my jaw.

They put me and another member of my crew in the village jail. Then six of us were placed on a train to be interrogated at Frankfurt am Main. Next stop was Stalag Luft III, Sagan, my home from June 1944 until January 1945. When we went into the camp, we passed a cemetery. The crosses bore the names of the fifty escapees who had been executed as spies at Hitler's orders. The Germans explained that we might expect the same if we tried to escape.

At the time I got there, Stalag Luft III held 10,000 men. I was Prisoner Number 5442. Sagan was no country club, but those of us who'd been through cadet training were fit and able to take the stress. The German doctors who examined me gave me a clean bill of health, all except one notation on my record: "GebiB gesund, Obkf. vorstehend." It was that same overbite that had almost kept me at home. I played bridge and volleyball, and had two lines in *The Man Who Came to Dinner*. I have a copy of a Labor Day program from the camp: The All Stars, north vs. south, in boxing, softball, track, and volleyball. We had instruments and played "The Air Corps Song," "The Jersey Bounce," "The Woodchoppers' Ball," and "The Bugle Call Rag."

In the winter of 1944 the Russians were pushing into Germany from the east. We were ordered to march southwest. It was a five-day march in terrible cold. Some of us made little sleds out of bed-slats to drag along our pots and pans and hoarded food. The Germans had dogs and armed guards alongside the column. Anyone who fell out was shot. I saw a heroic chaplain stride up and down the columns, urging the men on, pulling stragglers back in. At one point, he jumped between a falling prisoner and an attacking dog until the guard called the dog off.

In Nuremberg we were housed in old-fashioned 40/8 railway cars, the sort meant to hold forty men or eight horses. There were sixty of us in each car. They were soon filthy. Only the cold kept down the stink. Worse, the railyards were targets for our own planes. When a strafing run came across the yards, we were able to get out of our boxcars and wave our arms at the pilots, letting them know that we were the good guys.

We were marched to Moosburg. One morning we heard firing, and got down low to avoid stray bullets. It was Patton's armor, rolling in through the camp gates on the twenty-eighth of April 1945. I had been a prisoner of war for eleven months.

We were so thankful to have been set free, to see that glorious flag flying high on the antenna of a tank. Men were shouting, clapping, singing, yelling, smiling with tears running down their cheeks. What a wonderful feeling ". . . that our flag was still there!"

And we were free!

Steve Lewelleyn

From the Home Front

When World War II really began, we lived in Hyde Park at 5424 East 54th Street. I thought our apartment was unsuitable for our two small children so did not renew the lease in the fall of 1942. We found, to our surprise, that no one would rent to people with two children. After much searching, we moved into a duplex at 8513 St. Lawrence Avenue. This was war-built housing and there were fifty duplex houses on one side of the street. However, there was a large prairie back of us, and every child had room to dig a foxhole there. Also we had a small backyard where there was space to dry clothes, have a sandbox, set up a swing, have a homemade furnace to cook hot dogs, and still leave room for a small garden. It only took four tons of coal to keep the furnace going, and it had a coil to heat water during the winter. In the summer we used a sidearm heater for hot water.

My husband took the Illinois Central to his work in the sales office of Republic Steel at Van Buren and Michigan. His status was always 1A but the company kept sending in statements about how much they needed him, and thus he was not drafted. However, he worked from 7:00 A.M. until 11:00 or 12:00 each night trying to keep ahead of the orders. This left me with everything to do around the house and an 18-month-old daughter and a 3½-year-old son. Having no car, I bought a large, red secondhand stroller to use for errands and the children.

In the neighborhood there were two supermarkets, located at 83rd and Cottage Grove. They were six long blocks from the house, and the stroller got much service. The store on the East Side of the street always had the best meat so it was very, very crowded. Therefore, since the children were always with me, I became a regular customer of the West Side store. As the war continued and rations got tighter, the stores occasionally were sent a few pounds of this or that, which was hard to distribute equitably. My store solved this problem by putting a half pound of sugar, a quarter pound of butter, a package of cigarettes, or other rationed goodies in your grocery bag, with no comment, but charging for it. When the customers from the East Side store tried to shop at the West Side store so as to get some of these goodies, they never appeared in their bags. This annoyed them very much.

The school was only two blocks away, so when our son was in kindergarten the stroller came into use to trundle newspapers to the playground for recycling. We had belonged to the Hyde Park Union Church since 1934 and took the streetcar to 56th and Woodlawn for Sunday school and other services. We also took the streetcar and the El to Evanston to visit our relatives. Traveling with enough items for two children for a whole day was often a real nuisance, but was the only way.

Aileen Gordon

9

Getting Back to
Work and Family Life

In 1945, World War II finally ended, first in Europe—officially on
May 8, V-E Day—with the collapse of the German army, and then
with the surrender of Japan on August 14, following the bombing
of Hiroshima and Nagasaki. The men and women in the armed
forces returned home to resume educations and careers disrupted
by the war, or to pursue different paths as new horizons opened.
Marriages were celebrated, families reunited, new families begun.
Life gradually returned to peacetime status.

For most of our generation, the decades following the war were
devoted to work, family, and community. Work for the future members of Montgomery Place took many forms, comprising a range almost as diverse as that in the *Dictionary of Occupations*: archaeologist to
zoologist, with businessmen and -women, civil service employees,
doctors, engineers, nurses, secretaries, and teachers in between. The
location of Montgomery Place, near a major university, is reflected in
the number of university professors among its residents.

Almost all of the women have worked outside the home for a
major portion of their adult lives. If the women of this generation
were limited to the role of "homemaker" and denied the privileges
our daughters boast of, as today's young people tend to assume, the
residents of Montgomery Place are exceptions to the rule.

232

Inspired by Oscar Mayer

The year was 1944. In those days it was very easy to get a job. Companies were recruiting young girls from all over the country to come and work in the city. But it was difficult for a young girl to move around by herself, so it was only with much pleading that I convinced my parents to allow me to accept a position in Chicago.

Finally they agreed, and I went to live with many other girls at the Eleanor Club residence for women on Ashland Avenue. Soon after I arrived, I began working for the man whose name lends itself to one of the most widely known brands today—Oscar Mayer. It was a family-oriented business started by three brothers in a small butcher shop that quickly grew to serve customers throughout the entire Chicago area. It was exciting to work at that company—everything was so new and big. Oscar was a wonderful employer; working for him reminded me of my earliest experiences in my grandfather's butcher shop as a little girl, and also taught me important lessons that served me in my later career in management training and development.

Conventional training activities at the time too often permitted uneven participation, involved little or no feedback, and brought only temporary change. At the Oscar Mayer Company, by contrast, brainstorming and collaboration were integrated at every level. As a young woman, I learned these lessons well, and in the 1980s I developed a new training system that presumes that learners do better with active participation; meaningful content; constructive, immediate feedback; and small-group discussion.

The invitation I received to Oscar Mayer's birthday party in 1946 cited his "kindliness, keen sense of humor, and deep understanding of the world about him that provides great inspiration for those who know him as friend, employer, and associate." This certainly proved true in my life and in my work. I remember Oscar, and I thank him.

Marilee S. Niehoff

Working at Argonne Labs

When I was nineteen, I chose to spend my week's vacation visiting Chicago where my older sister Annie lived. We filled our days with free entertainment: museums, listening to records at Lyon and Healy's, sitting on the grass at Grant Park concerts. Some time during that wonderful week, I decided that Chicago was the city to live in. I phoned my father to send more money, so I could stay a little longer. Instead he sent me a one-way ticket from Chicago to Huntington, Indiana.

Many years later, I spent the spring and summer of 1963 writing letters of application for jobs. Finally I had a call from the employment agency to set up an appointment with Dean Dalquest at Argonne National Laboratory. I had two daughters living in Chicago and I had wanted to live there for years. Most of all, I was between husbands: I could go anyplace my heart desired. So I made the appointment. I was instructed to go to the University of Chicago to meet a man who drove out to Argonne every day. I started looking for the place on the map— it was way out in the sticks! It was a long way out on the Stevenson Expressway, which was still under construction. I kept thinking, "I don't want to work there! I like my job at Whirlpool, I like my boss, and I haven't given notice yet."

Bob Buchanan interviewed me for a job in the Chemistry Division. He made clear what was expected, and explained the functions of the division. He made little pretense of looking at my book of sample illustrations and drawings, which had taken me so long to assemble. I felt at ease when I had my interview with Mr. Dalquest. Perhaps it was because I had already made up my mind I didn't want to work there. For the first time in my life, I wasn't nervous at a job interview!

Finally, after several weeks went by, an offer was made. So I went back. Mr. Dalquest assured me that he preferred a man. As a matter of fact, he had been interviewing men, but he couldn't find one with my qualifications. In the meantime, I had been thinking about Argonne. It would be nice to live in the city and to work in the country. And, too, I could look for another job while working at Argonne. I thought I'd give myself about a year.

Soon I forgot about looking for another job. I had settled in. The work was mostly drawing graphs, but once in a while I had the opportunity to draw an exploded view or a cutaway. I remember spectrographs—I had to draw these in ink to ready them for publication. After several years I heard about an opening in the Graphic Arts Department for a "sort-of" artist. So I moved on from chemistry to graphic arts. There I painted posters and signs. One wag suggested that I go into business after I retired, as "The Old Lang Sign Company."

There were parties at Argonne; every time a scientist had something to celebrate, the wine and cheese would come out. In the week between Christmas and New Year's, we all gathered in D Wing for a Glögg party. A scientist from Sweden had taught the other scientists to make Glögg, a mixture of spices, raisins, orange peel, and laboratory alcohol, all heated to a heartwarming temperature. A tradition was born.

There were parties in Graphic Arts, too. Every time someone retired, a big party was given. It helped that the boss, Frank Gentille, played with a live orchestra. It was there to provide music for dancing. And food! Every year at Christmas, everyone would bring food, spread it out on a long table, and we'd eat all day long.

When it came time for me to retire, I had the biggest and fanciest party of my life. There were speeches, dancing, music, food, and presents! One speech I'll never forget was delivered by Ray Barnes, a scientist in the Chemistry Division, who had asked for the privilege. Ray said, "When Ruth came to Argonne seventeen years ago, she was short and stumpy. Now, seventeen years later, she's still short and stumpy."

Ruth Lang

Forty-three Years on the Telephone

During my last twenty years with the Illinois Bell Telephone Company I did market research, working for any department that requested a survey. At the time, I was the only woman doing customer attitude studies.

It may seem odd now, but there was a time when stand-alone public telephones were a startling innovation. One research project was the Model 50: an open, doorless public telephone booth. I remember seeing people visiting the Hilton Hotel lobby where demonstration models of these freestanding telephone booths were set up for people to use, and seeing other visitors carrying brown paper bags into which they planned to scoop any coins left in the return slots.

For nine years I worked for Mr. Howard Jones, forecasting operating revenues. Mr. Jones later joined the University of Chicago Graduate School of Business. In 1994, I won the Crystal Ball award given by the Northern Trust Bank for forecasting the price of gold a year in advance. Unfortunately, Mr. Jones had died by then, so I didn't have the pleasure of sharing my forecasting award with him.

Catherine German

Advances in Healthy Living During the Twentieth Century

I am a pathologist; pathology is the science of disease. All of us who study disease are challenged by wanting to do something about the terrible toll disease takes each year. My mother, father, sister, and brother all died of cardiovascular or cerebrovascular disease. For many years, these have been the number-one cause of death in our country.

The changes in medical knowledge and practice during the lifetime of most of the residents at Montgomery Place are impressive. We have seen and benefitted from advances in treatment and prevention of common infections that had shortened the life of many elderly Americans. I refer to tuberculosis and other chronic infections of the lungs, bacterial endocarditis, and many other fatal infectious diseases.

The one big disease area that we haven't conquered is cancer. If anything, its incidence is increasing as more and more of us live into our seventies and longer. There is more time for carcinogens to affect our cells over the twenty or more years that it usually takes for them to stimulate susceptible cells to grow out of control. Fortunately, we have learned enough to help avoid the chemicals and overexposure to the rays that can trigger the start of a cancer, and we now have various methods of treatment once cancer is recognized.

But what about the biggest killer of all for us old people: cardiovascular disease? We've learned a lot about prevention, and we know that most fatal heart disease is the result of atherosclerosis, the buildup of plaques on the inside of our most important arteries. This disease is almost completely preventable if we keep our cholesterol levels low enough. Can we as a population of elderly people slow or prevent athero-sclerosis? The evidence we have from clinical studies, such as the famous Framingham study on the East Coast, is that we can successfully prevent progression of this arterial disease and, in turn, prevent coronary thrombosis (heart attack) and cerebral thrombosis (stroke) .

At Montgomery Place, our food committee, working with the kitchen manager, has attempted to always have at least one "Heart Smart" entree on our luncheon and dinner menus, which is marked with a heart. That is excellent progress.

Robert Wissler

Family Life in the 1950s

In late 1951, when my husband, Tom Farr, was working on his doctorate degree and teaching part time at Wilson Junior College, we moved the family to Chicago from Dover, Illinois. We moved to an apartment building at 5450 Blackstone Avenue, and our two girls attended Ray Elementary School. I was on the Ray School PTA board, and I helped supervise the school lunch-room. It was in the basement and was very chaotic.

Tom had begun having epileptic seizures in the spring of 1950. He was alone in a roominghouse in Chicago when the first one happened, and he didn't recognize it for what it was. Not much later, he had a grand mal seizure one night while we were in bed. I thought he was going to die; I described it over the phone to the doctor and he told me what to do. During the months that followed, it was difficult for me to watch Tom in the mornings, trying to get ready for school, with a seizure coming on.

Tom's family lived in Idaho. In the summer of 1951, they wanted us to visit. We said if we could pick fruit with the migrant workers to earn money for the trip, we would come. We picked Bing cherries early in the mornings, up on three-legged ladders to reach the fruit. We earned seventy-five dollars at the rate of six cents per quart of cherries. That covered our car expenses to and from Idaho.

The trip to Idaho was really scary because Tom was having epileptic seizures from time to time. There was some question about his driving, so I had to sit in the front seat with Stanley, who was one year old, while the two girls were in the back seat quarreling. I have strong memories of a baby on my lap dribbling chocolate ice cream all over while I was trying to make sure nothing happened to the driver.

We continued the doctorate struggle. Tom's dissertation was on European federalism. He insisted that I learn to type; he wrote 600 pages of that dissertation and I typed it for him. I typed according to the rules of Kate Turabian, the great U. of C. authority on term papers, theses, and dissertations. In the end, the dissertation was turned down because it wasn't objective enough.

In 1953 Tom was working on it again. It took so long, he said if Stanley learned to say "dissertation" before it was finished, he was going to just quit. We sent Stanley to stay with my parents in Dover in the summer of 1953 so I could help Tom. I compiled a 36-page bibliography for him. Finally, Tom got his degree in December 1953. The day he came in and announced that his dissertation had been accepted, I was up on a ladder painting. I was so excited, I dropped a gallon of paint all over the floor.

Alta Blakely

A Nurse without a Country

I traveled many miles to get to Montgomery Place. My husband Kam and I were both natives of Canton, Kwantung Province, China. I studied pre-nursing at Yenching University in Peijing, and then enrolled in Peking Union Medical College School of Nursing, an institution supported by the Rockefeller Foundation, where I completed the five-year bachelor of nursing program. I was working there the day Pearl Harbor was bombed, December 8, 1941. (We were on the western side of the International Date Line and thus a day ahead of Hawaii.)

The Japanese, who had had forces in China since 1933, immediately took over the hospital. The soldiers identified and rounded up all British and American doctors, nurses, and technicians. They were marched off and spent the war as prisoners. The soldiers did not bother the Chinese in our work, although one of them would jump over the courtyard walls every now and then to check and make sure we were following their orders. We were cautious around these soldiers. I worked in the Tien Ho Hospital, four hours from Peking by train, as director of the department of nursing.

In 1946, an American cousin, who was a graduate of the same nursing school as I and whose husband was a pathologist, asked me to bring her two girls, 2½ and 4 years old, to the United States. We were ready to sail for San Francisco, but couldn't: The sailors in California were on strike. Not until January 1947 did our ship—one of the U.S. Army's Transport Command troop ships—lift anchor and head for the United States.

We arrived, only to be held by Immigration. Two shiploads of Chinese passengers, some 800 people, were taken ashore to a big building, where the men and boys went into one section, the women and girls into another. We had no change of clothes with us; in the heated barracks I wore the same heavy green dress that had been warm enough for North China. There were 120 women and girls in the room. We slept in army bunks stacked three high. We lined up for the shower and lined up for meals. The Americans in charge of this mob of people needed help, so they asked me—the girl in the green dress—to interpret for them. This life was grim.

I was visited by a missionary, to whom I gave a letter for a friend in Fresno to let the two little girls' parents know that we were in the country. Their mother came from Clarksburg, West Virginia, to take them home. I hitched a ride to Detroit with a nurse friend.

Having a fellowship at Wayne State University, I was able to transfer to the University of Michigan. The China Medical Board furnished me a stipend of $175 a month for seven months, and I finished my master of arts degree. Under the terms of my agreement with the China Medical Board, I was required to return to China. I had to go to Peking to teach again at my alma mater. However, the Communists had closed Peking Union Medical College because it was a capitalist-supported institution. As an American-trained nursing instructor, I could not feel secure in Mainland China, and I had no wish to go to Taiwan, where I had no family or friends. I had become a displaced person, a "DP," with no valid citizenship anywhere.

I stayed in the United States with my expiring visa. At the University of Chicago, I asked for admittance as a student at large, with a student visa, in the Nursing Education Department, and stayed at International House. After a semester of this, out of money, I had to leave.

It was my good fortune that the Cook County Hospital School of Nursing had a postgraduate program in pediatric nursing. I enrolled in this program, which gave me room and board, but no salary. After I'd been there for half a year, the dean of the school asked to hire me, but Immigration wouldn't allow it. I was still only a DP, a nurse without a country. They let me work as a nurse assistant, though, with the children in pediatrics at Bobs Roberts Hospital (later Wyler Children's Hospital). I applied for citizenship, citing the fact that the Communists had forced me to leave China, and, after 5½ years, I took my oath as an American in 1955.

Davina Wong

Korea Before M.A.S.H.

I first knew Korea through Jack London's novel, *Star Rover*. What that book led me to expect was, oddly enough, just what I saw in 1946. Korea had been frozen in time ever since it had become a protectorate of the Japanese empire in 1905.

We came into Yung Dung Po by landing barge. When the ramp slammed down, we American boys stepped ashore and transferred our barracks bags to A-frames carried by skinny Korean laborers. It was the first time any of us teenagers had employed a porter. The fee for carrying our gear a couple of blocks to the warehouse where we were to be processed was a pack of cigarettes. Even nonsmokers had learned that cigarettes were better currency than either military scrip or Korean won notes.

I was assigned as platoon sergeant to a rifle company at Pohang. We had a single battalion near this little city, which smelled of drying fish. (Today Pohang makes more steel than Chicago.)

The country was primitive. The Japanese, whom we replaced as occupiers, had, as policy, denied all professional and technical work to native Koreans. We could have been in the Korea Jack London knew, where dignified, bearded men wore snow-white robes and black horsehair hats like Stetsons, where the roads were dusty tracks raised above the rice fields, where night soil was spread on those fields by barefoot farmers using gourds as honey dippers. The houses appeared primitive, too, with their thatched roofs, but when we had opportunity to visit there, we discovered that, like the Romans, the Koreans had invented hypocaustic heating: pipes under the floors circulating heat from the big central stove, keeping the rooms cozy in winter. They also had a system of writing superior to that of any other culture: Koreans celebrate an annual holiday in honor of Hangul, a writing system so logical that any Korean speaker can become literate in a day.

The young men in Pohang were no happier at having us in their country than they had been with the Japanese, whose barracks we'd taken over. Our soccer games with the high school kids thus became rougher than usual: Every bump and intercept was a political statement. The Koreans had become xenophobic as a result of their history; they were for centuries the "Hermit Kingdom," sealed off from all the world, except for an annual tribute paid to the Emperor of China.

A romantic adolescent who carried Nietzsche's Superman legend in his backpack, I loved to climb the little mountains and look out to sea, thinking deep, important, adolescent thoughts. In training, my platoon marched across dry riverbeds that would, in the war years later, run red with the blood of United Nations, North Korean, and Chinese soldiers. What we did not realize, as we counted cadence marching through the villages, was that the Russians north of the 38th Parallel could have wiped us out in a day if they'd wanted to. We had enough ammunition to last just that long.

The men in my platoon returned to the Zone of Interior—Army-speak for our homeland—and civilian life. The men who replaced us weren't all so lucky.

I spent the Korean War in England.

Allen Lang

Civilian Life After WWII

After the war, I was offered a job with my old employer AT&T at a substantial salary increase, but decided to return to the University of Wisconsin for more education. Next a degree, a wife, and a job with the Wisconsin Department of Agriculture Fairs Division as manager of the Junior Fair, and assistant manager of the Wisconsin State Fair. In three years, I was moved to the top spot, general manager, a job I held for seventeen years. When I left the fair, I became the executive director of the Milwaukee World Festival. This was a research job and was the start of the now very successful Milwaukee Summerfest.

I left this position after two years and purchased the Muskego Beach Amusement Park, which Jessie and I, and our family of three girls, ran for the next seventeen years. We closed the park in 1984 and sold all the assets except the land. We subdivided the land in 1993 and learned a great lesson in real estate development: to buy by the acre, and to sell by the square foot.

We then lived in Las Cruces, New Mexico; Reno, Nevada; and Sun Lakes, Arizona. In spring 2001 we moved to Chicago and now are members of the Montgomery Place community.

Willard Masterson

Higher Education

Soon after my husband came back from World War II, we moved to Cambridge, Massachusetts, so Ned could go to graduate school and study American history. We had a house. We had a four-year-old and, very soon, another baby. But I began craving school for myself. I went to apply to Radcliffe, which was just around the corner. I explained that, because of the war, I'd been to the University of Chicago, Bryn Mawr, and the University of Wisconsin for a year each, and that I wanted to go to Radcliffe for my senior year. The dean I was talking to drew herself up and said, "You'll have to start all over from the beginning if you come to Radcliffe." I was furious.

Then I discovered that the U. of C. would give me a degree if I took four correspondence courses (very well taught by mail) and spent one summer quarter in residence. My dilemma was understood! With the help of a cousin, a freshman at Harvard, who tutored me through the physical science survey course that was still required; and with the help of my parents, who took on my two children during the week while Ned and I spent a summer quarter in Hyde Park; and with my husband's willingness to pay tuition, I finally finished the requirements. I had started college in the fall of 1939. Ten years later my undergraduate diploma came in the mail from the University of Chicago. Now I could go to graduate school!

Being female, I had to be admitted to graduate school at Harvard via Radcliffe. They were allowed six students a year in the Psychology Department, where I wanted to study. So I got together all my records and applied, but they said I was a "poor risk"—married with children. Heaven forbid that Radcliffe should take a chance on me! So I applied to the kinder and gentler Harvard Graduate School of Education.

By this time I had a six-year-old and a two-year-old, and a profound belief that mothers should stay home with their children at least until they went to school, that children shouldn't go to school until they were at least four, and that when older children came home from school their mothers should be there with the milk and graham crackers, ready to sit on the back steps with other mothers while the children played outside in the backyards. Above all, my children must never suspect that I was going to school, too. If they knew, it meant that I was a bad mother. So for ten more years and two more babies, I crept through graduate school, feeling guilty all the time. With morning classes and furtive trips to the library, and reading and writing papers after the children were asleep, and an occasional use of babysitters, I managed to make it through.

When I graduated and had a chance to wear a cap and gown at last, my bewildered children came with their father to see me graduate. I sat proudly under an open-sided tent with the other Ed. School graduates while my family stood outside watching and the dean gave out diplomas. After a while, my five-year-old son came and sat on my lap, and, though I could feel the disapproval around me, I ignored it. What a curious example I set for daughters!

A year or two later I read Betty Friedan's *The Feminine Mystique*. This book was the spearhead of the feminist movement. To me it was a revelation that wiped out twenty years of guilt. It was really okay for women to have some life outside their families. Wow!

I went out and got a job. It was part time, of course, so I could be there when the children came home from school.

Alice Hayes

A Family Camping Trip

September was our family's vacation time when our girls were growing up. The university was closed for the month, summer camp was over, school didn't open until October. We enjoyed camping, and this year decided a trip around Lake Michigan, camping in state parks and public campgrounds, would be fun and educational. A brand-new tent sleeping four, our beat-up but well-seasoned camp cooking kit, two new, bright-colored slickers with Sou'wester hats, and sleeping bags all around were packed in the station wagon. Family added—father, mother, nine-year-old daughter Dee, and three-year-old daughter Barb—we started our trip up the eastern shore of Lake Michigan.

Sunny and warm the first day, the weather the second day became rainy and the new slickers came into play. The guessing game "My Father's Grocery Store" began to pall as a challenging pastime. Boundary lines between the two girls in the back seat had to be drawn and patrolled. And then the little one started coughing. As any mother knows, there is a certain cough or wheeze or snuffle that means trouble. The next step is a flushed face, a hot forehead. At home with Barb, the next step was a call to the doctor, who took these things seriously, and a trip to the drugstore for antibiotics. Three hundred miles from home, on a windy shore of Lake Michigan, we couldn't do that.

We decided to wait till morning and find a doctor if indeed the cough and flushed face were followed by more serious symptoms. It was cold and windy in the campgrounds near the beach, and after an unsuccessful struggle with the tent, we asked about cabins available. There turned out to be one a ways away in the woods, and we gratefully moved in. It was furnished with two sets of bunk beds, a woodstove, a couple of chairs, and a table. A huge fireplace and stacks of firewood promised heat. Water was available at an outside faucet. Luxury accommodations on a chilly Michigan night. We settled in, planning to get to the nearest town in the morning, and in the meantime dispensing aspirin to the increasingly feverish patient. A roaring fire, candlelight supper, and cocoa made life look brighter.

In the morning, a warm fire and breakfast continued to seem auspicious, though Barb's cough had settled into its familiar pattern and her hot forehead made the situation clear: sick child. As we packed up to go to town, my husband went out to start the car. It wouldn't start. There were no cell phones in those days, and no phone closer than the camp office some miles away.

He walked. The children and I settled back in the cabin. I built up the fire, administered more aspirin, and tried to think of things for a nine-year-old to amuse herself with. The lakeshore nearby, with its beach of wave-smoothed pebbles kept Dee occupied for a while, but the cold wind drove her back inside. As always when we traveled, I had brought books for all, but Dee was not a reader. She preferred social activities, swimming, walks, and "doing things."

The hours went by, Barb hot and coughing in her sleeping bag in the bottom bunk bed, Dee fussing about being bored, poking the fire.

Rescue arrived with a tow-truck and a mechanic, and my husband. The men descended on the car, as men do, peering into the cavern under the hood, wiggling things. Screwing and unscrewing things until the culprit was found. It was not a time to rejoice, however. A new part had to be obtained from a distant source, and we had to wait until it arrived.

That was the low point. We had food enough, plenty of fire-wood and water and someone taking care of the car, but also a feverish child and a bored one. Another day went by.

And then our luck changed. Barb's fever dropped and she stopped coughing, and another small miracle occurred—small but important. Dee, bored beyond endurance, picked up one of the books I had brought for her, and, lying on her bunk bed, she began to read—and read and read. She discovered what most of us learn earlier, that there are people in books, and exciting things happen, which you can find out about by reading. The book she chose was one of a very popular series from my childhood, a series disdained by librarians everywhere, but loved by their young readers: The Bobbsey Twins.

The rest of the trip was almost anticlimatic. Barb continued to improve, the car was returned to us, and we continued on our way down the western shore of Lake Michigan. A rock thrown up by a passing car made a hole that required the purchase of a new windshield when we got home, and we heard the terrible scream-ing of an animal (caught by dogs?) in a Wisconsin state park, but we had survived worse. Dee was reading in the back seat, Barb singing out the window, and we were almost home.

Joan Swift

Family Wisdom

Family stories get handed down like family jewels, from generation to generation. My mother had a fund of stories from her college years which delighted us, especially when they featured a character known as the "Housemother" who gave Wednesday-evening lectures to her charges, known as "Young Ladies," on manners and other useful tidbits. One was on "How to Handle Unwanted Attentions from a Gentleman" and con-cluded with "When all else fails, use your hat pin."

Another favorite was "Never Insult Your Hostess by Not Eating the Food She Has So Graciously Prepared." The climax of this story came when its heroine found an inchworm measur-ing the salad leaves and calmly rolled it into a bit of lettuce and ate it to avoid causing her hostess any embarrassment.

Although I chose not to tell these stories to my children when they were very young, the occasion arrived when I needed to pass on a modicum of the basic wisdom from the inchworm story. My 3½-year-old was invited to go with her big first-grade sister to have lunch at a friend's home. It was her first social event without an adult manners monitor along. I was not so much concerned about "which fork" as I was about "table conversation." At home it was apt to be free and forthright, and might include such information as "I hate cooked carrots!" and *did* the day before the luncheon party. I took advantage of this opening and inserted my concern.

"What's the polite thing to say if your hostess serves cooked carrots to you tomorrow?" I asked as offhandedly as I could. I got suggestions from "No thank you" to "May I have my carrots uncooked, please," which I rejected as not the kindest way to reward a hostess who has made a special "company" effort.

"It seems to me," I mused, "that the most polite thing to do would be to eat them, with a smile. Don't you think a guest who declares dislikes and preferences at a party is really saying, 'You did it wrong—you should have done it better?'" I queried.

There was nothing but silence after this leading question, so I dropped the subject and didn't find out if I should have told about the inchworm until the next day, when the luncheon guests returned. My little one was in the lead, so filled with pride she fairly beamed.

"Mother, Mother!" she shouted as soon as she came in the door. "We didn't make a single declare!"

Ann Parks

DDT

The potent insecticide DDT was developed during World War II and applied by the U.S. Army in the early 1940s to combat insect-borne diseases. It was particularly effective in the control of typhus: Soldiers could be dusted with DDT powder to kill the infestations of lice that carried the disease. It was also used for mosquito control, particularly in the marshes of southwest Italy, where endemic malaria made some regions almost uninhabitable. In the final days of the war, the Army also wanted to explore the use of DDT for insect control in the United States. At the time, I was a curator of insects at the National Museum in Washington, working for the Bureau of Entomology, and was one of four insect specialists chosen to make a study on the effects of DDT on our local forests. What would be the damage to the environment if DDT were released for civilian use and widely sprayed over the countryside? Would the insecticide be effective on destructive forest pests such as the gypsy moth?

Many insects are remarkably sensitive to contact with DDT. The chemical is stable and completely insoluble in water, thus when it is dissolved in kerosene and sprayed on leaves, the droplets evaporate to transform a lush green woodland into a theater for insect death. Toxic crystals may continue to be potent for weeks and are not readily washed away.

In early spring of 1944, we spent several weeks getting ready for our studies. We chose two test plots, each one mile square, one to be treated and the other as a control. We started by getting a sample of all living things in our study area, all the plants, birds, and particularly the insects and spiders. There were a few frogs and minnows in the creeks, but as one would expect, almost all the living creatures we could find were insects. We had all manner of traps, some baited with molasses and some with decaying meat, light traps for night-flying insects, boards covered with sticky glue like flypaper, trays to catch insects that fell from above, and special funnels that forced out tiny mites from the leaf litter on the forest floor. Our efforts resulted in the collection of several thousand inhabitants of our area, and kept us up late in our field laboratory sorting and identifying our specimens.

In any natural area of woodland, a curious observer is bound to have lots of questions about the lives of organisms one meets. I had wished many times that I could someday have the time to stop and study some inviting area of field or woodland. My new job of investigating the effects of DDT on the environment seemed to provide just such an opportunity. With our temporary field lab set up in an old CCC [Civilian Conservation Corps] camp we had microscopes; all manner of equipment for sorting, identification, and storage; a small library of reference books; and, most important, colleagues who had spent much of their lives in the study of field ecology.

Then came the time for spraying. The United States Department of Agriculture (USDA) hired two crop duster airplanes for the application of the DDT, with a heavy dose of five pounds per acre. The pilots had some problems with the mountainous terrain and complex wind patterns, and it took two days for the light biplane to cross and recross our area. Results of the spray were dramatic. There was an almost continual rain of insects from the forest canopy into the trays we had set out, but we could capture only a tiny fraction of the billions of insects that came down. At first they were largely caterpillars and other insect larvae but, later, insects of almost any kind. Since the insecticide remained on the leaves for weeks, the more resistant insects continued to die.

On the morning of the second day, we found many wild birds dying among the leaves. Litter was thick, so we could find them only when we heard them struggling or trembling. We found thirty dying birds (warblers, vireos, and thrushes), but there were certainly hundreds more killed by the spray. They had clearly gorged themselves on the dying caterpillars and thus obtained a heavy dose of the poison. I called an ornithologist friend at the University of Pennsylvania and told him birds were dying in our treated area, and he came to see for himself. For this call I was strongly reprimanded by the regional USDA officer who was supervising our studies; he reminded me that our work was classified, and we were not allowed to talk with others. This officer had been assigned to control the infestation of gypsy moths that were doing damage to Pocono forests. I am sure that he felt that, after years of fruitless attempts, he might at last be able to eradicate this persistent pest, and he wanted no adverse publicity to stand in the way.

One day later, standing at the edge of our study area, I listened to the bird song. Outside was the usual chorus of spring voices from vireos, warblers, thrushes, and robins. Inside our plot there was no sound, only a deathly silence, except for the fall of dying insects from the trees. A few of the stronger fliers, crows and blue jays, occasionally ventured into the area from outside. The USDA confiscated my detailed report of bird death, and I was pledged to secrecy about birds being killed. In the next few days, we also found dead minnows and frogs in the small creek that flowed through the area. (A few years later, when Rachel Carson published *Silent Spring*, I felt that I knew better than most what a silent spring was really like.)

I have wished many times that I had more fully realized the danger of massive applications of DDT to our environment. Later in our studies we realized that the five-pound-per-acre applications of DDT were unnecessarily destructive, and that lower doses would still be effective in gypsy moth control. Also, spraying could be carried out later in the season, after young birds had left their nests, with much less damage to bird populations.

I returned to our area briefly the next year. The insect population was still depressed, but many birds and insects had repopulated our plot from outside. There were interesting shifts in insect population numbers. Moths and caterpillars were still very low, but some insects showed major infestations, particularly aphids and the insects that preyed on aphids, such as ladybug larvae. These showed higher resistance to the treatment, and doubtless became superabundant because many of their normal enemies had been killed.

As before, I became frustrated that there was so much to study, but no time to do so, since that summer the USDA closed out the project, concluding that spraying of controlled doses of DDT was an effective way to keep most insects under control. The substance was thus released for civilian use. But this was, unfortunately, before the much more subtle effects of DDT became known, in particular its effect on metabolism of the birds of prey (hawks and owls), which produced eggs so weak they often became crushed in the nest. This DDT effect resulted in the extermination of peregrine falcons in the eastern United States and necessitated the importation of falcons from abroad. This, more than anything else, finally resulted in strong new restrictions placed on the civilian use of DDT. Rachel Carson's *Silent Spring* at first met with strong protests from industry, and finally became an acclaimed voice for the protection of the environment. The web of life is indeed intricate, with many lessons yet to be learned.

Hewson Swift

Two Careers

At the end of the war, with a master's degree from the University of Chicago, I joined the faculty of Indiana University in Bloomington, in the Department of Social Service. For four years, I taught courses in probation and corrections, including prison management.

After Indiana University I became chief probation officer in the Chicago office, and also headed up a National Training Center under joint administration by the U.S. District Court and the University of Chicago. Planning for this center followed a conference between Chief Judge William Campbell of the Chicago Court, Dean Edward Levy of the U. of C. Law School, and Dean Alton Linford of the School of Social Service Administration; there was also financial and other support from the administrative office in D.C. I was honored to accept this position, and for the following twenty-five years experienced a stimulating career.

In 1973, having reached retirement age, I left the federal court system. Shortly thereafter Professor Phil Neal, dean of the U. of C. Law School, offered me a temporary position there as an administrator. I continued there for the next ten years. The law school's Center for Studies in Criminal Law was directed by the distinguished criminal law professor Norval Morris, with great assistance from Professor Frank Zimring. This was fortuitous for me, as both Morris and Zimring were old friends who had lectured regularly at the National Training Center. My job at the law school was primarily assigning research personnel, allocating research funds, and being sure that university research guidelines were complied with. Finally, I gave retirement a second try, and succeeded in retiring from active service in 1984.

Ben Meeker

10

Community Involvement and Troubled Times

During the 1960s and 1970s, many events occurred that were of major significance to the country and to the world: the assassination of one president, the forced resignation of a second; two military actions, the Korean and Vietnam wars; the build-up of the cold war with Russia; the assassinations of Dr. Martin Luther King, Jr., and Robert Kennedy.

These were times of turbulence and change in America. Many of the accepted values and social practices of earlier eras were being brought into question and redress was being sought, sometimes violently, sometimes through more peaceable means.

To our generation, the "hippies," the "flower children," the drugs, and the "dropping out" (out of college, out of conventional lifestyles) were largely phenomena of our children's generation. We were the "over thirty," seen as the obstacles to a freer society. Involved as we were in jobs and support of family, rebellion against the codes we grew up with was not an item on our personal agendas, except for those whose children, caught up in the acting out of the times, turned the home into a battlefield. There were, however, issues of a social and political nature that did engage our attention as concerned adults, especially the environment and the Civil Rights Movement.

Inadvertent Urban Renewal

In 1954 there was talk of urban renewal in Chicago. Our apartment building at 5450 Blackstone was one that was going to be torn down. When the Queen Anne duplex at 5418 Blackstone came up for sale, our block group was afraid it would be bought by someone who would chop it up into a rooming-house. Since my husband and I were the only people in the block group who did not own a home, we were designated to "case" the situation. We were supposed to pretend we wanted to buy the house . . . in fact, we fell in love with it, but we couldn't afford it. We had all of $1,000 in the bank. We made a really low bid on the north side (twelve rooms) and forgot about it. A few months later the Leonard sisters, who owned the house, called and said they would like us to buy it. We couldn't get a first mortgage from any bank in Hyde Park—but Talman came to our rescue. We borrowed money from family members, and the Leonard sisters gave us a second mortgage.

We moved in the summer of 1954, carrying stuff up the street from the old house to the new one. Now that we had possession of the house, the question was how we were going to pay for it. Our daughters wore cardboard in their shoes for some months, and we took in a roomer, a French-speaking Jamaican girl named Andrea. Since teaching was the only thing I could think of that I could do to make money, we decided I ought to be a substitute teacher. In the fall of 1954 I started subbing at Harper High School. By 1957 I was a full-time teacher at Hyde Park High School, and, from 1960 to 1969, the chairman of the English Department.

Alta Blakely

The Cleaner Air Committee

How many people remember when Chicago was considered one of the least desirable places in which to live because of air pollution and dirt? The South Side was particularly bad because when the prevailing winds came from the south, they brought pollution from the steel mills, and when winds came from the west, they brought pollution and odors from the stockyards. Two current residents of Montgomery Place and one former resident played a part in improving the quality of the air we breathe today. This is our story:

In the spring of 1959, when Laura Fermi, the widow of the distinguished nuclear scientist Enrico Fermi, returned from a trip to Europe, she was appalled at the dirt and soot that had collected on her back porch. Gathering a sample, she submitted it for analysis to the Armour Research Foundation (now Illinois Institute of Technology). The foundation's report showed that the sample consisted of 10 percent unburned coal, 75 percent cinders and fly ash, and 15 percent old-fashioned dirt or dust. Mrs. Fermi concluded that most of her airborne dirt was of local origin. Perhaps she could reduce it by enlisting the help of friends who were discouraged and depressed by the constant fight that Chicago housewives waged against filth. And so the Cleaner Air Committee of Hyde Park–Kenwood was formed, at the beginning consisting of only seven women.

Our first aim was to educate ourselves about air pollution and its specific problems as related to Chicago. We knew that the mechanics of keeping clean were unending and frustrating, but we also were concerned about the effect breathing dirty air had upon our families. Living near the University of Chicago, we were able to gather much information on air pollution and its problems from experts in engineering, meteorology, and medicine. We obtained copies of the city's Air Pollution Control Ordinance and, with the help of a law professor, reduced it to simple language. We prepared a pamphlet, *Cleaner Air for Our City*, which presented the air pollution problem, explained the ordinance, and suggested methods by which citizens could help with its enforcement. With the help of the Citizens Information Service, an affiliate of the League of Women Voters, thousands of the booklets were distributed.

In our first enthusiastic months, we naively expected that through education and appealing to the conscience of the general public we could get compliance with the city's air pollution laws, which were going to be made stricter in May 1964. We wrote letters to real estate companies suggesting it would be in their best interest to upgrade their apartment buildings' heating equipment, which burned coal and garbage. We talked with officials of the janitors union, suggesting that all janitors be cognizant of correct procedures for firing furnaces, the majority of which then burned coal and garbage.

We soon became more realistic and faced the fact that enforcement could be obtained only through sustained legal action against violators. So we recruited volunteers and trained them in smoke watching. We used the Ringelmann chart, a cardboard chart with a circular diagram showing degrees of smoke density. When the chart was held up to one's eye, the degree of pollution could be ascertained. Our volunteer smoke-watchers jotted down the address and duration of smoke violations, information we sent to the city's Air Pollution Control Department. This reporting of violations made us very unpopular with the janitors in the neighborhood, who called us, derisively, "smoke-watching housewives." We campaigned to get landlords to convert coal-burning furnaces to natural (clean) gas. It wasn't until the two buildings on Blackstone Avenue, in which two members of the committee lived, and which shared the same janitor, installed new furnaces using natural gas, that we found one of our most outspoken supporters. That janitor helped convince others in the neighborhood to get their buildings converted to cleaner heat.

In January 1964, the special United States Senate Subcommittee on Air and Water Pollution under the chairmanship of Senator Muskie of Maine came to Chicago for hearings on the proposed tightening of pollution control laws by Congress. The Cleaner Air Committee of Hyde Park–Kenwood was asked to testify about its role in trying to reduce air pollution in our community. We all felt that Laura Fermi should be our spokeswoman; however, she was a very modest person and hated speaking in public, partly because of her foreign accent. I was delegated to make our statement. The morning that I was to appear, on an impulse I took one of my husband's clean linen handkerchiefs and ran it across the windowsill of his study. I began my speech by waving the handkerchief before the subcommittee and the audience, and explaining why we felt Chicago needed stricter air pollution rules. That evening my picture was on the front page of the metropolitan newspapers with the caption "Housewife displays dirty linen in public." *The Hyde Park Herald* picked up the story and we got more publicity in our community. We also got more supporters. Our little group of "smoke watchers" certainly can't take all the credit for making Hyde Park a better community in which to live, but we do feel we played a role in making it a cleaner, healthier, and more pleasant place.

Edith Y. Harris

Park Reminiscences

The Hyde Park Historical Society Bulletin of September 1990 included an article about sculpture in the small parks of Hyde Park. The article said that the Park District "responded enthusiastically" to the willingness of community residents to participate in the plans for the parks. Since I was chair of the Hyde Park–Kenwood Community Conference Parks Committee in the 1960s, when all of this was going on in the process of urban renewal, I think the record should be set straight.

It is not exactly the case that the Park District "responded enthusiastically" to the willingness of community residents to participate in the plans for the parks. At first district personnel were defensive, as they thought we were just being difficult and impractical, and it was a case of amateurs interfering in professional affairs. The neighborhood parks they were installing in other areas of the city were flat expanses of grass with swings and seesaws, and maybe a baseball diamond. We put hills in our models, so children could coast on their sleds in winter and fly kites in the summer. The Park District engineers said hills were impractical for their motorized, ride-on mowers. In the end, they built a low hill in the park by the Neighborhood Club. At the park dedication, the Park District chief engineer asked me, "Aren't you pleased about the hill?"

I said, "We're glad you put in a hill, but it's not high enough."

He said, "Well, next time maybe we can make a higher hill." (So far, they haven't.)

Nancy Hays and John Hawkinson made enchanting wood and clay models for the various urban renewal parks, complete with seating areas shaded by miniature trees and shrubs. We held neighborhood meetings to get reactions and suggestions and then we ceremoniously took the models to the Park District offices to present them. It was a good thing our family had a station wagon then, because the models were fairly large, one of them the size of the top of a bridge table. Since they were not blueprints, the Park District couldn't file and forget them and had them out in their planning workspace. I was told that they were disregarded until visiting professionals from other cities saw them.

"What are those?"

"Oh, just something from a neighborhood group."

"You mean they care enough about the parks to go to all that trouble? These are kind of interesting ideas."

Then the *New York Times Magazine* published an article about neighborhood committees helping to plan parks, and the next thing we knew the Park District people were saying to us, "Those New Yorkers. Always thinking they're first. You know, we had the idea long before they did."

So in the end they used the committee's ideas for all the new small parks except the one behind the shopping center at 53rd and Woodlawn. The Park District produced its own model for that. It was not exactly what we had thought appropriate for that spot, but John Hawkinson said we should give them credit for having come up with something original and charming, and should accept it. So we did. I read recently that park was being redesigned!

Sculpture was included in some of our models. Nancy Hays said the Art Institute had a fund from a bequest for outdoor sculpture, and the trustees had been using it for building renovation instead of contemporary sculpture. Chicago sculptors felt deprived of the opportunity. We thought if we had a competition for Art Institute students, the Art Institute might help fund the sculptures. We were wrong about that.

So we set up a prestigious committee that raised the money and oversaw the competition. We finessed the idea that outdoor sculpture would be ruined by children climbing on it by making a requirement that the sculpture designs actually invited being climbed on.

Incidentally, one of the parks we planned was next to the old Church Home, between it and a school playground. I helped with the discussion of the model at the Church Home. Some of our committee members have said that the old folks would just love to watch children at play. It turned out that might be so, but "watch" was the operative word, not "hear," and not "get a baseball through the window." So we redesigned to make a quiet area next to the Church Home, but with a clear view so the residents could see the children at play.

Barbara Fiske

Lunch with Mayor Daley

A native New Yorker, I grew up thinking of local politics as one of those subjects that were the province of serious newspaper articles in the *New York Times*—slightly indecent and filled with scandals of the financial variety—not something that the ordinary citizen had access to except on Election Day. Even then one understood it was the politicians in the smoke-filled rooms of Tammany Hall who made the decisions. In Chicago, on the other hand, I found that local politics were as close as one's front door and as friendly as one's local precinct captain or ward committeeman.

Coming to Chicago, I was prepared for gangsters, the Mob and the Mafia; I was not prepared for politicians I could reach out and touch, who greeted me as I got off the Illinois Central train on my way to work, or shook my hand during dinner at Jimmy Wong's restaurant. I wasn't prepared for ordinary citizens taking stands on local issues and getting away with it, tying themselves to trees to modify a city plan, for example. And I certainly was not prepared to find myself elbow to elbow with the Mayor of Chicago, Richard J. Daley, at lunch in the Grand Ballroom of the Palmer House with some 300 people watching our every bite. Well, *my* every bite: Mayor Daley did not necessarily eat at those elegant lunches. He would arrive part way through such ceremonial lunches, escorted by his staff and bodyguards. He sat at his appointed place on the dais, and stood up at the podium to give his obligatory speech when introduced.

Then he marched out, staff and bodyguards ahead of and behind him, to the applause of the diners, leaving them to finish their desserts and coffees under the supervision of the master—or mistress—of ceremonies.

In my case, it was the mistress of ceremonies who had initiated and managed the luncheon to celebrate the publication of a handbook on day care centers. My claim to fame on that occasion was that I had served as chair of the Handbook Advisory Committee—a committee typical of local politics in Chicago. It was made up of twenty educators, day care owners and directors, and agency staff, representing all segments of the local professional community. My selection as chair of the committee also was typical of Chicago politics in those days: The mistress of ceremonies knew me; we had cooperated on a program on the South Side that had benefitted us both. She knew my personal and professional agenda, and both were compatible with hers. She could trust me to do the job that needed to be done without threatening her personally or professionally. That was the way the system worked, and the way Chicago worked. Serving on a local neighborhood committee to boost some plan favored by the city administration (or at least not antagonistic to some city plan), and providing assistance, if appropriate, was likely to result in an opportunity to serve on a committee made up of citizens. Local politicians in Chicago needed the backing and assistance of their constituents and involving them at the grassroots level paid off—for the politicians and the constituents.

This was not my first personal contact with Mayor Daley. The first time he and I shared an occasion was shortly after his hard-fought electoral campaign against Charles Merriam, a Hyde Parker, for the office of mayor. It was my introduction to Chicago politics, and I had been prepared for violence, Syndicate kidnapping, cement-encased bodies dragged from the lake—none of which seemed to have occurred, to my relief but bewilderment, considering the charges that had been assaulting us through the media. The occasion was a meeting of the Hyde Park–Kenwood Community Conference, an overwhelmingly Merriam-supporting group. In the midst of the meeting, it was announced that His Honor, our new mayor, would be coming to speak to us.

And there he came, a short, stout little person, marching firmly down the center aisle, accompanied by an aide or two, up to the podium. I expected boos and hisses, shouts of disapproval. Instead, there was polite clapping; people rose to their feet.

Daley made a short but strong speech about his respect for our community and the great University of Chicago, and marched out again to perhaps a little more enthusiastic applause. I was amazed. What had happened to all that rhetoric about corruption and gangster tactics? Chicago politics—much sound and fury—and life goes on.

It was several years later, when I was a little less naïve, that I had my next encounter with His Honor. I was working with the Welfare Council of Metropolitan Chicago's Committee on Health, and a small group of us had set up an appointment to meet with the mayor to present a plan for a new hospital on the South Side that would augment the medical services provided by Cook County Hospital. After an appropriate time spent in the large outer office of the mayor on the fifth floor of City Hall, we were invited into His Honor's presence. Sitting behind his huge desk, under the seal of the City of Chicago, he greeted us politely as a figure hurried out the door behind his desk. Dr. Bundeson had briefed the mayor on the situation and departed. Our spokesman said his piece, the mayor listened politely, expressed concern over the conditions brought to his attention, and thanked us for coming. That was it; our spokesman left a carefully prepared report filled with persuasive facts and figures, and we all filed out. There is still no county hospital on the South Side.

My third encounter with the mayor occurred when the professional organization to which I belonged wished to have the mayor dignify our efforts on behalf of children by proclaiming a week in April as the "Week of the Young Child." After suitable diplomatic negotiations with City Hall underlings, we were notified that His Honor would meet with us for a formal signing of the proclamation in his office on the appropriate day. Five of us attended the ceremony, with a rather bored-looking cameraman present to record the occasion. The mayor signed our proclamation, I signed the proclamation, we held up the carefully inscribed proclamation, smiled for the camera, shook hands, and left. The photograph did not make the front page of the morning papers and, unfortunately, I have no copy.

And my five minutes of fame elbow to elbow with Richard J.? My mouth full of lunch, my brain paralyzed by the presence of His Honor the mayor at my side, I could only stammer stupidly in response to his attempt at conversation. "This child care—it's important, isn't it? It's good for da kids." I agreed it was good for the kids and in his three- to five-minute speech, that's what he said—"It's good for the kids," though I think he added something about "the fair City of Chicago."

Joan Swift

Volunteering for the Agápe Victim Assistance Program

"Case continued!" called out the judge, as he banged down his gavel. Those were words we heard over and over again as we stood in the courtroom with a victim of a crime. The "we" were volunteers with the Agápe Victim Assistance Program of the United Church of Hyde Park.

The program (*agápe* is the Greek word for love, usually meaning "spiritual love" or "Christian love" or "love for humanity") grew out of a Sunday-morning class studying the problem of criminal justice and developed into a two-part volunteer help program, including court escorts for victims of crime and "Neighbors-on-Call."

As court escorts, we would accompany a crime victim to court, explain ahead of time courtroom procedures, and give moral support during questioning, especially when the perpetrator was present in the courtroom—sometimes sitting behind the victim while waiting for the case to be called.

A Neighbor-on-Call volunteer was scheduled to be close to the phone and available when a victim (more often than not, a woman) needed emotional support or information as to where to find further help. There is much to be said for a listening ear!

Two organizations helped us set up the Agápe Assistance Program. Initially, Eileen Murphy of Attorney General Neil Hartigan's office helped by training our volunteers, and Hartigan's office gave us a $4,000 grant a year to hire a director for a program which was basically made up of volunteers from the congregation.

Then Agápe and Bob Mason of the South East Chicago Commission (the SECC, a neighborhood watchdog organization) developed a symbiotic relationship. Gradually the commission was able to turn over to the Agápe volunteers some of the SECC court cases. We did not take murder cases, but cases of domestic violence, sexual assault, battery, armed robbery, and so forth.

Someone stole a copper downspout from a home managed by Hyde Park Realty. A waitress at the House of Tiki was assaulted by a customer who was angered because she refused his advances. A young woman who was walking to a friend's house at three o'clock in the morning was raped in Nichols Park.

There were always jobs to be done. My responsibility was as court escort. I also served as a Neighbor-on-Call, a trainer of volunteers, director of neighbor relations, and sometimes interim director of the general program.

According to Agápe records, in our first ten years we assisted with 397 court cases and responded to innumerable Neighbor-on-Call requests. We talked to senior citizen and block groups, participated in the 57th Street and Community Art Fairs, and the Windermere Health Fair, and sponsored annual community Safety Days.

In February 1992, we celebrated fourteen years of helping "Neighbors in Need."

Alta Blakely

Troubled Times

The Civil Rights Movement was not a product of the rebellions of the 1960s, but part of a longer struggle against racial discrimination and bigotry.

Discrimination against individuals and groups of different cultures, races, ethnic backgrounds, or genders was not a new feature of American life; it had been a fact of life, "the way things are." Each new group of immigrants coming to America was stigmatized by demeaning nicknames, refused jobs, and confined to menial roles. Discrimination against certain religious groups was formalized in the bylaws and observed in the practices of many organizations. Gender, too, was subject to discriminatory practices; women's right to vote had been a hard-fought battle of our parents' generation. For African Americans, despite generations of living in America, discrimination was an ongoing reality in housing, in employment, in public accommodations. Legislation correcting some discriminatory practices, effective at a federal level, often needed local reinforcement.

The death of Dr. Martin Luther King, Jr., was a defining point in the Civil Rights Movement. Some of us observed the violence in Chicago that followed, as all of us have observed the changes that have been a legacy of those times.

Two Secrets

When I graduated from high school, I found a job with a company situated in the Palmolive Building at 919 North Michigan Avenue. In those days it was the tallest building in Chicago.

My job was in the bookkeeping department, where I was taught to operate a posting machine. The keyboard was too high for me to sit down while I worked, so I had to stand up to operate it. My boss, Mr. L., liked that.

After I had had the job for a few months, the Jewish High Holidays came. I told Mr. L. that I had to take two days off for the holidays. He said okay, but it had to be a secret between us, because the company wasn't hiring Jews at that time. In my ignorant innocence, I agreed.

A few years later, my admirer and I decided to get married. Again I told Mr. L., and again he cautioned me it would have to be a secret between us. It seems they were not hiring married women at that time.

In 2001, the building is no longer the tallest in Chicago. It stands dwarfed and obscured by the Hancock Building and other giants. For many years it was known as the Playboy Building, and now it is being refurbished as the Palmolive Building. Through these changes Mr. L. and I still have the two secrets about my employment hidden deep in our minds.

Lillian Century

Welcome to Atlanta, Georgia!

In September 1941, I left Philadelphia for Clark College in Atlanta. My mother and a host of friends saw me off from the Pennsylvania Railroad station. I was elated and just a little anxious. It was my first time away from home. I was dressed in beige gabardine slacks, a chocolate-colored blazer, a white shirt, a tie, and brown and white shoes. After much hugging and kissing (I really tried to look, as well as act, manly), I boarded the train. As it pulled away from the station, I settled back in my seat, trying to hide the tears that slowly coursed down my cheeks and clouded my vision. The first stop was Washington, D.C., where I had to change trains.

Crossing the station, I headed for the Southern Railroad train depot. At the train gate I started down the long line of coaches. At each coach, a trainman told me, "Keep going." So I arrived at the baggage car, coal car, and engine. I started back up the line and at the baggage car I was stopped by a conductor who said, "In here." I entered. It was a dingy car. A few African Americans were sitting quietly, watching me. I took a seat by the window, biding my time until I could see the conductor and change coaches. The train slowly left the station; soot and smoke seeped through the windows. After what seemed like hours, the conductor entered the coach. I complained to him and requested a change of coaches. He said, "This is where you belong." I was crushed, already beginning to regret this adventure, but I calmed myself down and philosophically looked forward to the future that would begin for me in a matter of hours.

It was a long, hot, and restless trip. I couldn't sleep. I feared the roaches crawling down the walls of the coach. Finally, Atlanta was only a few moments away. I tried to clean myself because I was now a sorry mess. I was no longer the dapper young man, the gay vivant, of only a few hours ago. My trousers were dull, wrinkled, and soot-streaked. My handsome white shirt was dirty and disheveled. But I was not going to allow anything to dim my arrival. I eagerly left the train, walked through the terminal to the taxicab stand, set my luggage down, and waited. Cabs were lined up at the curbside. Gradually they filled up with passengers and left. I was still standing.

No taxi came for me. I was a little anxious, but did not know what to do. Nobody from the school met me. There was no one I could ask for help. I was a little scared, too.

"Nigga, whatcha doin' out here? Nigga, dontcha hear me talking to ya?"

I dared not respond because he wasn't talking to me. Yet I knew in my gut that the challenge was directed to me. I turned, full of growing resentment and anger.

Then I saw him. He was like me. Black. I was utterly and completely devastated, crushed.

He saw my consternation, the tears beginning to run down my face unheeded. "You just get off that train?"

I don't remember what I answered.

Picking up my luggage, he said, "Boy, you don't belong here; you belong on the other side." He led me back through the station to a small waiting area in the back. Black drivers were there!

How I got out to Gammon Seminary on the old Clark College campus, I don't remember. Mine was a journey begun in hope and excitement and now filled with uncertainty. Such was my arrival in the sunny South. Welcome to Atlanta, Georgia!

Phillip Harley

Integrating the Watering Holes

Orlando was chief of our NAACP branch, which met in a corner of a dentist's office. We worked to get technical jobs for African American high school grads; at a Civil Rights rally we countermarched the pitiful troop of Fort Wayne Nazis. We took field trips, too, the splendidest being our bus ride to Washington to dangle our feet in the reflecting pond by the Lincoln Memorial as we heard Dr. Martin Luther King, Jr., deliver his "I Have A Dream" speech.

Not all our activities were so uplifting.

Orlando worked hard as branch chief, but he kept his perspective. During one Saturday meeting, he asked my wife Ruth, me, and the others, "Why do we have to spend our time defending the Constitution, when there's baseball to watch? If the [expletive deleted] would only give in, we could be seeing a game."

Orlando was black, big, and athletic. Those latter traits made me feel a little less apprehensive when he decided that it was time for us to integrate another Hoosier tavern. We'd go in together—I most unwillingly—and order beer.

On one such expedition in the summer of 1963, the bartender at the Magic Bar pointed us toward the door. "We don't serve your kind," he told Orlando.

"My kind? You mean Presbyterians?" Orlando demanded. "Boy Scout Troop Leaders? Cubs fans?"

"You know what I mean," the bartender said.

Orlando requested change for a dollar. The bartender slammed the coins down on the bar. Orlando used a dime to call the police on the pay phone right by the bar. "I want to report illegal activity at the Magic Bar," he said. "That's at Broadway and Taylor." He hung up.

Orlando sat quietly on his barstool. In the dark corners of the room, grim men sat over their beers, glaring at us and muttering. I sat, too, hoping that my blood type was in stock that afternoon.

When the cops came and demanded to know the nature of the illegal activity, Orlando explained. "I have been denied service here," he said. "That is in violation of the Indiana Public Accommodation Acts of 1865. You could look it up." The cops, gritting their teeth, wrote a ticket charging the Magic Bar with a misdemeanor. We each got a beer on the house. I have never relished a glass less. Orlando finished his and said, "We've got time to check out another place."

I remembered another engagement.

Allen Lang

Urban Renewal in Hyde Park

When I moved to Chicago in June 1943, I had no idea that I was moving into a potential urban renewal site. We started out in a third-floor apartment on Blackstone Avenue, a few doors south of 55th Street, and were quite happy to discover that within one block we would have a ma-and-pa grocery store, a good bakery, a fine shoe repair, a hardware store, and a toy shop; in an additional two blocks, we had access to the Hyde Park Co-op and a drugstore as well as two chain groceries. It did not bother us at that time that, in the three blocks between Blackstone and the Illinois Central tracks, there were about ten bars open until the early morning, or that above many of the stores were three or four floors of antiquated walk-up apartments.

In the spring of 1950 we bought a third-floor apartment containing five bedrooms, four baths, a mahogany-paneled dining room, and forty-three windows to be washed. It was a three-family co-op, and the second-floor owner, who was the chairman of the English Department at the U. of C., insisted that the third floor could be sold only to a person who had permanent status in the community. Hence the price was only $11,000. The reason it had become available was that during the winter of 1949–50 the Supreme Court had declared restrictive covenants illegal. We had never known of these covenants, which prevented African Americans from buying property anywhere in the Hyde Park–Kenwood area. The seller was unwilling to live in a block where African Americans were expected, and indeed the first black family moved in one week before we did.

In Chicago real estate lore, it was a certainty that when one black moved into a block, all whites would leave the block within one year. This principle was not accepted as certain by either the university or the residents of Hyde Park. The university set up a program for neighborhood protection, which included drawing up laws for the federal government to create urban renewal areas. This included provisions for the purchase of property that was deteriorating and reselling the land at a loss for specified uses that would renew the community. It also provided that the university could supervise the drawing up of plans for the renewal and could get credit for property it purchased in pursuit of its general aims for renewal.

The program was divided into two stages: Hyde Park A and Hyde Park B. This continued until about 1970. On 55th Street, for example, when the process was completed, there were only three blocks where the buildings were not completely torn down: the south side of the block between Harper and Lake Park, the north side between Kenwood and Ridgewood Court, and the north side between Woodlawn and University. The result was that 55th Street, which had formerly been the principal shopping area of Hyde Park, became a residential street occupied by families and institutions, except for the new shopping center on the north side adjacent to Lake Park Avenue.

The citizens of Hyde Park took a different stance from the university, and organized the Hyde Park–Kenwood Community Conference. Its principle aim was to encourage new residents to join in preventing the creation of slums. The whole community was divided into block groups to welcome new arrivals—persons seeking to get out of the slums—and urging them to join with the established residents in enforcing the laws that were intended to preserve the character of the neighborhood.

Specifically, neighbors were to watch for any sign of illegal conversion of large apartments into smaller ones. The Conference would then get the city to send in a building inspector, who could file a detailed report on the illegal construction and thus enforce the law. Block leaders met regularly as a group to exchange reports. We were quite encouraged when a black resident of the northwest quarter of Hyde Park (and editor of the *Chicago Defender* newspaper) told his block leader, "I am moving to Washington to become vice chairman of the Democratic Party. I want you to find a white purchaser for my house. It's time for a change from black to white."

I served as chairman of our block group for much of the twelve years we lived in the 5100 block of Ellis Avenue, welcoming new neighbors, some of whom became good friends. At the end of that period my three-flat was the only all-white building in the block, and there were 2 two-flat buildings that were jointly owned by white and black residents. The block was in better condition physically than it had been when I moved into it, and it has remained in that state ever since.

During that period, I had a treasurer's responsibility for some several hundred thousand dollars of endowment money belonging to the Western Unitarian Conference. The man who served as the broker to help me make appropriate investment decisions in those years was an Episcopalian, Francis Butler, who happened to be a trustee of the Church Home at Ingleside and 54th Street, three or four blocks from my home. In 1952 or 1953, he mentioned to me that his Board of Trustees were about to decide to sell the Church Home and move to a whiter neighborhood because they assumed Hyde Park would soon be all black. I immediately told him about the way we were working through the Community Conference to create a really integrated community. He thanked me for the information and apparently was able to persuade his fellow trustees to keep the Church Home in Hyde Park. For this reason, I feel that I had some part in the later decision to build Montgomery Place in its present location.

When our children were through college and had established themselves a thousand miles away, my wife and I moved to a smaller apartment closer to the university. We decided on a six-flat co-op at 5515 Woodlawn. That put us in the proper place to observe the second phase of the Hyde Park Urban Renewal. The buildings on 55th Street between Kenwood and Woodlawn avenues came down during our first year in the Woodlawn apartment, and planning was beginning at that time for new constructions in several locations. One of these was the development of the Harper Court shopping center, which had been designated by the approved plan for that area as a shopping center for special artisans and other proprietors who required low rentals. Community leader Muriel Beadle had chaired the committee that formulated plans.

The plan for the shopping center was so specific that no one else bid on the site, and the Harper Court Foundation's bid for the land was accepted. Financing was arranged so that the Small Business Administration agreed to provide 80 percent of the required capital on twenty-five-year mortgages. Each mortgage was specific to a particular small businesses, and we were required to give that business a twenty-five year lease. The other 20 percent was financed by hundred-dollar bonds purchased by individual residents of Hyde Park. Barbara Fiske and I were among the persons who solicited bond purchases. Our bond holders were surprised when, a year later, they actually received a six-dollar check for interest on each bond. They had thought of their bond as a contribution to a good cause. Muriel Beadle remained as Chairman of the Board for about twelve years. By that time, her husband had retired from the presidency of the University of Chicago.

Without Muriel's steadying hand, the foundation quickly developed serious problems. A year later I accepted the responsibility of becoming Chairman of the Board. After four years, things were running smoothly again, and I recognized that I could not continue any longer. At that time, too, the Treasurer of the Board, a successful lawyer, decided he wanted to become an Episcopal cleric. So I persuaded Barbara Fiske to succeed me as chairman by promising to take on the job of Treasurer. After another four years, I allowed Barbara to take on the Treasurer's job.

Harper Court completed payment of its mortgage and redemption of its bonds at the end of its twenty-fifth year. It continues to provide the services it was created to make available and it is now able to underwrite additional artistic endeavors.

Albert Hayes

A Test Case

On a warm Saturday evening in 1953, six of us, all Elgin State Hospital employees, decided to go out for dinner. We were all professionals: two were married to each other and the remaining four were single men and women. One was a young black psychologist; the rest of us were white.

We entered a restaurant around 6:00 p.m. and were directed toward a table for six. We sat and waited to be served. Everyone around us seemed to get service, and after about half an hour we wondered why we were still waiting. After a brief discussion we realized that it was because of our black friend. So we quietly left the establishment. The following Monday we asked for time off from work to visit the state's attorney. Our superintendent didn't like the publicity.

While we were in the attorney's office, the first thing he asked each of us was, "Where are you from?" None of us was originally from the Chicago area—we were outsiders! The attorney suggested that, instead of suing the restaurant for violation of the Civil Rights law, we make a "test case" of it.

We were able to motivate another six employees, black and white, to go to the restaurant the following Saturday, together with our original group. The restaurant had been notified of our coming by the attorney. We were promptly seated and served. We considered our efforts a success, although the owner or manager had said we seemed to be drunk on our first visit and he therefore had the right, under the Dram Shop Act, not to serve us. That was, of course, a lie. None of us had been drinking.

Renate Vambery

Reflections on a Decade

During the 1960s, the world I knew changed from a place where kindly Boston policemen ushered ducklings across Beacon Street in *Make Way for Ducklings* to a world where, at the same crossing, I saw policemen chasing terrified hippies out of the Public Garden with dogs. I think of a scene in Harvard Square with a squadron of police with shields, helmets, and clubs marching across the street toward Harvard Yard while I waited at the crossing with my groceries. I think of a daughter working for the Liberal Party in South Africa and carrying papers to London hidden in her underwear, and I think of her putting her life on the line in Mississippi. I think of another daughter getting weaker and weaker on a hunger strike at college. I think of my husband talking to a bus driver all night in order to keep him awake as he drove a busload of people to a demonstration in Washington, D.C.

And I think of my nine-year-old son walking home from school one day, past Harvard Yard, where the striking students were locked inside. As he looked through the fence, a young man came up to him, said he was hungry, and passed a dollar through the bars, asked the boy to get him a chocolate milkshake. "I'll wait here," said the prisoner. So off my son went, feeling proud to be of use, but when he came back nobody was there. He waited hopefully, holding the milkshake for an hour and a half, but nobody ever came, so he walked home, almost in tears, still carefully holding the untouched drink.

In October 1962, during the Cuban Missile Crisis, I spent hours pacing the basement of our house, imagining how I could make it secure against a nuclear attack: the canned food would go there, mattresses and blankets over there, and I would fill the old laundry tubs with water. We would bring down the radio and plenty of candles. We'd use the old toilet that had been for the servants in this nineteenth-century house. We'd be okay. And when my six-year-old came home from kindergarten I comforted myself by reading *The Little House in the Big Woods*. See, I thought to myself, if Laura Ingalls Wilder's family could do it, so could we. We could surely find a convenient forest to survive in. My innocence was monumental.

One day five of us, teachers of a new little school in the basement of a church, were meeting one afternoon when the custodian burst into the room saying, "Kennedy's been shot. I think he's dead." I drove home numb, amid the tolling of all the church bells in Cambridge.

In 1965, my husband started a small alternative high school. Students were dropping out of high schools, both public and private, all over the Boston area. There were drugs and protests, the Civil Rights Movement and the Vietnam War, and these, mixed with ordinary adolescent rebellion, made for a tumultuous educational scene. The schools tried to control the ferment by conventional rules and demands, but, one after another, the students were dropping out.

We had all kinds of kids coming to this unconventional school; they felt respected here and at home, where the adults were on their side. There were bright ones, remedial readers, white ones, black ones, eager and reluctant ones, suburban and city kids. Very quickly this became a school community where no one was pushed to go to Harvard or to live up to someone else's expectations, and where the usual high school subjects were taught without tracking of any kind. The classes weren't easy but they were small. Nobody dropped out and everybody graduated. It was a highly successful maverick institution and its graduates, though many didn't go straight to college, have become lawyers and professors and writers and artists just as they would have if they'd gone to a conventional high school.

In April 1968, after Dr. King was shot, desperate for some way to show my horror, I went out and bought an American flag so I could hang it at half-mast in front of our house. But the message was unclear. When my husband came home, he said, "What's *that* for?"

and I realized it looked like a celebration instead of a cry of grief as I had intended, and I quickly took it down.

I think of a friend my age at a demonstration against the Vietnam War. There were thousands of people on Boston Common chanting in chorus, "Stop this fucking war!" My friend turned to the young man next to her and said, "I'm with you all the way; I just can't say that word."

Alice Hayes

Breakfast with JFK, November 1963

News that President Kennedy was going to be in Dallas on November 22 caused a furor among Fort Worth Democrats, who feared that they were being bypassed. Senator Ralph Yarborough was contacted. Strings were pulled, and Fort Worth Democrats were informed that the President would, after all, make a brief stop in their city the night before going on to Dallas.

President Kennedy was to arrive at the Texas Hotel in Fort Worth late Friday night, November 21. He'd have breakfast the following morning, and then fly from Meacham Field to Dallas's Love Field, then to the Dallas Trade Mart for lunch with Dallas and other Texas Democrats.

Early on the morning of November 22, we gave our sixteen-year-old son permission to cut school in order to go down to the hotel with the hope that he'd get to see President Kennedy up close. It now seems ironic, but there was extended discussion among the President's advisors as to the safety of his facing a crowd without proper protection. Nevertheless, he decided to just go out; not make a speech, but shake a few hands and chat with some of the young people.

Our son and his friends attended Pascal, one of the two main high schools. The other was Arlington Heights High School. Two weeks earlier, the schools had held a rally before their big football game at Arlington High. One of the boys from Pascal "borrowed" his father's airplane and flew over the rally, dropping toilet tissue. When the president shook hands with the Pascal contingent, he asked, "How is your air force?" which question astounded the young people. (Kennedy's staff combed

the city papers before each of his appearances to cue him in for
these topical, offhand references.)

In the meantime, inside the hotel about 5,000 people gathered.
Everyone waited patiently, and finally the President, Vice President
Lyndon Johnson, Texas Governor Connally, Senator Yarborough,
and Representative Jim Wright all came marching in. The President apologetically explained that Jackie was delayed because it
took her longer to get dressed and ready than it took Lyndon and
him. "However, the results are much better and nicer to look at."
Then Jackie appeared. He was right.

At last we all ate. At one point, my husband nudged me and
whispered, "Look at the way Lyndon is eating." It was a strange
sight. Johnson was bent over his plate, and literally shoveling food
into his mouth. Very strange. So tense, so nervous. After the breakfast was over, my husband and I went down to the street to watch
the President's entourage drive by on their way to Meacham Field,
where their plane would make the twenty-minute flight to Dallas.

We drove home. As we got to our back door and were about to
enter, Air Force One flew over our heads on its way to Dallas. I went
in and started to fix lunch for my elderly mother-in-law, who lived
with us. As I worked in the kitchen, I heard an announcement
coming from the TV: "The President has been shot!"

Ruth Rapfogel

Mississippi Summer

In the summer of 1964 somebody came to me and said, "Will
you join a group of women who are going down to Jackson,
Mississippi, to show their support for the young people who are
down there running Freedom Schools and registering voters in
black communities all over the state?"

That was the summer that Andrew Goodman, James Chaney,
and Michael Schwerner, driving to work in what was known as
"Mississippi Summer," were dragged out of their car and shot
because they were a racially mixed group traveling together from
the North. In Ohio, hundreds of college students were briefed
about the work they had volunteered to do in Mississippi, and even
before the three prospective workers were murdered, the students

in Ohio had been warned about the danger they faced and given a chance to change their minds about going. A few remained home, but my daughter Susan decided to stay the course. They were taught how to avoid being beaten or killed, what to wear, and how to relate to hostile whites.

At the time I was invited to go to Jackson, Susan was living with a brave black family and registering voters in a town called Moss Point on the Gulf Coast. We were the second of several groups of northern women who went as observers. We had a training session before we left; we were told that we were to wear hats (there was even some discussion of gloves) and that we were to be "ladies" in order to show the southern whites that it wasn't only wild radicals and hippies who supported the work the students were doing. There was one black woman in the group, but we had been instructed that as soon as we got off the plane in Jackson we were to act as though we didn't know each other. This was part of the plan not to be confrontational. We stayed in separate motels and mostly remained separate during the two days of our trip. This was disturbing.

The first evening we met with a group of white women from the League of Women Voters to talk about the summer project. Their opinion of the summer volunteers ranged from suspicion to outright hostility. However, one woman made a moving speech about how she hadn't wanted to believe that blacks were being intimidated or oppressed, but that she had come to believe that it was so. It came out that I had a child registering black voters in the southern part of the state, and one of the ladies said, "How could you let her go?" I said I couldn't have stopped her if I'd wanted to, and that I was proud of her courage. The good ladies were aghast. But they were there to talk with us even though it developed that some of their husbands had been told to have their wives withdraw from that "commie organization"—the League of Women Voters!

Actually, I was very much afraid for Susan. I would have liked to go down to Moss Point, but I was afraid to attract attention to her so I made do with a telephone call, which we arranged with some difficulty. I wasn't sure the motel would let me know when she called, but they did.

The next day we were driven in two cars to a town called Canton, outside Jackson. On the way, the driver got lost and stopped at a store to ask the way. From then on we were closely followed by a small white pickup truck with two men with guns in it—the sheriff. All day they were behind us until we got back to the motel in Jackson.

First we visited the nuns who ran a parochial school in Canton. The local priest came to talk with us, too, wearing civilian clothes because he didn't want to be recognized. The nuns were sympathetic but extremely anxious about being seen with us so we didn't stay long. Then, closely followed by the white pickup, we visited two Freedom Schools in Canton where the volunteers were trying to offset the poor schooling and the messages about inferiority that the children had gotten in their regular schools. We were very impressed by the innovative summer programs developed by the northern students. Some of the children in those Freedom Schools had their lives totally changed by the experience. When Susan went to an anniversary meeting of Mississippi Summer in the late 1990s, some of the people who had been children in those schools were there, educated men and women who talked about how the schools had transformed their lives.

That evening we met in someone's home with a group of women, not all white, from the Jackson YWCA. These were people committed to the cause of civil rights, but they too were worried about how the students dressed (badly) and whether we had seen things the way they really were. However, they asked us to go back up north and speak out about what we'd seen. We had learned how courageous these women were.

Other groups of northern "ladies" went to Jackson every week that summer. In 2000 there was a meeting in Boston of all the women who could be located who had taken part in these trips. Many of them, both black and white, have spent their lives as activists working for civil rights. I was sorry I couldn't go, but a friend who was there reported that it made her feel as though our trip had meant something important to the students risking their lives for change. Perhaps also the people we talked with in

Jackson were a little bit influenced by those crazy ladies who came down from the north to show their support for the students working on such an important project.

Alice Hayes

The Night the West Side Burned

It was an evening in April 1968, soon after Martin Luther King, Jr.'s, death. The fires of protest had begun earlier in the day and accelerated as darkness grew. I sat listening to the radio broadcasts when a request came over WBBM: the Catholic Interracial Agency requested help from social workers. The agency offered assistance to the families being evacuated from the fires on Chicago's West Side, and the need for food and shelter was temporarily being met by this single resource. No formalities were being observed—just come to the agency office.

I called Jean Battle, a black woman and a close friend, a fellow social worker at the Chicago Child Care Society. She agreed to go. My husband offered to drive us since we had been asked not to bring vehicles into the area unless they could be quickly driven away. As we drove to North Clark and Superior streets, we saw National Guard troops on patrol—six to a jeep and with bayonets on their guns; the exposed bayonets underlined the city's need for help.

At the old mansion on Superior Street that housed the Catholic Interracial Agency we were hurriedly brought inside and given instructions. Jean was to oversee the telephones receiving incoming appeals for help from families in the burning areas. All the phones were covered by black volunteers, who spoke with understanding to the callers.

I was ushered to the second floor of the house. There were two bare rooms; one had stacked cots available for children and other weary victims of the burned-out areas. The other room was to provide food; adjacent to it was a very large closet whose shelves were stacked with all manner of canned foods. A small shelf held an electric frying pan and a one-burner electric unit.

The frying pan and I became inseparable. I gave choices to incoming refugees as to which can of food they would like to "enjoy." I would heat and serve it, wash the pan in a nearby bathroom and start again with newcomers. For children frightened by this change from home, I spread a sheet on the floor to designate the "picnic area," and the children and their parents sat on the floor in small circles, alternating the routine of eating with singing.

Jean coordinated calls from those needing evacuation and those offering to help. Many people called to offer food, contributions, and shelter in their homes. We worked with many others through the night. The grim experience was lightened only once, when an irate donor to the agency called requesting information as to how her money was being used. She wanted "to speak to the Cardinal." Quickly, one of the male workers was designated. He assumed the necessary role, reassured the caller, and we all laughed for the first time that long night.

About 8:00 a.m. the following morning, a fellow worker and board member of the agency offered to drive Jean and me home. His car's windshield had been shot out during the night and the shards of shattered glass abounded. When we arrived at my home, we sat briefly. Solemnly, we shook hands and muttered, "I'm so happy to meet you." Then we both laughed. What could be more ridiculous than exchanging these niceties after the preceding twelve hours!

Elizabeth Jones Borst

Sit-in at Wilson College

Compared to the rioting on the West Side of Chicago following the death of Martin Luther King, Jr., and the protracted and sometimes violent student sit-ins at major universities during those turbulent times, our student sit-in and rebellion at Wilson College was a small ripple, but it did transform a racially integrated institution into a predominantly black one in a short time. The president resigned, and the vice president transferred to another campus, as did the entire administrative office staff who had been with the college since its days as part of the

Chicago Public School system. A black president and vice-president were selected from the black faculty by a committee of students and installed in the administrative offices.

The issues were typical for the times: complaints about specific teachers as "unfair," lacking in respect, and failure to include books by black authors on the assigned reading lists.

The most substantial issue was a demand that the college eliminate a program that was the pride of the faculty members involved. Called the Basic Program, it had been set up to meet the needs of students who came with high school diplomas but whose entrance test scores indicated their academic skills were not adequate for college-level classes. The Basic Program paralleled the regular first-year college curriculum but did not earn full college credit. It was essentially a remedial program and, in those contentious times, was looked at as demeaning and a waste of the students' time. The program, they felt, should be eliminated, the students allowed to enroll in regular classes and take their chances: sink or swim. To educators, this is a perennial and controversial issue, not easily dismissed by caveat, but these were not the times for educational theory or compromise.

For those of us not involved in the particular program under fire, the "troubles," as they came to be called, were pretty much confined to dismissed classes and disrupted work. Fire alarms set off by students and bomb threats that emptied the building were a nuisance, especially to campus security and the Chicago Fire Department, which had to respond each time.

Our student sit-in in the administrative offices—two cubicles, three or four secretarial desks, and a small office for the comptroller—did provide our department with a minor role to play. The students had planned to take over the administrative offices until the chancellor of the City Colleges came and talked with them about their demands. But these were young students, not too sure of themselves or their roles as rebels; they asked some of our faculty members to stay in the building after it was officially closed "in case the police come." They thought the police would not beat them up if there were white faculty members as witnesses. We stayed through that long, hot afternoon, receiving reports from "the front" at intervals via student messengers.

Four hours later we were free to go home: an emissary from the chancellor had come out to the campus and met with the student leaders. The police had not been called.

There was a mixture of relief and a little disappointment as the students reported the outcome: no bruises or broken bones, but no headlines either.

The integration of the campus that we lost that day was replaced by something possibly of greater relevance to the times: Black Pride, reflected in body language and the slogans: "Black is Beautiful" and "I Am Somebody!" Some dead white poets were replaced by live black authors on the reading lists. Integration is a two-way street, as those of us who stayed learned. There is much to be gained in both directions.

Joan Swift

Eighties Vignettes

My older grandchildren grew up in the shadow of the cold war in an atmosphere of apprehension. My oldest grandson told me one morning that he had had a wonderful dream: "All the nuclear weapons were gone out of the world and we were safe!"

My grandchildren also grew up during the Vietnam War, in an atmosphere of protest. My seven-year-old grandson and his mother and brother were being interviewed by Studs Terkel. Toward the end of the interview Studs turned to Sandy and asked what he'd like to be when he grew up. Sandy said, "I hope I'll be old enough to go to jail, too, someday." Studs, that kind man, didn't laugh; he just nodded.

How different from my childhood, when I felt completely unthreatened by the world beyond my own.

Alice Hayes

11

Avocations, Retirement, and Beyond

Our lives have not been spent exclusively at office desks, in classrooms, on assembly lines, or attending to the needs of patients. Important and involving as one's work has been, life for most of us has been enriched by activities and special interests beyond the workplace, beyond the routines of family duties as well. Hobbies, special interests, and travel have added color and enjoyment to our lives.

Travel, especially, abroad or at home, has been a popular and enriching experience for many of us. Travel today is a different proposition than it was during our childhoods or even our early adult years. Most of us can remember our first plane ride, and remember travel by train as well. Trips that took an overnight train ride—in a Pullman berth if you were lucky, or sitting up in a coach seat, or, during the war, sitting on your suitcase in the aisle—today are a short plane ride away. In those days, going to Europe meant a steamship voyage of many days, its comfort and glamour a matter of class and financial means. Today, travel to Europe is a matter of hours and not much glamour. Even Asia is a one-day flight at most. Commercial adventure travel has brought the most remote areas of the earth—areas we marveled over in the *National Geographic* in our childhoods—within range of our cameras; neither the penguins of Antarctica nor the tigers of Nepal are out of our range.

281

Epiphany

To begin with, I grew up indifferent to life forms of the animal kingdom other than human beings. We never had pets when I was a child, and while I loved Albert Payson Terhune's *Lad, A Dog* stories, I knew and cared little about dogs. I visited the Lincoln Park and Brookfield zoos as a child, but didn't know or understand anything about the zoos' inhabitants.

In March 1978, a friend invited me on a whale-watching trip to Baja California in Mexico with his young son and some of the son's friends. We were to spend nine days camping (another aspect of life I knew nothing about) and driving down to Laguna San Ignacio, a mating- and birthing-ground for the endangered gray whale.

Our first trip out on the Zodiac raft was very exciting, watching the whales do what whales do, oblivious to our presence. On the second trip came the epiphany. Our guide cut the motor of the Zodiac to idling speed, and as we quietly sat there, a mother and her calf came alongside us, peering at us with their enormous eyes. Joined by another whale, they swam all around the Zodiac. Then our guide suggested we touch them.

Touch them?

Yes, go ahead. They won't hurt you.

Touch wild animals?

We gingerly did, and—or so we thought—they enjoyed it! They kept coming back for more. They did not bump the Zodiac, but swam under it and next to it, looking at us. We were excited beyond description! After some forty-five minutes, they jostled the raft. Our guide said it was in a playful way, but since these twenty-five-ton mammals do not know their strength, he thought it was time for us to leave.

When we arrived back in camp, I was still dazed and moved—so much so that I cried. From that day to this, much of my life and care and respect have focused on animals, conservation, and environmental issues, and all because a wild animal let me touch it.

Ann Marcia Lee

Four Months in Malaysia

It was 1977 and I had reached the age of mandatory retirement after nineteen years of social work. Departure from a
position I had thoroughly enjoyed and separation from colleagues who were now close friends left me unsure of what
interests and activities I would find to replace them. Our children had grown, married, and moved to distant cities. My husband had interests and associations that occupied much of his
time and would continue to do so.

Speculating about what came next, I received, providentially,
a phone call from an old friend. Through her association with
the University of Wisconsin she was offered a place in the international studies program. My friend invited me to join her as
there was a second place available. We would spend four months
in Malaysia, where we could take courses of our choice at the
University of Malaya at Kuala Lumpur. We would live with the
students and have few specific responsibilities except as a kind
of senior advisor to the students.

What an opportunity! A complete change in a new land of
strange people with young students whose enthusiasm would
negate the doubts of, and offer stimulation to, an older person.
I saw it as irresistible. I persuaded my husband that four months
wasn't that long, urged my children to "stand by," and began to
plan my departure.

My friend and I left the day before my sixty-fifth birthday
and flew to London. We spent three days in London in the
poorly heated Peace House, and then flew Air India to
Singapore. I well remember the large sign in the Singapore
airport: "Waving Deck." My question: What waved? Explana-
tion: The people on the deck could wave to departing
friends. The deck itself was secure!

For two weeks we lived in Changi, a suburb of Singapore, in
the quarters occupied during World War II by the Royal British
Engineers. We had tennis courts, a large outdoor swimming
pool, good bus service to Singapore, excellent food—this was
the closest to luxury we would come in the four months we were
in Southeast Asia.

We took frequent sightseeing trips in and around Singapore, usually by public bus. Since none in our group spoke Chinese, communication was difficult—sometimes impossible. To visit the frequent street fairs, where apparel was cheap and suited to the intensely hot weather, we would board a bus, point to our clothing, and display some money. The bus driver got the idea. When we arrived close to the fair, the driver would shout "Go!" and hasten our exit with a push. We learned very quickly that the clothes that fit our slender Chinese neighbors didn't fit us at all!

If not the bus, then the rickshaw. This often was pulled by an elderly man. The rickshaw seated two Chinese but only one American! Since we usually traveled in pairs this meant one rode and one trotted behind the rickshaw, while the rickshaw driver labored, pulling twice the weight of an Asian passenger.

We learned to cover our heads and to remove our shoes when we entered a temple. To escape the ceaseless heat we would take a rickety bus carrying passengers and farm animals— all in one section of the bus—to small inns, *bukits,* located on a miniature mountain, where the heat was less but the language difficulties greater.

After Singapore we went a short distance north to the University of Malaya. The students were housed in two- and three-story buildings, two students per bedroom. My friend and I had an "apartment" with two bedrooms, one bath, and a large central room with a refrigerator—luxury! The central room also served as a common room for all the students. We had a great deal of company.

Each night as we retired, we lit a large bowl of incense designed to burn all night and discourage spiders and mosquitoes descending from the ceiling. Geckos were on every wall of the bedroom, protecting us from flying menaces. The incense and the hungry lizards discouraged the wildlife, but a second problem came each day at sunrise—the tireless, monotonous, tuneless voice of the muezzin calling the faithful to prayer. Our apartment was only a short distance from the muezzin's tower.

We visited the zoo and rode a camel. Later I visited a park and rode an elephant. We went to museums and saw the *wayang kulit* shadow puppet plays. At the Hindu religious festival Thai Pusam we went to the Batu caves to watch the penitents inflict torture on themselves. Also to be seen were tin mines, rubber plantations, yards of batik in process, endless shops, and food stalls that sold a variety of vegetables and fruit. One fruit, the durian, famous in Malaysia, has a vile odor when it is cut, but once the seeds are removed the meat is delicious.

The University of Wisconsin charged a flat fee covering transportation; housing in University of Malaya dormitories, where food was provided; some travel expenses; and tuition for courses at the university. In return we gave aid and comfort to the students as needed. Occasionally we were asked to speak about American life to student groups or at one or more of the embassies.

We were free to travel at our own expense on school holidays and we took advantage of this, spending one week at Sanur Beach in Bali, Indonesia, another week in Bangkok and Chang Mai, Thailand.

At the end of four months I returned home and was shocked when, on a familiar street, I felt strangely displaced. Reverse culture shock is a reality.

Elizabeth Jones Borst

Around the World in Fifteen Months

My thirty-five-year teaching career at the University of Chicago began in 1943, when I was invited to join the faculty of an experimental college devoted to a four-year program of "general education" beginning after the second year of high school and designed to prepare citizens to be capable of functioning in a democratic society where specialists could share their knowledge with one another. This program led to a bachelor's degree with no major field of study. It was to be followed by three years of specialization leading to a master's degree; the curriculum breadth and the provisions for placement tests and comprehensive examinations were well adapted to the years when students were being inducted into military service and, later, to the needs of the veterans returning from their military years. The concept of general education became a major topic in educational theory for a few years.

In early 1955, I learned that the University of the Philippines had asked the Fulbright Foundation to send them a professor who could help them set up a good education program in the humanities. It sounded to me as if they were looking for someone from our Chicago college, so I applied and was quickly accepted. I soon learned that in the Philippines only ten years of schooling preceded college, and that from the fourth grade on, all schooling was in English.

At that time my daughter, Judith, was a sophomore at Oberlin, and my son, Knox, was four years behind her, at the University of Chicago Laboratory Schools. Their birthdays were both in June; in 1955 they would become nineteen and fifteen. They could easily fit into the University of the Philippines system. Moreover, since April and May were the "summer months" (hot and dry) in the Philippines, their year as well as mine would end about April 1. That meant we would have five months for leisurely travel before a September return from Europe. The whole family could go together on a trip around the world.

Our trip began on the *California Zephyr* to Oakland; then we took a freighter, the *President Harding*, to Manila, with a short stop in Tokyo Bay, where the ship unloaded military supplies for the troops there and picked up ten airplanes to be repaired in Manila. In the middle of the Pacific Ocean, the captain took the ship off automatic pilot so that Knox could steer it for an hour.

The University of the Philippines had been partially destroyed during the war, and it had been rebuilt in a suburban area east of Manila called Diliman, easily accessible to the city but higher in elevation and less crowded. Our house, made of native materials by the Army Corps of Engineers for MacArthur's staff, was on a slope above the university buildings and commanded a view of Manila Bay. The neighbors were a mixture of university employees and other Fulbright families. We were within walking distance of the university buildings and the buses going to Manila. It was a very easy kind of foreign experience because everyone spoke English. The children were soon able to go into the city without us, and we had a houseboy, who shopped in the markets and cooked for us. In addition, we quickly became acquainted not only with Filipinos but with students from China, Indonesia, Thailand, India, and Pakistan.

The American Embassy arranged several special daylong trips to interesting sights so that we quickly acquired an understanding of the native patterns of living outside Manila. In November, during the week vacation between semesters, we went to Camp John Hay, a mile-high Army resort in cool Baguio. My wife, Elizabeth, and the children went to Hong Kong for Christmas with an American family from Chicago; I used my travel allowance to visit the southern Philippines at Christmastime and Tunghai University in Taiwan in March.

Our five-month trip home, completing a circuit of the globe, began on the S.S. *Bronxville* (of Norwegian ownership) because that ship took the longest time to travel from Manila to Suez of any freighter we could locate. We left Manila around the first of April. Our itinerary began with Hong Kong and went on to Saigon, where we departed from the ship to fly to Cambodia to see Angkor Wat. After three days there, we flew on to Bangkok where we spent a week in a hotel while the ship went to Singapore and then up to Bangkok. From Bangkok we sailed to Jakarta and then back to Singapore, where we were scheduled to spend an additional week. (On this leg of the trip, we were the sole passengers on the *Bronxville*.)

Another weeklong stop came at Penang, where the ship loaded ingots of tin from small boats out in the harbor. From Penang, we crossed the Bay of Bengal to Colombo, and then another long sea voyage took us to Italian Eritrea at the foot of the Red Sea. On these long sea passages, the days that Judith on her flute and Elizabeth on her violin played Bach duets for a chorus of seabirds were a special joy.

Our last stop before Suez was Port Sadam, where "fuzzy-wuzzies" scrambled over our decks for their stevedorian duties, and near the harbor we saw a camel parking lot. The ship's carpenter made a special crate to fit the many interesting objects we had acquired during our passage across South Asia and added that box to the others we were to pick up in New York. At

Suez we took a train to Cairo, where we visited museums and pyramids, and arranged for the first leg of our European tour. From Cairo we flew to Athens, which had not yet succumbed to gasoline pollution; it was wonderful to look out the hotel window across the rooftops to the Acropolis, where the Parthenon was lit up at night. We took an automobile tour through the Peloponnesus to Olympia and back to a ferry across the Gulf of Corinth and up to Delphi. Our guide and driver spoke only French, but Elizabeth and I were able to translate for the others in our party.

From Athens we flew to Rome, where we stayed in an inexpensive pension run by the Vatican, and took delivery of an Opel station wagon, which would carry us for the remaining months of our tour. Our route included Florence, Ravenna, Venice, Vienna, Salzburg, Zurich, Basel, Dole (included on the itinerary because Knox had written a paper on Louis Pasteur), Dijon, Chartres and Paris, Bruges, the Hague, Delft, and Rotterdam, where we turned in our Opel and boarded the S.S. *Rotterdam*. We started out from Athens about June 1 and boarded the ship in Rotterdam in early September.

We were met on arrival in New York by my brother Francis. After we reclaimed our piles of luggage and started them back to Chicago with Judith and Knox, Elizabeth and I went on to Haddonfield, New Jersey, for a week with my mother. Meanwhile, back in Chicago, Judith and Knox straightened out the mess that our fifteen-month tenants had left in our apartment.

Albert Hayes

Gardening at Vista Homes

Before I moved to Montgomery Place, I lived in Vista Homes for more than twenty-five years. It was probably the best-managed and best-maintained co-op in Hyde Park. One of the nicest amenities of Vista Homes was the gardens. There are forty of them, ten by twenty feet, with smaller flower plots along Stony Island and 59th Street. I have always had an interest in gardening, so I became active in Vista Homes'

Garden Club, serving as president for eight years. I started tomato and cucumber seeds in my lighted planter every February, so had plants ready for the garden when it warmed up. In the plot there was also room for lettuce, beans, broccoli, and carrots, as well as flowers. Usually there was sunshine from sunrise to four o'clock; tomatoes did very well and even six plants would produce more than enough for a family. I have tried a garden here at Montgomery Place, but I was spoiled by the better growing conditions at Vista Homes. So now I've turned to singing instead of gardening.

Alex Coutts

Every Day is Saturday!

When I was in school and college, I painted a lot, mostly watercolor sketches, usually of rural areas. This had the advantage of getting me out of doors, and also required intense concentration, which was restful and refreshing.

When it became necessary to choose a major in college, I debated long and hard. I had finished an art course and had just cleaned up and turned in my microscope for a biology course with great regret. I finally settled on biology. When I retired as a biologist at the age of seventy, which was mandatory at the time, I went back to painting full time. I took art courses, and I had a series of studios, some shared with other artists. I was connected with a couple of galleries and several art groups. I made a lot of new friends. In short, it was a very busy time.

All this time, I lived on or very near 57th Street in Hyde Park, but I did see something of the rest of the world. In a community of scholars there is plenty of opportunity to travel and attend conferences throughout Europe and Asia. One can give lectures in places like Hangzhou, Aberystwyth, and Alicante. In a community of artists one can also travel, or at least one's work can travel. I was in art a shorter time than I had been in science, and my range was more limited, reaching only east to New York and New England, south to Missouri, north to Wisconsin, and west to Iowa.

I am now truly retired. I travel at most only a few blocks north, south, east, or west from my retirement community, but the world tries very hard to come to me. There are numerous lectures and concerts, there are people who have lived and traveled all over the world. There are museum walks, there are gardens and receptions and dinners.

I had a friend who said that when you retire, every day becomes a Saturday; that's the day you relax. And how to relax? Montgomery Place has many answers.

Jane Overton

Appendix A: Continuing Care Retirement Communities

Just as the Church Home for Aged Persons and other philanthropic institutions were founded to answer the needs of the elderly in nineteenth-century America, so continuing care retirement communities (CCRCs) are springing up throughout the country to meet the requirements of today's seniors.

Already the significant shift to an older America has begun, as U.S. Census Bureau statistics reveal:*

- In 2000, individuals age 65 and older numbered 35.0 million, an increase of 3.7 million or 12.0% since 1990.

- Americans 45–64 years of age—those who will reach 65 over the next two decades—increased by 34% since 1990.

- By the year 2030, the older population will more than double to about 70 million, creating an "elder boom."

- The 85+ population is projected to increase from 4.2 million in 2000 to 8.9 million in 2030, and represents the most rapidly growing demographic in the U.S. population.

---

* Administration on Aging, *A Profile of Older Americans 2002*, U.S. Department of Health and Human Services.

With lengthening life expectancy come concerns about maximizing the quality of life during these final years. What has been termed "successful aging" is characterized by 1) length of life; 2) biological health; 3) mental health; 4) cognitive efficacy; 5) social efficacy; 6) social competence and productivity; 7) personal control; and 8) life satisfaction. In recent years, successful aging has been aided by many factors, notably "a decrease in overall disability and poverty" among mature Americans.*

Housing is a key consideration in successful aging. "Many studies document the remarkable stability of elders and their desire regarding housing choices. Overwhelmingly, elders choose to live independently and remain in their homes rather than to move in with children or other relatives."**

Aging in place—not having to move from one's present residence in order to secure necessary support services in response to changing need***—"is not a new expression but is an idea with greater salience as American society moves toward the elder boom of the 2020s. Although many successful aging theories elaborate the potential for individual successes, they fail to address the social, needed structural aspects of 'elderly friendly' communities that can foster the well-being of residents so that they can age in place."****

Healthier, more active, and more educated than their counterparts of earlier eras, Americans seeking appropriate housing for their senior years are turning increasingly to "elderly friendly" CCRCs, providers that offer more than one level of care—independent living, assisted living, and/or skilled nursing facilities—on a single campus.

---

* P. B. Baltes and M. M. Baltes. "Psychological Perspectives on Successful Aging: The Model of Selective Optimization with Compension," from Balthes, P. & Balthes, M. (Eds.) *Successful Aging: Perspectives from the Behavioral Sciences.* Cambridge: Cambridge Univerity Press, 1990.

** Ibid.

*** *The Journal of Housing for the Elderly,* cited on www.epill.com.

**** Baltes & Baltes, op cit.

These communities accommodate seniors' preference for independence and the option to age in place; here, an individual can enjoy independence as long as physically and mentally able, and then transition to an assisted living arrangement or nursing facility as needed without the disruption of transferring to another provider. The average age at which such a transition is needed is increasing:

While a relatively small number (1.56 million) and percentage (4.5%) of the 65+ population lived in nursing homes in 2000, the percentage increases dramatically with age, ranging from 1.1% for persons 65–74 years to 4.7% for persons 75–84, and 18.2% for persons 85+.

Limitations on activities because of chronic conditions increase with age. In 2000, among those 65–74, 26.1% reported a limitation caused by a chronic condition. In contrast, almost half (45.1%) of those 75 years and over reported they were limited by chronic conditions.

Disability, too, was shown to increase with age; 73.6% of those aged 80 or older report at least one disability. Over half —57.6% — of those age 80 or over.*

In 1998, 77% of providers responding to a survey by the American Association of Homes and Services for the Aging and PricewaterhouseCoopers reported offering all three levels of care; 12% offered independent living and nursing facilities, 8% provided independent living and assisted living, and 3% assisted living and nursing facility care.

The contracts offered residents by CCRCs represent a wide range of options, as well. "All-Inclusive" contracts, commonly called "Type A contracts," require an initial entry fee at move-in and a monthly fee that stays the same regardless of the resident's level of care. Type A contracts were reported by 42% of survey respondents in 1998. "Modified Contracts" (Type B), reported by 16%, require an upfront entry fee and a monthly fee that stays the same for a limited period and/or increases as services increase, but

---

* *Continuing Care Retirement Communities Industry 1998 Profile.* American Association of Homes and Services for the Aging, 1999.

remains less than market rates. "Fee-for-Service Contracts" (Type C), reported by 25%, call for an upfront entry fee, plus monthly charges that directly reflect the level of care provided. Two other options are less common: Rental Contracts (reported by 11%), where residents pay no significant fee at time of move-in and pay market rates for the level of care provided; and Ownership (6%) where "residents 'purchase' their interest in real estate and pay a monthly service fee that may either be at market rates or discounted rates."*

* Ibid.

Appendix B:
Design for Community Living

In It Together concerns the backgrounds, interests, and activities of the residents of Montgomery Place, and how they have combined to enrich people's lives and address important needs. As outlined in Chapter 1, these needs include the ability to achieve meaningful accomplishment, to enjoy social contact, and to maintain personal independence and control. The building's facilities also assist this effort.

Montgomery Place is a fourteen-story high-rise apartment building located on the South Side of Chicago, overlooking Lake Michigan. The first floor (see Floor Plan on p. 42) contains the public rooms and administrative offices; the second and third floors constitute the Health Care Pavilion, including a skilled nursing facility and a dementia unit. The remaining eleven floors comprise one-, two-, and three-bedroom apartments for independent living. The basement includes the garage, laundry room, and individual storage units for residents, as well as maintenance and housekeeping staff areas. A garden, built over the garage, runs along the length of the building on the north side and provides space for individual flower and vegetable gardens for residents as well as walkways and sitting areas.

The common rooms on the first floor, designed and maintained for maximum flexibility, each serve a number of functions and play a variety of roles. (See Calendar of Events on pp. 298 and 299.)

The East Room, located at the end of the corridor opposite the Lobby, runs the width of the building. It contains no permanently arranged furniture except for the grand piano in the north corner. Before a given event, stacking chairs are set up in appropriate configurations: in rows facing the piano for concerts, facing the east wall for lectures and slide shows, or arranged more informally for audience participation activities. Tables can be brought in as needed.

The East Room is used for major residential gatherings such as Residents Association meetings, Friday night lectures, presentations by outside speakers on topics of special interest, and musical concerts. Activity groups such as Carpet Bowlers and fitness exercise groups regularly use the room. All residents are invited to these events.

In addition, the East Room serves as a meeting place for neighborhood community groups, such as the League of Women Voters and the East Hyde Park Committee. On Election Days it serves as a polling place for local precincts.

The **Activity Room** is adjacent to the East Room on the north side of the building and overlooks the garden. Equipped with a sink and a closet for storing materials and furnished with movable tables and chairs, the Activity Room is used for art classes and individual art projects, as well as by smaller groups for meetings and events. Among the groups regularly using this space are activity groups such as the Book Discussion Group, Playreaders, Needlecrafters, and Card Recyclers, and resident committees such as the Activities, Food, Health Care, Maintenance, and Music committees.

St. Anna's Chapel, the only legacy from the old Church Home, is located on the south side of the building. Services to meet the spiritual needs of people from every faith are sponsored by the Episcopal Diocese through the continuing work of the Church Home. The chapel also offers solace for individual meditation and memorial services.

Next to the Chapel, the independently operated **Beauty Shop** provides services to men and women residents, including patients in the Health Care Pavilion, as well as people from the neighborhood.

The **Exercise Room** (since moved to the fourth floor) is adjacent to the Activity Room and contains a variety of exercise machines such as treadmills and stationary bicycles, and is available for resident use on an individual basis.

The **Library** provides materials of all varieties to meet a wide range of tastes, interests, and purposes. Several daily newspapers, reference books, and fiction and nonfiction titles are available, as well as a special section of materials written by residents. Large-print volumes, books on tape, and a closed circuit television are provided for the visually impaired. A computer with Internet access and a printer are also available for resident use.

The **Lounge,** furnished as a comfortable living room with small tables convenient for refreshments, serves as a social gathering place for receptions, celebrations, the weekly Wine and Cheese Social, Coffee and Conversation, an occasional birthday or going-away party. The large TV is used on a regular basis for movies, and a special sound system serves the Music Committee during its weekly recorded music program.

The **Dining Room** is set up predominantly with tables for four, with some smaller tables for two and the possibility of combining tables to provide for larger groups. Families and friends of residents are welcomed. An area partitioned off at one end of the dining room serves as a buffet for lunch and a salad bar for dinner. Windows on three sides look out into the garden.

Typical Calendar of Events from the
Montgomery Messenger

REGULAR EVENTS IN DECEMBER _____

SUNDAYS	8:30 and 9:30 a.m.		Church transportation
	11:00 a.m.	Chapel	Holy Eucharist
	2:00 p.m.	Lounge	Movie
	7:00 p.m.	Lounge	Movie Encore — Closed Caption
MONDAYS, WEDNESDAYS, FRIDAYS			
	8:15 a.m.	Fitness Walks	Museum of Science & Industry
	11:30 a.m.	East Room	Physical Exercise with Dana
TUESDAYS & THURSDAYS			
	8:30 a.m.	East Room	Strength Training with Amr
	1:00 p.m.	Activity Room	Resident & Caregiver Group
WEDNESDAYS & FRIDAYS			
	10:30 a.m.	Exercise Room	Exercise Machine Instruction
MONDAYS	10:15 a.m.	Library	Poetry Group
	2:00 p.m.	Activity Room	Trivia Group
TUESDAYS	9:30 a.m.	Activity Room	Needle Crafters
	10:00 a.m.	Conference Rm	Hyde Park Bank
	10:00 a.m.	Bus Trip	Water Aerobics Class
	5:00 p.m.	Lounge	Wine and Cheese
Dec. 4, 11	7:15 p.m.	East Room	Playreaders
Dec. 18	7:30 p.m.	Chapel	Unitarian Service
WEDNESDAYS	10:00 a.m.	Chapel	Midweek Eucharist
	2:00 p.m.	Lounge	Afternoon Film Series
Dec. 12, 19	2:30 p.m.	East Room	Dance Therapy
	7:00 p.m.	Lounge	After-Dinner Music
THURSDAYS	11:00 a.m.	Chapel	Rosary Prayer Group
	2:00 p.m.	Lounge	Coffee and Conversation
	7:00 p.m.	Exercise Room	Parlor Games
FRIDAYS	1:00 p.m.	Activity Room	Open Studio — Arts & Crafts
Dec. 7, 21	5:00 p.m.	Chapel	Shabbat Service
	7:30 p.m.	Apt. 1402	Poker and Games
	7:30 p.m.	East Room	After-Dinner Program
SATURDAYS	9:30 a.m.	Apt. 1402	Bridge and Games
	1:30 p.m.	East Room	Carpet Bowling
	2:00 p.m.	Activity Room	BINGO *(see p. 4)*
	7:00 p.m.	Lounge	Saturday Evening Movie

SPECIAL EVENTS IN DECEMBER _____

SATURDAY	1	1 - 3 P.M.	EAST ROOM	HOLIDAY PARTY FOR CHILDREN OF MONTGOMERY PLACE STAFF *(SEE P. 1)*
SUNDAY	2	11:30 AM-1 PM	DINING ROOM	SUNDAY BRUNCH
MONDAY	3	3:00 P.M. 7:00 P.M.	EAST ROOM EAST ROOM	TOWN MEETING COUNCIL MEETING
TUESDAY	4	1:00 P.M.	BUS TRIP	RIVER OAKS SHOPPING TRIP (SEE P. 2)
WEDNESDAY	5	3:00 P.M.	EAST ROOM	HOLIDAY TEA RECEPTION *(SEE P. 1)*
THURSDAY	6	1:00 P.M.	EAST ROOM	HOLIDAY BAZAAR
FRIDAY	7	5:00 P.M.	EAST ROOM	SHABBAT CHANUKAH SERVICE *(SEE P. 1)*
SATURDAY	8	11:00 A.M.	EAST ROOM	CHICAGO AREA SONATA/SONATINA RECITAL *(SEE P. 2)*
SUNDAY	9		🕎 CHANUKKAH BEGINS	
TUESDAY	11	1:30 P.M.	BUS TRIP	GARFIELD PARK CONSERVATORY: "CHIHULY GLASS EXHIBIT" *(SEE P. 9. $2 DONATION)*
WEDNESDAY	12	1:00 P.M.	BUS TRIP	WATER TOWER PLACE SHOPPING TRIP *(SEE P. 2)*
THURSDAY	13	1:30 P.M.	EAST ROOM	LEAGUE OF WOMEN VOTERS MEETING — TOPIC: PUBLIC EDUCATION IN CHICAGO
		6:00 P.M.	BUS TRIP	LINCOLN PARK ZOO LIGHTS ($4)
FRIDAY	14	7:30 P.M.	EAST ROOM	GRETEL BRAIDWOOD SPEAKS ON "DIGGING BEYOND THE TIGRIS AT CHRISTMAS" *(SEE P. 1)*
MONDAY	17	3:00 P.M.	EAST ROOM	TOWN MEETING
WEDNESDAY	19	NOON	BUS OUTING	TATRA INN LUNCH OUTING
THURSDAY	20	2:00 P.M.	BUS TRIP	"HOLIDAY OF LIGHTS" AND "CHRISTMAS AROUND THE WORLD" AT THE MUSEUM OF SCIENCE AND INDUSTRY
FRIDAY	21	7:30 P.M.	EAST ROOM	"METRA ELECTRIC" BY JOHN ALLEN
SATURDAY	22	7:30 P.M.	EAST ROOM	UNITED CHURCH OF HYDE PARK CAROLING *(SEE P. 1)*
MONDAY	24	7:00 P.M.	EAST ROOM	CHRISTMAS EVE SERVICE WITH THE UNION CHURCH OF HYDE PARK *(SEE P. 1)*
TUESDAY	25		🎄 CHRISTMAS DAY	
WEDNESDAY	26		KWANZAA BEGINS	
THURSDAY	27	11:45 A.M.	DINING ROOM	RESIDENTS' BIRTHDAY LUNCHEON
MONDAY	31	7:30 P.M.	EAST ROOM	NEW YEAR'S EVE PARTY *(SEE P. 2)*

Appendix C:
List of Contributors

Allen, Beverley 157
Anderson, Jean Bowman 63, 73, 170
Anderson, Linnea 125
Bensema, Virginia 107
Bibler, Grace 76, 148
Blakely, Alta 237, 253, 261
Borst, Elizabeth Jones 12, 32, 110, 151, 160, 162, 186, 209, 277, 283, 302

Brock, Mary 9, 74, 179
Cade, Elise 175, 210
Carroll, Clement 172
Century, Lillian 263
Coleman, Dorothy 164
Coutts, Alex 38, 171, 288
Ellison, Emily 302
Ellison, Jack 67, 80, 164, 302
Fish, Laurie 76
Fiske, Barbara 119, 161, 256
Fiske, Donald 85, 154, 221
German, Catherine 152, 235
Gordon, Aileen 142, 230, 303
Gray, Alberta 76
Hadra, Ruth 205
Harley, Phillip 172, 264
Harris, Chauncy 200
Harris, Edith 253
Hayes, Albert 21, 266, 285, 303
Hayes, Alice 16, 72, 86, 95, 135, 136, 150, 159, 167, 173, 180, 213, 242, 271, 274, 280, 303

Members, Montgomery Place Historic Book Committee

Elizabeth Jones Borst was born in Chicago, Illinois, on January 3, 1912, and has lived on the South Side of Chicago her entire life. She attended the University of Chicago School of Social Service Administration in the mid-1930s and worked at the Chicago Child Care Society as a social worker and administrative aide from 1958 to 1977. Before beginning her career with Chicago Child Care, she married Charles D. Borst and spent twenty years raising her two daughters. She has lived at Montgomery Place since June 1994.

Emily Ellison received her early education in a small town in New Hampshire. She attended Wellesley College and graduated with a B.A. degree, after which she was awarded a graduate teaching fellowship. A few years later she moved to the Midwest and joined the faculty of the Francis Parker School, where she met her husband, Jack. After several years of teaching high school English, she took time out to study linguistics. Following the birth of two children, she began a full teaching schedule in linguistics at Northeastern Illinois University, where she continued to teach in the undergraduate and graduate programs for twenty years. Emily and Jack moved to Montgomery Place in 1999.

Jack Ellison was born in 1910 in Toronto, Canada. His early education was in the Toronto schools, and later at Trinity College at the University of Toronto. He moved to the United States where he continued his studies at an experimental college in Winnetka, Illinois. Subsequently, he began a long teaching career at the Francis Parker School in Chicago. It was there in the 1950s that he found the encouragement to develop a course in Cultural Anthropology for high school students, a unique course at that level. For five years he was principal of the Francis Parker School, which continues to be a leader in the development of progressive education.

Aileen Howell Gordon was born in 1907 in Marion, Indiana. She attended Franklin College in Franklin, Indiana, where she met the love of her life, Noel Marion Gordon. They were married in 1932 and moved to Chicago, residing in Hyde Park and Chatham. When the younger of her two children entered second grade, Aileen returned to the workplace part-time as a secretary. From 1950–1969, she worked full-time in the office of South Shore High School. Aileen moved to Montgomery Place in December 1992, where she lived until her death in April 2002. An active member of the Historic Book Committee, the Sewing Group, and the Welcoming Committee, and contributor to the *Montgomery Messenger*, Aileen's sharp good humor enlivened many of our meetings.

Albert M. Hayes, born in 1909, spent most of his first twenty-four years getting an education, chiefly in New England (A.B. Dartmouth, 1930; Ph.D. Princeton, 1933). From teaching jobs in the east, he moved west to Chicago in 1943, where he taught English and Humanities at the University of Chicago for thirty-five years. He spent a year in the Philippines on a Fulbright, and has traveled widely with his family. His first wife died in 1979, a year after his retirement. He and his second wife, Alice, were among the first people to move into Montgomery Place in the fall of 1991.

Alice J. R. Hayes was born in Chicago. After World War II, she and her first husband moved to Cambridge, Massachusetts, where she became a school psychologist, raised four children, and helped to start two schools. Later she volunteered on several digs in the Middle East and in Illinois, but her efforts to be an archaeologist were interrupted by a call back to the Midwest to start the Ragdale Foundation, a place for artists of several disciplines to come to work. She has published five books of poetry. She married Albert Hayes in 1981 and moved with him into Montgomery Place.

Allen Lang was born in 1928, sharing his end-of-July birthday with look-alike Arnold Schwarzenegger. The U.S. Navy airship *Akron,* flying over his hometown of Fort Wayne, Indiana, inspired his lifelong, if unrequited, love of lighter-than-air craft. After military service in Korea and England, Allen managed a blood-bank laboratory for the Red Cross. He received a Master of Public Administra-

 tion degree from Roosevelt University, and was employed as safety officer for the United States Environmental Protection Agency. Allen and his wife, Alberta Ruth, moved to Montgomery Place in 1999. In retirement he is very slowly completing his third novel.

Joan Swift, a former community college administrator, and her husband, Hewson, a University of Chicago professor emeritus of Biology, came to Montgomery Place in November 1994. Originally from New York City, they moved to Hyde Park in 1949. Joan

 spent the early retirement years writing a biography of her grandaunt, a missionary to Burma, which was published in 2003. At Montgomery Place, she has been an active member of several committees and activity groups.